The Nineteenth-Century Sonnet

The Nineteenth-Century Sonnet

Joseph Phelan

First published 2005 by
PALGRAVE MACMILLAN
Houndmills, Basingstoke, Hampshire RG21 6XS and
175 Fifth Avenue, New York, N.Y. 10010
Companies and representatives throughout the world

PALGRAVE MACMILLAN is the global academic imprint of the Palgrave
Macmillan division of St. Martin's Press, LLC and of Palgrave Macmillan Ltd.
Macmillan® is a registered trademark in the United States, United Kingdom
and other countries. Palgrave is a registered trademark in the European
Union and other countries.

ISBN 13: 978–1–4039–3804–6   hardback
ISBN 10: 1–4039–3804–0   hardback

This book is printed on paper suitable for recycling and made from fully
managed and sustained forest sources.

A catalogue record for this book is available from the British Library.

Library of Congress Cataloging-in-Publication Data
Phelan, J. P. (Joseph P.), 1963–
      The nineteenth-century sonnet / Joseph Phelan.
         p. cm.
      Includes bibliographical references and index.
      ISBN 1–4039–3804–0
      1. Sonnets, English–History and criticism. 2. English poetry–19th century–
History and criticism. I. Title.

      PR509.S7P48 2005
      821'.042'09–dc22   2005051250

10   9   8   7   6   5   4   3   2   1
14 13 12 11 10 09 08 07 06 05

Transferred to digital printing in 2007.

For Giovanna

Contents

Introduction

One of the pastimes of the Rossetti siblings was a game called 'bouts-rimés', in which they would compete with one another to compose sonnets from a set of rhymes. Many of the resulting poems were of fairly low quality, as William Michael Rossetti admits in mitigation of one of his own efforts which found its way into the Pre-Raphaelite magazine *The Germ*: 'This sonnet was one of my *bouts-rimés* performances. I ought to have been more chary than I was of introducing into our seriously-intended magazine such hap-hazard things as *bouts-rimés* poems: one reason for so doing was that we were often at a loss for something to fill a spare page.'[1] Sometimes, however, the spontaneity of the exercise produced a freshness and immediacy absent from more studied performances:

> The spring is come again not as at first
> For then it was my spring; & now a brood
> Of bitter memories haunt me, & my mood
> Is much changed from the time when I was nursed
> In the still country. Oh! my heart could burst
> Thinking upon the long ago: the crude
> Hopes all unrealised; the flowers that strewed
> My path, now changed to painful thorns & curst.
> And though I know the kingcups are as fine
> As they were then, my spirit cannot soar
> As it did once: when shadows of a wood
> Or thinking of a blossom that soon should
> Unfold & fill the air with scent, would pour
> Peace on my brow now marked with many a line.

This is one of a group of 'bouts-rimés' sonnets preserved amongst Christina Rossetti's papers, all composed (according to her own annotation) in between five and nine minutes.[2] The result in this case has, partly due to the sparing use of punctuation, something of the appearance of a piece of 'automatic writing', an impression reinforced by its reworking of some of Christina Rossetti's most characteristic themes and motifs. Her poetry is full of the kind of repetition with variation introduced in the opening lines and developed throughout the poem; spring returns, but a different spring which merely reminds the poet of all that she has lost in her life. There is a very characteristic suggestion of Christ-like suffering in the Miltonic-sounding 'painful thorns & curst', without the answering moment of consolation which appears in almost all of her published poetry. And the last line, with its reference to the speaker's own physical appearance, may contain an implicit equation between the 'lines' on her brow and the 'lines' inscribed on the page – a possibly unconscious suggestion of a connection between her vocation as a poet and her unfulfilled personal life.[3]

The 'bout-rimés' sonnet encapsulates many of the complexities and contradictions of the nineteenth-century use of the sonnet form. It is both spontaneous and rule-governed, both personal and conventional. It is a throwaway form of little intrinsic value, written to fill up a spare page, and at the same time the most intrinsically valuable of poetic utterances. Wordsworth lamented the amount of time he had wasted writing sonnets, but also characterised the sonnet as the 'key' to Shakespeare's 'heart'.[4] It is an ephemeral and occasional form, and at the same time a 'monument' which will immortalise both poet and subject. These contradictions reflect the sonnet's ambiguous position within nineteenth-century poetics. As a conventional and arbitrary form it runs counter to the prevailing belief in the necessity of an organic connection between form and content, leading to a series of attempts to 'organicise' the form and demonstrate its indissoluble connection with certain states of mind and feeling. Again, as a form proverbial for its insincerity it seems to conflict with the very strong post-romantic emphasis on sincerity as a criterion of poetic value, and the result of this conflict is a sustained endeavour to position the sonnet as the most sincere and personal of poetic forms, sometimes (as in the case of Keble) by virtue of its very conventionality.[5] The story of the nineteenth-century sonnet is the story of the exploration of these tensions and contradictions. Some poets, of course, use the form inertly, imitating the gestures and techniques of others; but the most innovative and interesting sonnet writers of the century – Wordsworth, Elizabeth Barrett Browning, Gerard Manley Hopkins, George Meredith, Christina Rossetti – use the form with a full sense of its uneasy relation to prevailing beliefs and assumptions about poetry, and with an awareness of the ways in which they can exploit the resulting tensions for their own ends.

One of the difficulties in tracing this story is the miscellaneousness of the nineteenth-century sonnet. For many poets, this miscellaneousness was an integral part of the form's appeal; Wordsworth, for instance, saw it as an expression of the 'Fancy', 'as capricious as the accidents of things', and called his first sustained effort in the form 'Miscellaneous Sonnets'.[6] This emphasis on the capricious and occasional nature of the form means that there are sonnets on every conceivable topic; sonnets addressed to friends and to enemies, sonnets on war and on peace, sonnets on profound spiritual or metaphysical topics and sonnets on trivial matters. It is, under these circumstances, very difficult to make generalisations about the nineteenth-century sonnet, and impossible to say that it always does one kind of thing. For every subtle exploration of the form's dialectic of freedom and limitation, there is an obtusely rhetorical blindness to it; for every example there is a counter-example. It is, however, possible to trace certain recurring themes and motifs in the use of the sonnet which help us to understand what it signified at various points throughout the century, and why poets continued to be drawn to it.

The phenomenon of the 'sonnet upon the sonnet' is one such motif; almost every sonnet writer of note 'be-sonneted The Sonnet' at some stage, as Dante Gabriel Rossetti puts it.[7] Some of these efforts, such as Wordsworth's 'Scorn not the Sonnet', are apologetic or defensive in tone, attempting to justify the use of the form in the face of real or imagined critical hostility to it; others, like those of Rossetti, Symonds and Watts-Dunton towards the end of the century, are more like poetic manifestos in which a particular view of the sonnet is advocated. All of them suggest an attention to and an awareness of the structure and resources of the form itself typical of an age obsessively interested in the technicalities of verse. They highlight the reflexive quality of much nineteenth-century sonnet writing. For some poets the sonnet is a kind of default mode of poetry, something to which they could turn in their less inspired moments; noted sonnet-refusers like Robert Browning tend to use it in this way.[8] But others are fascinated by the symbolic and iconic possibilities of the form, and attempt to make an awareness of its difficulties and limitations a constitutive part of the reader's experience. The exemplary 'sonnet upon the sonnet' is the 'Prefatory Sonnet' in

Wordsworth's *Poems in Two Volumes* of 1807. In this poem, discussed at length in the first chapter, Wordsworth transforms the sonnet itself into an iconic representation of freely chosen imprisonment, establishing an implicit analogy between the rules of the form and other kinds of moral and social rules. This analogy allows Wordsworth to explore some of the most keenly contested moral and political questions of his time, and to justify his own complex and occasionally contradictory shifts of political position. The sonnet is seen as illustrating the paradoxical relationship between liberty and restriction; its example shows that true rule-governed 'liberty' is different from and superior to mere 'licence', or what Matthew Arnold later in the century calls 'doing as one likes'.[9] Wordsworth's example resonates with significance for a number of his successors, most notably Elizabeth Barrett Browning and Gerard Manley Hopkins, in ways which demonstrate the profound continuities between the Wordsworth of the *Poems in Two Volumes* and his Victorian successors. It is in these poems that the 'Victorian' Wordsworth, the Wordsworth who helped to forge and sanction the attitudes and beliefs of Victorianism, comes into being.

In these sonnets Wordsworth turns for guidance and example to Milton. *Poems in Two Volumes* represents not only a return to the formal discipline of the Miltonic sonnet after the 'licence' of the previous thirty years, but also a return to Miltonic values of earnestness, Puritanism, and a proper, sober, responsible liberty. Wordsworth's appropriation of Milton was so successful that the resulting Miltonic-Wordsworthian sonnet acquired massive cultural authority, an authority which was not seriously challenged until Wordsworth's death. During the years after 1850, however, poets began to look to Shakespeare and the Elizabethans, to Keats, and to the Italian originators of the sonnet in the search for alternatives to the Miltonic-Wordsworthian model and everything that it implied. The sonnet, in fact, played an important part in the broad cultural reaction against Victorian earnestness and Puritanism which characterised the latter part of the nineteenth century; poets turned to the history of the sonnet for instruction in and sanction for dissenting attitudes and beliefs. The story of the nineteenth century's engagement with the sonnets of Michelangelo illustrates the way in which sonnet history could modulate into a challenge to the dominant culture. Wordsworth's 'Miscellaneous Sonnets' in *Poems in Two Volumes* includes three translations from Michelangelo's sonnets, translations which emphasise the artist-poet's high-minded Neo-Platonism. As an artist who wrote poetry only when prompted by some occasion or private passion Michelangelo's example helped Wordsworth develop the idea of the sonnet as the most intimate and confessional of poetic forms. Many of Michelangelo's sonnets were assumed to have been written late in his life to Vittoria Colonna, a noblewoman who had herself composed a set of Petrarchan sonnets on the death of her husband. Colonna came to be seen as a model and an inspiration by a number of women writers throughout the century, most notably Elizabeth Barrett Browning; her combination of poetic talent and subordination to the towering genius of Michelangelo perfectly reflects Barrett Browning's own mixture of self-assertion and self-denigration as a woman poet. The 1860s, however, saw the publication of a new Italian edition of Michelangelo's sonnets, which demonstrated that some of his poems had been bowdlerised to conceal the fact that they were addressed not to Vittoria Colonna but to his friend Tommaso de' Cavalieri. This revelation not only prompted comparisons with Shakespeare, most of whose sonnets are also, of course, addressed to a man, but also helped Walter Pater and John Addington Symonds develop their understanding of the Renaissance as the partial and limited revival of 'Platonic' values, including the celebration of love between men. By the end of the century, then, Michelangelo's sonnets look like a cuckoo in the Wordsworthian nest, a source of values antithetical to those nurtured in the rest of the collection.

This shift away from the Miltonic-Wordsworthian model also produces an increasing interest in the 'sonnet sequence', a term coined by Dante Gabriel Rossetti late in the century to describe *The House of Life*.[10] This was the dominant mode of sonnet production during the medieval and Renaissance periods, and one sign of the new moral and cultural climate of the last quarter of the nineteenth century is the exponential growth of the Petrarchan-inspired amatory sonnet sequence during this period. The relative importance of the sonnet sequence at the end of the century should not, however, be taken as implying its absence from earlier periods. Throughout the century the sonnet is both a freestanding structure in which a single thought can be housed and (potentially at least) a unit in a larger-scale development, and this produces an uncertainty about the status of the individual sonnet which is never fully resolved either in Wordsworth's work or in the work of his successors. Wordsworth follows Milton in liberating the sonnet from its position as a mere stanza in a larger poem, but then cautiously regroups his sonnets into larger structures which subtly redefine their significance; and he is imitated in this respect by Felicia Hemans and Elizabeth Barrett Browning amongst others. Many of these groupings are loosely (if usually also enigmatically) biographical in orientation; Elizabeth Barrett Browning's sonnets in *Poems* (1844) hint at an unspecified source of private grief, and invite us to read them as the narrative of the poet's movement from grief to acceptance and resignation. In this respect the sonnet sequence closely resembles the 'lyric sequence', that characteristically nineteenth-century attempt to fuse the lyric intensity of poetry with the interest and social range of narrative.[11] The affinities between them are demonstrated by the existence of a number of collections which it is difficult to place securely in either category. Wordsworth's *Memorials of a Tour on the Continent* (1820), for instance, includes both sonnets and other kinds of lyric; Shelley's 'Ode to the West Wind' (1819) is a lyric sequence which may or may not consist of sonnets; Tennyson's *Maud* (1855) includes a small number of sonnet-like poems; and George Meredith's *Modern Love* (1862) is a lyric sequence consisting of uniform sixteen-line poems designated 'sonnets' by Meredith. Perhaps the most significant of these borderline cases is Tennyson's *In Memoriam* (1850), which is clearly not a sonnet sequence, but is equally clearly based on one – Shakespeare's – and in its turn becomes a major influence on the amatory sonnet sequences of the last quarter of the century. The sonnet sequence differs from the lyric sequence, however, in preserving the integrity of its component parts; the sonnet is never (in John Addington Symonds' words) allowed to become a mere 'strophé'.[12] In both the loosely biographical groupings of the early part of the century and the more formally patterned sequences of the later part, such as Christina Rossetti's 'sonnet of sonnets' *Monna Innominata* (1881), there is a delicate and ineradicable tension between the claims of the individual poem and those of the sequence as a whole.

As a sequence written from the point of view of one of the many unknown women addressed by the sonnet-writers of Medieval and Renaissance Italy, *Monna Innominata* illustrates the way in which the form becomes for most of the century the site of a contest (albeit a decorous and literary one) between male and female writers. The century opens with Wordsworth's blatant 'remasculinisation' of a form cultivated with notable success by women poets, and continues with similar acts of appropriation and realignment by both sides. In spite of Wordsworth's efforts women writers continue to find the form congenial for a number of reasons, amongst them its apparent modesty and humility, its ability to offer them a level playing field, and perhaps most importantly its association with an interior and often secret life of longing and desire. Because it necessarily implies some view of the nature of the relationship between men and women, the amatory sonnet becomes particularly contentious in this respect. Both its chivalrous elevation of women to the status of unattainable near-divinities (Dante's Beatrice) and its tendency to objectify the recipient of the poet's attentions (Petrarch's Laura) render it complicit with patriarchy in certain obvious ways, and produce on the part of many women poets a desire to subvert or reverse its habitual gender roles and characteristics.

Due to its tremendous popularity and instant availability to un-tutored and non-professional poets, the form also had the potential to serve as a site of class conflict; but class divisions are less obviously inscribed in its history than divisions of gender. There are a number of possible reasons for this. One is that relations between social classes are not basic to the form in the way that gender relations are; Elizabeth Barrett and Christina Rossetti can challenge social convention simply by making the previously silent partner in the amatory sonnet speak for herself. Again, adoption of the sonnet by working-class poets meant the adoption of an alien vocabulary and a partial (if also partially resisted) acquiescence in a genteel literary tradition from which they had usually been excluded. And, by virtue of the form's associations with the Middle Ages, its use by politically motivated working-class poets is bound up with those aspects of the radicalism of the nine-teenth century which seem most obviously and bafflingly reactionary to the contemporary reader; the deference to patrons and 'genuine' aristocrats, the doomed attempt to produce love between social classes, and so on. Its widespread adoption does, however, bring to light certain connections and affinities obscured by the more familiar pathways through nineteenth-century poetry. There is, for instance, a link between the jingoism of the sonnets produced by a number of working-class poets in response to the Crimean War and the attitudes adopted by the speaker in Tennyson's *Maud*, whose final vision of a country rushing to its appointment with fate comes in the form of a series of pseudo-sonnets.

This ability to make new connections is one of the main benefits of studying the sonnet across the whole of the nineteenth century. From the point of view of the sonnet, the boundary between 'Romantic' and 'Victorian' fades in importance. The key date in this story is not 1830 but 1850, the year of the publication of *Sonnets from the Portuguese* and *The Germ*, both of which illustrate some of the possibilities latent in alternatives to the Miltonic-Wordsworthian form. The effect of this new configuration can be seen with particular clarity in the case of Keats, who becomes important primarily as the precursor of the neo-renaissance sonnet-writers of the last third of the century. In overriding period boundaries in this way, the sonnet provides an exemplary instance of the way in which a literary medium interacts with broader social, cultural and ideological transformations. It begins the nineteenth century as the bearer of what Raymond Williams calls 'emergent' cultural values, those of Victorianism, carries these values through to dominance, and then becomes the site both of these values in their 'residual' form and of the new 'emergent' values of aestheticism, decadence and proto-modernism.[13]

The period of study chosen is not, however, intended to suggest that moments of significant innovation and transformation in the form can be precisely correlated with the beginning, middle and end of the century. The pivotal significance of 1850 does not imply a neatly symmetrical history. In many respects the movement is rather more like the 'ebb' and 'flow' discerned in the sonnet's asymmetrical structure by Theodore Watts-Dunton.[14] There is a reasonably clear moment of origin in the poems written by Wordsworth during the first decade of the nineteenth century, but there is no corresponding clarity in the response to this initial movement which plays itself out at the end of the century. Although it is possible to detect a kind of end-point in the reaction against the 'Decadence' which sets in in the wake of the Oscar Wilde trial and the Boer War, it would be equally possible to argue that many of the characteristic features of the late-nineteenth-century sonnet survive well into the second decade of the twentieth century. The arch-Modernist Ezra Pound, for instance, who blamed the sonnet's 'dirty work' for the 'decline of metric invention', began his career like Dante Gabriel Rossetti by looking to the early Italian sonnet for inspiration in his translations from Guido Cavalcanti;[15] and Wilfred Owen's anti-war sonnets acquire a significant additional dimension when placed in the context of the 'imperialist' sonnet of the turn of the century. Conversely, the roots of the Modernist rejection of the sonnet, and indeed of most of the traditional forms and metres of English poetry, can be detected in the sceptical attitude of the 'Decadent' poets of the late nineteenth century towards a form which their immediate precursors had embraced as their own. The untidiness of this upper boundary could not, then, have been avoided by making the end-point twenty years earlier or later; and it means that this study, like many of the best sonnets, ends on something of an interrupted cadence, gesturing towards the diminished but certainly not insignificant role of the form in twentieth-century poetry.

1
The Wordsworthian Sonnet Revival: *Poems in Two Volumes* (1807)

It was until fairly recently possible to argue that Wordsworth 'resurrected the sonnet from the virtual oblivion in which it had lain for more than a century and re-established it in a position of eminence', but such assertions have become increasingly implausible.[1] It is now clear that when Wordsworth produced his first sustained exercise in the form in *Poems in Two Volumes* (1807), he was rather belatedly adopting a form that had already been rediscovered and popularised during the last quarter of the eighteenth century. Thanks to recent scholarship the story of the sonnet revival has become a familiar one, from the role played by Percy's *Reliques* in disinterring this apparently moribund poetic form to the work of women poets, especially Charlotte Smith, in developing the 'elegiac sonnet' into a vehicle for the articulation of a certain type of intense and personal experience.[2] The sonnets in *Poems in Two Volumes* do not even represent Wordsworth's own first attempt at sonnet-writing; in spite of his claims to the contrary, we now know that he wrote and published sonnets before 1807, and that these sonnets were heavily indebted to the elegiac sonnet tradition that he later disowned. Under these circumstances it seems a severe distortion of literary history to credit Wordsworth with having 'revived' the sonnet, a distortion complicit with the general tendency of literary history to appropriate women's achievements and innovations and reassign them to men. It is, however, still possible to see Wordsworth's intervention in the form in 1807 as a decisive moment in the history of the nineteenth-century sonnet. He did not rediscover the sonnet in any straightforwardly antiquarian sense, but he did produce sonnets which alerted his contemporaries and successors to the latent power and potential of the form. His sonnets hit the resonant frequency of the form, and continued to reverberate for the rest of the nineteenth century. He summarised and surpassed the achievements of the sonnet-writers of the late eighteenth century with such completeness that he succeeded in transforming potential rivals into largely forgotten precursors. It was, in short, Wordsworth himself who appropriated the form; and the task of literary history is not to replicate (or indeed deprecate) that appropriation, but to try to understand the appeal of the Wordsworthian sonnet for his contemporaries and successors.

In the notes that he dictated to Isabella Fenwick towards the end of his life, Wordsworth gives the following account of the development of his interest in the sonnet:

> In the cottage of Town End, one afternoon in 1801 [1802], my Sister read to me the Sonnets of Milton. I had long been acquainted with them, but I was particularly struck on that occasion by the dignified simplicity and majestic harmony that runs through most of them, – in character so totally different from the Italian, and still more so from Shakespeare's fine Sonnets. I took fire, if I may be allowed to say so, and produced three sonnets the same afternoon, the first I ever wrote except an irregular one at school. Of these three, the only one I distinctly remember is 'I grieved for Buonaparté'. One was never written down: the third, which was, I believe, preserved, I cannot particularise.[3]

His assertion that these sonnets were 'the first [he] ever wrote except an irregular one at school' is, however, somewhat less than the whole truth. His very first published poem was the profoundly un-Miltonic sonnet 'On Seeing Miss Helen Maria Williams Weep at a Tale of Distress':

> She wept. – Life's purple tide began to flow
> In languid streams through every thrilling vein;
> Dim were my swimming eyes – my pulse beat slow
> And my full heart was swelled to dear delicious pain.
> Life left my loaded heart, and closing eye;
> A sigh recalled the wanderer to my breast;
> Dear was the pause of life, and dear the sigh
> That called the wanderer home, and home to rest.
> That tear proclaims – in thee each virtue dwells,
> And bright will shine in misery's midnight hour;
> As the soft star of dewy evening tells
> What radiant fires were drowned by day's malignant power,
> That only wait the darkness of the night
> To cheer the wandering wretch with hospitable light.[4]

This is an exemplary elegiac sonnet. In writing about his own response to Helen Maria Williams's response to someone else's distress, Wordsworth illustrates the tendency of this form to feed upon suffering; Miss Williams's tears 'proclaim' her possession of 'virtue', and her response causes the poet's organ of benevolence to dilate under the influence of 'dear delicious pain'. His poem is, moreover, typical of the elegiac sonnet in its formal irregularity. The revival of the term 'sonnet' in the late eighteenth century did not entail any attempt to revive the strict Petrarchan form, with its intricate and closely-wrought rhymes. As Mary Robinson notes with some disdain in the Preface to her *Sappho and Phaon* (1796), '[so] little is rule attended to by many... that I have seen a composition of more than thirty lines, ushered into the world under the name of Sonnet'; and Anne Radcliffe uses the term to describe a pair of elegiac quatrains in her 1790 novel *A Sicilian Romance*.[5] This refusal to adhere to the antique rules of the form was perceived by a number of critics as one of the positive virtues of the new sonnet. A reviewer of the 1786 edition of Charlotte Smith's *Elegiac Sonnets* argues that '[a] very trifling compliment is paid to Mrs Smith when it is observed how much her sonnets exceed those of Shakespeare and Milton' adding that she has 'undoubtedly conferred honour on a species of poetry which most of her predecessors in this country have disgraced.'[6] Similarly Nathan Drake, in his *Literary Hours* of 1798, praises 'Charlotte Smith and Mr. Bowles' for their success in cultivating the sonnet, and in particular for abandoning any vestigial attachment to the Petrarchan origins of the form. By 'assuming the elegiac measure' they have freed the sonnet from the artificial restrictions and limitations which cramped the efforts even of Milton.[7] Wordsworth's is not a radical departure from Miltonic precept – he does not exceed the allotted number of lines – but he allows himself the metrical licence of not one but three Alexandrines (in lines 4, 12 and 14) to mimic the 'swelling' of his feelings and sensibilities in the presence of Miss Williams's suffering.

This sonnet might, of course, be the 'irregular' one Wordsworth claims to have written at school, but it is by no means the only sonnet he wrote or published in the years before 1802. There are at least four other sonnets belonging to this period, and one of these, a translation from Petrarch, was also published.[8] We know, in addition, that he was extremely interested in and even (according to one recent account) obsessed with the work of Charlotte Smith, the originator of the elegiac sonnet: 'As early as 1789, when he was an undergraduate at Cambridge, Wordsworth obtained a copy of the fifth edition of Smith's *Elegiac Sonnets*, in which he made some notes, added his name to a list of late subscribers, and copied by hand early versions of two sonnets that would not appear until the sixth edition'.[9] Wordsworth visited Smith on his way to France in 1791 in order to procure a letter of introduction to Helen Maria Williams.[10] And, according to Dorothy Wordsworth's Journal, he was still reading Smith's sonnets in 1802, at the very moment when he was claiming to have been converted to the form by Milton's example.[11]

It seems extremely unlikely under these circumstances that Wordsworth could have forgotten his familiarity with the elegiac sonnet, so the most likely explanation of his statement to Isabella Fenwick is that it constitutes a conscious misrepresentation of his past. Some of the reasons for this 'deliberate erasure of the sonnet of Sensibility'[12] from his own personal history are suggested in a letter of November 1802 praising Milton's sonnets and discussing the technical challenges they offer the poet:

> Milton's sonnets... I think manly and dignified compositions, distinguished by simplicity and unity of object and aim, and undisfigured by false or vicious ornaments. They are in several places incorrect, and sometimes uncouth in language, and, perhaps, in some inharmonious; yet, upon the whole, I think the music exceedingly well suited to its end, that is, it has an energetic and varied flow of sound crowding into narrow room more of the combined effect of rhyme and blank verse than can be done by any other kind of verse I know of.[13]

In aligning himself with Milton's 'manly and dignified' sonnets, Wordsworth is attempting to place some distance between himself and the female-dominated elegiac sonnet tradition of the late eighteenth century; and there is no doubt that part of his aim in returning to Milton was to 'remasculinise' the sonnet.[14] Where the elegiac sonnet is emotional, excessive and formally undisciplined, Milton's sonnets are characterised by a properly masculine self-discipline exemplified in their unswerving adherence to the rules of the Petrarchan or 'legitimate' sonnet. Coleridge does something similar when he singles out William Lisle Bowles as his precursor in the elegiac sonnet, and praises the 'mild and manliest melancholy' of his poetry; but, as was so often the case, Wordsworth's gesture is both more comprehensive and more productive than that of his friend.[15] In turning to Milton, Wordsworth is not making small-scale distinctions between elegiac sonnet writers but retrospectively feminising and rejecting them all (his earlier version of himself included) in one sweeping movement.

In this respect, then, Wordsworth seems to participate in the widespread denigration of the cultural products of 'Sensibility' during the most intense years of the conflict with Napoleonic France which saw other genres like the Gothic novel come under suspicion in similar ways. Wordsworth's realignment of his relation to the sonnet tradition cannot, however, simply be labelled reactionary. The phrase 'narrow room', used in the letter cited above, is one which Wordsworth employs repeatedly in connection with the sonnet, and its uses provide some important clues about the attractions of the form for him at this time.[16] Michelangelo's sonnets are difficult to translate because 'so much meaning has been put... into so little room'.[17] And Wordsworth uses the phrase again in the Preface to the 'River Duddon' sonnets of 1820:

> Hail, ancient Manners! sure defence,
> Where they survive, of wholesome laws;
> Remnants of love whose modest sense
> Thus into narrow room withdraws;
> Hail, usages of pristine mould,
> And ye that guard them, Mountains old! (ll. 55–60)

The 'little room' is, in all these instances, a place of safety and refuge during times of adversity. Both Milton and Michelangelo maintained a severe and principled republicanism in the face of extremely hostile political circumstances. In the same way, the valley of the River Duddon, cut off and guarded by the mountains from the march of civilisation, maintains the 'ancient manners' of an earlier and more wholesome period; the 'remnants of love' which these manners represent have withdrawn into 'narrow room' in order to preserve themselves from corruption. These examples of strategic limitation and withdrawal fortify Wordsworth, the republican and revolutionary of the 1790s, when he too finds himself '[on] evil days... fallen, and evil tongues;/ In darkness, and with dangers compassed round'.[18] Entering the 'narrow room' of the sonnet represents a way of sealing himself off from potentially corrupting influences. The form's association with personal authenticity and political radicalism render it an appropriate vehicle for the preservation of 'feelings all too delicate for use' in the current hostile political climate.[19]

Wordsworth's turn towards the Miltonic sonnet is, then, a complex gesture which fuses together a number of contradictory impulses, and its complexity is apparent in the 'Prefatory Sonnet' which he uses to introduce and justify the two sonnet sequences in *Poems in Two*

Volumes. Here the 'narrow room' is both a place of refuge from a per-plexing and intractable reality, and an emblem of the paradoxical rela-tion between freedom and imprisonment. The heavily rule-governed Petrarchan or 'legitimate' sonnet becomes an iconic representation of the poet's own freely chosen confinement; both his acquiescence in the rules of the form and his minor creative infractions of them acquire an almost immediate moral and political resonance, reinforc-ing or counterpointing the poem's explicit discussion of the relative merits of liberty and submission to authority.[20] Moreover, the images used in the poem are carefully chosen to blur the boundary between engagement and withdrawal, indeed to present withdrawal as the most productive form of engagement available at the present moment. The poem attempts to construe these acts of submission and disengage-ment as temporary expedients; but, as Wordsworth's successors recog-nised, it also signals a subtle but permanent shift in the poet's outlook. He comes to like the 'narrow room' of the sonnet too much to ever want to leave it, and begins to accommodate his opinions to his new surroundings.[21]

The images in the octave both resist and gesture towards the world of social and political conflict from which the poet claims to be with-drawing:

> Nuns fret not at their Convent's narrow room;
> And Hermits are contented with their Cells;
> And Students with their pensive Citadels:
> Maids at the Wheel, the Weaver at his Loom,
> Sit blithe and happy; Bees that soar for bloom,
> High as the highest Peak of Furness Fells,
> Will murmur by the hour in Foxglove bells:
> In truth, the prison, unto which we doom
> Ourselves, no prison is: and hence to me,
> In sundry moods, 'twas pastime to be bound
> Within the Sonnet's scanty plot of ground:
> Pleas'd if some Souls (for such there needs must be)
> Who have felt the weight of too much liberty,
> Should find short solace there, as I have found.

To the meditation and prayer of the nun and hermit are added the bookishness and erudition of the students in their 'pensive Citadels'. Unlike his great precursor, Wordsworth apparently can praise a 'fugit-ive and cloistered virtue', even in wartime.[22] However the word 'Citadel', with its military connotations, incorporates in a very understated way the poet's acknowledgement of the war going on in the real world; the apparently unproductive student is, by a kind of chiasmus, made the guardian of the fortress. There is a similarly understated allusion to the outside world in the figure of the weaver at his loom. The weaver was, at this time, the embodiment of those threatened by the industrialisation of manufacture. During the eighteenth century northern weavers were generally independent, self-employed people who worked for a number of masters or (more commonly) a single master, and enjoyed the status of skilled artisans in the community. During the period 1780–1830, however, their status was 'greatly debased' into that of the 'proletarian outworker, who worked in his own home, sometimes owned and sometimes rented his loom, and who wove up the yarn to the specifications of the factor or agent of a mill or of some middleman. He lost... status and security... [and] was exposed to conditions which were, in the sense of the London artisan, wholly "dishonourable"'.[23] The idealised image of the weaver sitting 'blithe and happy' at his loom is, then, one loaded with ideological significance, a vision of the potential self-sufficiency and contentment of the skilled labourer.[24] The final image of the octave is the most explicit in its combination of the ideas of freedom and limitation, sublimity and beauty; the bees soar to the 'highest Peak of Furness Fells' only to imprison themselves in the foxglove's flowers.[25]

The volta or turn of the sonnet comes in lines 8–9, with the pivotal assertion that 'the prison unto which we doom/ Ourselves, no prison is.' This enjambment across the major structural divide of a strictly observed Petrarchan sonnet becomes a formal (and Miltonically sanctioned) echo of the statement made in the lines themselves.[26] Moreover, in describing the sonnet as a 'scanty plot of ground', Wordsworth once again ushers in the world of social and political conflict which he is ostensibly trying to exclude. The sonnet is the equivalent within the poetic sphere of the 'little tract of land' which, according to Wordsworth, both symbolises and guarantees the moral well-being of society:

> The domestic affections will always be strong amongst men who live in a country not crowded with population, if these men are placed above poverty. But if they are proprietors of small estates, which have descended to them from their ancestors, the power which these affections will acquire amongst such men is inconceivable by those who have only had an opportunity of observing hired labourers, farmers, and the manufacturing poor. Their little tract of land serves as a kind of permanent rallying point for their domestic feelings, as a tablet upon which they are written which makes them

objects of memory in a thousand instances when they would otherwise be forgotten.[27]

By returning to his 'scanty plot of ground', then, Wordsworth is implicitly demonstrating what can be achieved by the cultivation of these
'domestic affections'. And the poem ends by looking forward to the
moment when these carefully preserved and reinvigorated virtues can
once again take their rightful place in the life of the nation. The withdrawal and self-restraint praised in the poem provide 'short solace' at a
difficult moment; when circumstances are more propitious, the poet
can return to untrammelled personal and aesthetic self-determination.

However, the very isolation and self-containment praised in the
poem as necessary virtues during a period of extreme reaction establish
counter-currents which transform the poet's principles in the act of
seeming to preserve them. One of these counter-currents can be
glimpsed in the striking indifference to gender displayed by Wordsworth in his choice of images of freely chosen imprisonment in the
octave; he is happy to compare himself to a nun and a maid as well as
to a student and a hermit. Such indifference to gender suggests that the
poet's 'remasculinisation' of the sonnet is not a straightforward matter.
By projecting himself into these feminine roles Wordsworth ends up
articulating a new and in many ways radically altered version of masculinity, one which includes not just self-restraint and fortitude in
adversity, but also domesticity, seclusion and passivity, and in so doing
anticipates some of the key features of the 'monastic discourse' which
Herbert Sussman identifies as an important vehicle for the analysis of
'the problematics and the contradictory possibilities of manhood'
during the Victorian period.[28] And Wordsworth's Victorian successors
also saw much to admire in the poem's apparent inversion of the qualities of freedom and restriction. Unlimited freedom comes to be seen as
a burden, a restraint, a kind of imprisonment; while submission to
authority – even the arbitrary authority of poetic tradition – is increasingly seen as a kind of liberation or release. The poet's joy at casting off
'the weight of too much liberty' is paralleled in another of the poems
of 1807, the 'Ode to Duty':

> Me this unchartered freedom tires;
> I feel the weight of chance desires:
> My hopes no more must change their name,
> I long for a repose which ever is the same.

('Ode to Duty', ll. 37–40)[29]

It is these suggestions of an alternative scale of values which make the Prefatory Sonnet, and indeed the turn towards the Miltonic sonnet which it announces, important elements in Wordsworth's gradual but inexorable transition from youthful radicalism to moralistic conservatism. The sonnets are the crucible in which the 'Victorian' Wordsworth is formed, and they were recognised as such by his Victorian admirers and imitators. In his 1841 review of Wordsworth's sonnets Sir Henry Taylor describes the Prefatory Sonnet as a 'doctrinal poem', and goes on to draw out its message in plain terms:

> [No] enlargement of a man's liberty of action can take place without a corresponding aggravation of his moral responsibility, and... there must needs be some souls which 'feel the weight of too much liberty,' – such, that is, whose liberty of action is disproportionate to their strength of judgment or of self-control, and must therefore either oppress their conscience, or vex them with the perplexities of an undetermined choice or the consequences of an ungoverned will... Such, then, are the views of moral restraint indicated in this poem; and the drift of it is to bring this species of restraint into a comparison mutually illustrative with the restraint imposed by the laws of the sonnet upon an exuberant and discursive imagination. As of the moral will, so of the intellect: as in life, so in art. The law to which the sonnetteer submits himself, substitutes the restraint of a mechanical limitation for restraint by effort of judgment.[30]

Taylor highlights the reflexive dimension of the poem; the rules of the sonnet find their moral equivalent in the notion of duty, which provides the individual with a prefabricated set of moral imperatives. Taylor, indeed, goes on to note the similarities between the Prefatory Sonnet and the 'Ode to Duty', and finds other parallels in Wordsworth's later work, such as this passage from 'The Pass of Kirkstone' (1820):

> And I (as all men may find cause,
> When life is at a weary pause,
> And they have panted up the hill
> Of duty with reluctant will)
> Be thankful, even though tired and faint,
> For the rich bounties of constraint;
> Whence oft invigorating transports flow
> That choice lacked courage to bestow! (ll. 53–60)

In reading the Prefatory Sonnet as a 'doctrinal' poem, however, Taylor omits any sense of its delicate balance of forces; and a similarly coarsened or simplified response can be seen in Leigh Hunt's observations on the poem:

> It is a very bold general proposition to say that 'nuns fret not at their narrow rooms' and that 'hermits are content with their cells'. Thousands of nuns, there is no doubt, have fretted horribly, and do fret; and hermitages have proved so little satisfactory, that we no longer hear of their existence in civilised countries. We are to suppose, however, that the poet alludes only to such nuns and hermits as have been willing to be solitary. So also in regard to the spinning maids, and the weavers. The instances are not thoroughly happy; for the spinning and the weaving are too often anything but voluntary, however cheerfully made the best of.[31]

Writing during the 1850s, Hunt seems oblivious to the possibility that Wordsworth might have intended us to notice the ambiguity of his 'instances' in the octave. His Wordsworth is the sage and moraliser who presided over and sanctified the pieties of Victorian England, not the perplexed revolutionary caught at a moment of transition between two selves.

In the 1807 volume the Prefatory Sonnet introduces two series of sonnets: the 'Miscellaneous Sonnets' and the 'Sonnets Dedicated to Liberty'. In grouping his sonnets together in this way, even under the heading 'Miscellaneous', Wordsworth departs from Miltonic precept and indicates a residual allegiance to the elegiac sonnet tradition. Milton's sonnets are autonomous and free-standing entities; the liberation of the individual sonnet from the Petrarchan sequence is one of the most significant aspects of Milton's legacy for Wordsworth. And he imitates Milton to the extent that each of his poems is robust enough to stand alone without the support of a sequence, as the frequency with which individual sonnets from these two series have been anthologised indicates. However, unlike Milton, Wordsworth remains highly sensitive to the possibility of interaction between individual sonnets, and it is this sensitivity which leads to his restless grouping and regrouping of them into different formations. A number of the 'Sonnets Dedicated to Liberty' first appeared (in a different order) in the *Morning Chronicle* during 1802–3, and seem in that incarnation to form a series with what

Alan Liu calls 'a calculated interlacing of theme and imagery'.[32] There is, moreover, some evidence that the 'Westminster Bridge' sonnet was originally part of a series of poems commemorating Wordsworth's visit to Calais in 1802, and that it was separated from the other 'Calais Tour' sonnets in a typically Wordsworthian act of repression and displacement designed to obscure his personal engagement with the public events discussed in the other poems.[33] The 1807 ordering is not definitive either; both series are broken up, recast and assimilated to larger groupings in Wordsworth's later work. This obsessive revisiting and recasting of the legacy of the past gives the poems something like an organic connection to Wordsworth's life – each new constellation reveals new aspects of familiar experiences and connections between apparently disparate events – and its most obvious precursor is Charlotte Smith's *Elegiac Sonnets*, which went through a similar process of revision and expansion throughout her career.

To describe the 'Miscellaneous Sonnets' and the 'Sonnets Dedicated to Liberty' as 'sequences' is, then, somewhat misleading, as it implies a degree of premeditation and formal organisation which neither possesses.[34] Both work, rather, by exploiting what Wordsworth calls 'lurking affinities' between different sonnets to produce an oblique record of the poet's endless re-examination and revision of his personal history.[35] Alan Liu suggests that Wordsworth is drawn to the Miltonic sonnet at this period because it allows him to articulate his conflicting impulses; the form 'virtually demands thematic opposition between octet [sic] and sestet', and so enables him to stage arguments between the different aspects of himself. But Liu adds that this form is 'especially suited to reifying turns of mind', and 'tends to freeze the antithetical moment into glacial composure'.[36] Wordsworth's 'elegiac' use of the Miltonic sonnet, however, introduces an element of fluidity and instability beneath this apparently immobile surface; the connections he establishes within and between the two series of poems allow them to become a living record of these contradictions and unresolved tensions rather than simply a monument to them.

The twenty 'Miscellaneous Sonnets' have little obvious connection with one another; personal reminiscences and observations are mingled with sonnets 'To Sleep' and translations from Michelangelo. They are, as the first of them makes clear, avowedly products of the 'Fancy' rather than the imagination, and therefore 'as capricious as the accidents of things' in their choice of subject matter:[37]

How sweet it is, when mother Fancy rocks
The wayward brain, to saunter through a wood!
An old place, full of many a lovely brood,
Tall trees, green arbours, and ground flowers in flocks;
And Wild rose tip-toe upon hawthorn stocks,
Like to a bonny Lass, who plays her pranks
At Wakes and Fairs with wandering Mountebanks,
When she stands cresting the Clown's head, and mocks
The crowd beneath her. Verily I think
Such place to me is sometimes like a dream
Or map of the whole world: thoughts, link by link
Enter through ears and eyesight, with such gleam
Of all things, that at last in fear I shrink,
And leap at once from the delicious stream.

Jennifer Ann Wagner uses this poem to illustrate what she calls the 'synecdochic' relation between the sonnet and the epic; the sonnet is construed as containing a 'miniature version' of the 'visionary gleam' which it is the job of Wordsworth's more ambitious poems to explore at length.[38] But this reading overlooks the fact that what we see in this poem is not an embracing of the 'visionary gleam' but a turning away from it. The emphasis throughout is on precisely that 'wayward' or (to use a word Wordsworth uses in talking about one of the other 'Miscellaneous Sonnets') 'wanton' power of the mind to make forced links between disparate objects characteristic of the fancy rather than the imagination.[39] The poet's 'wayward' brain is 'rocked' by 'mother Fancy' as he wanders through a wood, and the immediate product of this state is a highly fanciful image of the wild rose as a young girl looking down at a crowd from behind a clown's head at a country fair. When, however, the characteristic Wordsworthian vocabulary of visionary experience begins to appear in the sestet – 'link by link', 'gleam' – the poet, prompted by 'fear', beats a hasty retreat from this 'stream' of thought. The poem is determined to remain within its self-assigned limits. There is a similar emphasis on playfulness and the refusal or avoidance of the higher imaginative powers in 'Beloved Vale!' (sonnet 15) which deals with one of the commonplaces of the elegiac sonnet tradition, the 'revisit' to a place of significance.[40] In some of Wordsworth's poetry this 'revisit' motif yields moments of profound insight, but in this instance there is no visionary gleam: 'no fears/ Distress'd me; I look'd round, I shed no tears;/ Deep thought or awful vision I had none' (ll. 6–8). In the absence of the imaginative sublime, the 'fancy' has licence to play across the poet's mind;

the trees of his childhood become '[mere] dwarfs', and the rest of the landscape is reduced to 'Juggler's Balls old Time about him toss'd' (ll. 11, 12). This underlying metaphor (or 'underthought', to use Hopkins's terminology) of the circus is shared by both sonnets, and strongly suggests that the sonnet is not the appropriate medium for the exercise of the most exalted powers of the mind. Wordsworth's ambivalence about the status of the sonnet was to be one of his most enduring and troubling legacies for his nineteenth-century successors in the form.

Beneath this surface miscellaneousness it is, however, possible to detect some common themes and motifs which give shape and direction to the group. The three translations 'From the Italian of Michelangelo', for example, reiterate the Prefatory Sonnet's implicit equation between submission to the rules of the sonnet and moral self-restraint. They put forward a severe and uncompromising asceticism; the soul expresses its desire to soar beyond the visible world and discover the spiritual: 'For what delights the sense is false and weak,/ Ideal Form, the universal mould' (11, ll. 7–8). This 'universal mould' is, of course, imaged in the 'Ideal Form' of the sonnet itself; and Michael Angelo's submission to it is all the more impressive given the evident capacity to respond to the world of the senses provided by his work in the visual arts.[41] Similarly, in sonnet 17, 'To the —', the poet implicitly compares the activity of sonnet writing to the framing of beds for winter flowers during the early days of spring, an image which has a 'lurking affinity' with the Prefatory Sonnet's representation of the form as a 'scanty plot of ground'. Such structures are, the poem suggests, appropriate for times when 'the sun of life more feebly shines', and promise thoughts of 'solemn gloom' to their inhabitants. Moreover, as in the Prefatory Sonnet, this submission to the rules of the form is more than simply a temporary expedient; the poem ends with the idea that the 'perennial bowers', in spite of their less immediately attractive appearance, might eventually prove as 'gracious as the music and the bloom/ And all the mighty ravishment of Spring'. Far from being simply a 'short solace' during unpropitious times, the certainties of the sonnet might become for the poet a permanent shelter even when the longed-for spring has returned. This theme of self-restraint is also explored in the poem 'To the Memory of Raisley Calvert', the last of the 'Miscellaneous Sonnets'. Calvert was a friend of Wordsworth's who died at the age of 21 in 1795, leaving the poet a legacy of £900 so that he could devote himself to poetry. The 'early liberty' which this gave the poet was, however, a paradoxical and 'frugal' liberty which found its highest expression in self-denial:

> This care was thine when sickness did condemn
> Thy youth to hopeless wasting, root and stem;
> That I, if frugal and severe, might stray
> Where'er I liked... (ll. 4–7)

The poet could 'stray/ Where'er [he] lik'd'; but the very existence of this sonnet, and indeed the poet's voluntary subjection to the sonnet form, illustrate how willing he is to be appropriately 'frugal and severe' in the enjoyment of his liberty. And throughout the collection there is an emphasis, consistent with the Prefatory Sonnet, on remaining within limits and boundaries. The poet is anxious at the sight of ships about to set sail for unknown foreign lands, and wishes them in a 'Haven' rather than on the perilous sea (2, l. 9). Even the sonnets addressed to Sleep, which might be seen as the most obviously derivative in the collection, drawing as they do on one of the commonplaces of the Renaissance sonnet, praise sleep as a 'blessed barrier twixt day and day' (6, l. 13) and as '[a] Captive never wishing to be free' (5, l. 4).

In the second of the sonnets 'To Sleep' the poet tries to lull himself into unconsciousness by thinking about an image from the Prefatory Sonnet: 'A flock of sheep that leisurely pass by,/ One after one; the sound of rain, and bees/ Murmuring...' (ll. 1–3). This typifies the tendency of the 'Miscellaneous Sonnets' to recycle and amplify one another's images and motifs; and the poem in which this kind of allusion is most obvious is the sonnet 'Composed Upon Westminster Bridge'. This much anthologised and endlessly imitated poem, probably the most famous sonnet of the nineteenth century, perfectly illustrates the ineradicable tension between the individual sonnet and the series in Wordsworth's writing. Its ability to survive without the other poems in its group – whether we take that group to be the 'Miscellaneous Sonnets' or the reconstructed 'Calais Tour' to which Liu assigns it – is self-evident, and yet reinsertion into these contexts adds resonance to almost all of its features:

> Earth has not anything to shew more fair:
> Dull would he be of soul who could pass by
> A sight so touching in it's majesty:
> This City now doth like a garment wear
> The beauty of the morning; silent, bare,
> Ships, towers, domes, theatres, and temples lie
> Open unto the fields, and to the sky;
> All bright and glittering in the smokeless air.

Never did sun more beautifully steep
In his first splendor valley, rock, or hill;
Ne'er saw I, never felt, a calm so deep!
The river glideth at his own sweet will:
Dear God! the very houses seem asleep;
And all that mighty heart is lying still!

The list of features in line 6 looks at first like the product of observation, in a poem which owes a great deal to the 'loco-descriptive' and meditative sonnets of late-eighteenth-century sonnet-writers like Bowles. Yet the '[ships]' also recall sonnets 2 and 8, and look forward (as we shall see below) to the various uses of the motifs of sailing and seafaring in the 'Sonnets Dedicated to Liberty'; the 'towers' look back to the 'pensive Citadels' of the students in the Prefatory sonnet; the 'domes' are associated with Michelangelo, architect of St Peter's in Rome; while a 'Grecian Temple' features in the two sonnets dealing with the journey across the Hamilton hills taken by Wordsworth on the day of his marriage.[42] Moreover, the poem as a whole allocates a new place to London within the symbolic economy of his poetry. In *Lyrical Ballads* and in the (as yet unpublished) *Prelude*, London is represented as a place of social and personal disintegration, the very antithesis of the stable and knowable rural community which represented for Wordsworth the source of civic virtue. This association of London with corruption is obscurely but powerfully connected with the influence of London on Wordsworth himself; London was the place where he learned his political radicalism and associated himself with people sympathetic to the aims of the French Revolution.[43] In 'Westminster Bridge', however, London is presented far more positively. It is not only compared to natural phenomena, but is more beautiful than 'valley, rock or hill' in the early morning light; it earns the magical Wordsworthian epithet 'glittering'; and the river Thames 'glideth at his own sweet will', unforced by the pace of industry or commerce. Far from being a cancerous growth on the healthy body of the nation, London is seen as its 'mighty heart'. Perhaps most interestingly, Wordsworth commends the 'majesty' of the city. This word is always loaded with political significance; to anticipate for a moment, the second of the 'Sonnets Dedicated to Liberty' condemns the French people for rushing to celebrate Napoleon's 'new-born Majesty'. The use of the term in 'Westminster Bridge' has about it a studied political neutrality; the 'majesty' inheres in the people and the city, not in any individual; but it nevertheless leaves open the possibility of an identification of the two kinds of majesty.

As this poem makes clear, there is a latent political dimension to the 'Miscellaneous Sonnets'; the images developed in them leak into and colour the 'Sonnets Dedicated to Liberty', reinforcing and occasionally contradicting the overt political message of the latter. Wordsworth seems to have regarded the 'Sonnets Dedicated to Liberty' as the more unified and integrated of the two groups, even going so far as to describe it as a single connected poem:

> [The sonnets] to Liberty, at least, have a connection with, or a bearing upon, each other, and therefore, if individually they want weight, perhaps, as a Body, they may not be so deficient, at least this ought to induce you to suspend your judgement, and qualify it so far as to allow that the writer aims at least at comprehensiveness. But dropping this, I would boldly say at once, that these Sonnets, while they each fix the attention upon some important sentiment separately considered, do at the same time collectively make a Poem on the subject of civil Liberty and national independence, which, either for simplicity of style or grandeur of moral sentiment, is, alas! likely to have few parallels in the Poetry of the present day.[44]

In these sonnets Wordsworth presents himself as nurturing and pre-serving a national tradition of virtuous republicanism derived, above all, like the sonnets themselves, from the work and example of Milton; but this representation merges insensibly with a puritanical, national-istic and ultimately conservative rhetoric. England is both admonished for failing to live up to its heritage, and celebrated as a haven of liberty in a Europe increasingly dominated by Napoleonic tyranny. The series translates into overtly political terms the fundamental paradox of the Prefatory Sonnet, praising the self-restraint and acceptance of the 'low-liest duties' necessary during the national emergency of the war with Napoleonic France as manifestations of the highest and most enduring form of liberty.

The Prefatory Sonnet is, as we have seen, designed to emphasise the peculiar appropriateness of the sonnet form for the task of articulating the benefits of the voluntary renunciation of freedom. This inbuilt res-onance can be heard in the background of many of the 'Sonnets Dedicated to Liberty'. The sonnet beginning 'There is a bondage which is worse to bear', for instance, contrasts the misery of imprisonment with the much worse misery of those who 'must wear/ Their fetters in their Souls':

> For who could be,
> Who, even the best, in such condition, free
> From self-reproach, reproach which he must share
> With Human Nature? (ll. 6–9)

The word 'free' at the end of the line is allowed to release its full range of connotations before being reined in by the adjectival phrase which follows it, reiterating the poem's message that the ability to '[walk] about in the open air' is not, in itself, a guarantee of genuine freedom. Moreover, the rhyme on the word 'free' represents a licence within the Petrarchan sonnet; we should, in lines 6 and 7, be continuing the forbidding rhyme 'wall/ thrall', but Wordsworth allows the poem to break free of this convention in order to emphasise the liberty that can still be achieved by someone 'who breathes, by roof, and floor, and wall,/ Pent in'. The Miltonically sanctioned overflowing of the octave/ sestet division is, in a by-now familiar gesture, employed to emphasise the message that true freedom is compatible with certain forms of confinement.

Wordsworth suggests throughout these sonnets that it is France that has changed, not him; he is keen to stress the continuities between the different versions of himself, and equally keen to stress the French people's willingness to ignore or override the logic of organic growth. This is the key to Wordsworth's condemnation of Napoleon, or rather of the French people for their unseemly willingness to participate in Napoleon's apotheosis. In the second sonnet – headed 'Calais, August, 1802' – Wordsworth reflects on the overwhelming popular vote which allowed Napoleon to assume the title of First Consul for Life. He accuses the French people, in a resounding pun, of being 'to slavery prone', and castigates them for their willingness to worship the 'new-born Majesty'. This phrase deliberately parallels the 'new-born Liberty' remembered and celebrated in the next sonnet (3, l. 4); it also recalls (by contrast) the politically neutral but sublime 'majesty' of London celebrated in the 'Westminster Bridge' sonnet. This weakness in the French people derives from a failure to distinguish between mere prostration before power and the loyal virtue of 'seemly reverence' that cannot be 'sown in haste' or spring up overnight. Sudden change is compared unfavourably with gradual, nature-like transformation; the private and domestic spheres are the 'stalk/ True power doth grow on' (4, ll. 13–14). The use of organic tropes to undermine the rhetoric of revolution was, of course, one of Burke's most successful strategies in

his *Reflections on the Revolution in France*; and Wordsworth might seem
to be aligning himself here with an explicitly counterrevolutionary discourse. But he is criticising France not (as Burke did) for having a revolution at all, but for failing to live up to the ideals of its revolution. The
sonnet 'To Toussaint L'Ouverture', for instance, and the following one
describing the fate of a 'Negro Woman driv'n from France', both
emphasise the extent of the French government's apostasy. The rhetoric of liberty, equality and fraternity has given way to a reinstatement
of the most barbarous and unjustifiable forms of discrimination against
fellow human beings; the proneness to slavery imaged in the submission to Napoleon has resulted in the revival of the institution itself.
France has not allowed its revolution to mature into full liberty.

The poet's attitude towards Britain is altogether more complex and
ambivalent, but again there is a strong suggestion that Wordsworth's
patriotism is continuous and even identical with his earlier Jacobinism.
Some of the sonnets paint an idyllic and sentimentalised portrait of
'England' ideally suited to the task of generating national sentiment.
The tenth sonnet, 'Composed in the Valley, near Dover, On the Day of
landing', celebrates an England of small villages and boys playing
cricket, and explicitly contrasts English freedom with the fact that
'Europe is still in Bonds'.[45] Similarly the poems written during the
invasion scare of late 1803 occasionally employ a deliberately archaic
diction designed to emphasise the origins of English liberty in an idealised medieval past:

> Vanguard of Liberty, ye Men of Kent,
> Ye children of a soil that doth advance
> Its haughty brow against the coast of France,
> Now is the time to prove your hardiment!
> To France be words of invitation sent!
> They from their Fields can see the countenance
> Of your fierce war, may ken the glittering lance,
> And hear you shouting forth your brave intent.
> Left single, in bold parley, Ye, of yore,
> Did from the Norman win a gallant wreath;
> Confirm'd the charters that were yours before; –
> No parleying now! In Britain is one breath;
> We are all with you now from Shore to Shore: –
> Ye Men of Kent, 'tis Victory or Death!

Wordsworth is, of course, invoking the Norman invasion of 1066 in
this sonnet, and attempting to mitigate the unfortunate aspects of this
parallel by alluding to the tradition that the Men of Kent east of the

Medway remained unconquered by the Normans. This invocation of the Saxon/ Norman conflict is, however, slightly more complex and politically ambivalent than it at first sight appears. During the early 1790s Wordsworth was almost certainly in contact with the Society for Constitutional Information, an organisation established to promote political discussion and to press for constitutional reform. One of the tenets of the SCI's creed was the idea that 'the "great Founders" of the English constitution were the Saxons, but the yoke of "arbitrary kings" since the Norman Conquest had destroyed its former charters and liberties'.[46] 'Charters' is a word that Wordsworth uses frequently, often, as here, in close connection with the language of political and civil liberty; it signifies a controlled and orderly liberty, not the 'unchartered freedom' lamented in the 'Ode to Duty'. The historical allusion in this sonnet is, then, nicely poised between two types of 'patriotism'; a new celebration of England and Englishness, and a continuing adherence to the old radical creed.[47] The Men of Kent are the embodiment of English patriotism and warlike spirit, and at the same time the defenders of the ancient liberties of the English constitution against monarchical usurpers. Seen in this latter context, Napoleon begins to appear simply the latest in a long line of such usurpers, and the critique of Napoleon becomes continuous with the radical rhetoric of Wordsworth's earlier self.

Throughout the 'Sonnets Dedicated to Liberty', Britain is both the bulwark of liberty – 'the only light/ Of Liberty that yet remains on Earth!' (18, ll. 13–14) – and the target of Wordsworth's increasingly stern moral admonition for its failure to live up to its own heritage of liberty. This ambivalence is woven into the metaphorical fabric of the sonnets. The opening sonnet of the collection sees the poet standing on the sea-front near Calais and looking back longingly towards his own 'dear Country'. In a typically Wordsworthian manoeuvre, this gesture is mediated by reflections on the 'Fair Star of Evening', which seems to the poet to have become the 'Star of my Country' and 'a glorious crest/ Conspicuous to the Nations':

> Thou, I think,
> Should'st be my Country's emblem; and should'st wink,
> Bright star! with laughter on her banners, drest
> In thy fresh beauty. There! that dusky spot
> Beneath thee, it is England: there it lies. (ll. 6–10)

The star should be the emblem of Britain – it should, indeed, takes its place on Britain's flag. There were, of course, stars on the flag of the recently founded American Republic, a Republic often seen as the harbinger of the French Revolution and indeed of democratic reform throughout Europe. In the last line and a half of this extract Wordsworth almost seems to be urging the star to recognise its true home; the 'dusky spot' of England needs the guidance of the star, but does not, at the moment, seem to have it. The poem, then, implies that Britain needs to change in order to become worthy of the emblem; and the kind of change required is indicated most clearly in 'London, 1802':

> Milton! thou should'st be living at this hour:
> England hath need of thee: she is a fen
> Of stagnant waters: altar, sword and pen,
> Fireside, the heroic wealth of hall and bower,
> Have forfeited their ancient English dower
> Of inward happiness. We are selfish men;
> Oh! raise us up, return to us again;
> And give us manners, virtue, freedom, power.
> Thy soul was like a star and dwelt apart:
> Thou hadst a voice whose sound was like the sea;
> Pure as the naked heavens, majestic, free,
> So didst thou travel on life's common way,
> In chearful godliness; and yet thy heart
> The lowliest duties on itself did lay.

Milton is the 'star' whose soul 'dwelt apart' from his selfish fellow countrymen; but it is not Milton the republican and apologist for regicide who is celebrated here so much as Milton the Puritan. The first surprise in this sonnet comes in the sixth line, a surprise emphasised by the full stop at what seems an oddly disruptive moment in the sonnet. One might expect the 'ancient English dower' forfeited by Wordsworth and his contemporaries to be freedom, but instead it is the curiously anodyne 'inward happiness'. Milton is charged with giving us back our 'freedom' a few lines later, but the word is concealed in a list of moral qualities: 'manners', 'virtue', and 'power'. The Milton of the sestet, for all his metaphorical majesty, is a stoical figure who '[travels] on life's common way' and accepts the 'lowliest duties' with 'chearful godliness'. The political implications of Wordsworth's invocation of Milton are, then, muted and transformed by the emphasis on his moral and personal qualities.

These complexities are underscored by frequent internal allusion of the kind seen in the 'Westminster Bridge' sonnet. The sonnet to Milton, for instance, gestures with almost telegraphic abruptness towards the nation's heritage in its third line: 'altar, sword and pen' signify respectively the church, the hereditary knighthood, and the ancient universities. It is the voluntary forfeiture of their birthright by these estates which signifies the moral bankruptcy of the nation; hence (to return to the Prefatory Sonnet) the need for students to remain in their 'pensive Citadels' and not 'desert/ The Student's bower for gold' (17, ll. 3–4). The most striking example of this kind of 'lurking affinity' occurs in the twenty-first sonnet:

> England! the time is come when thou shouldst wean
> Thy heart from its emasculating food;
> The truth should now be better understood;
> Old things have been unsettled; we have seen
> Fair seed-time, better harvest might have been
> But for thy trespasses; and, at this day,
> If for Greece, Egypt, India, Africa,
> Aught good were destined, Thou wouldst step between.
> England! all nations in this charge agree:
> But worse, more ignorant in love and hate,
> Far, far more abject is thine Enemy:
> Therefore the wise pray for thee, though the freight
> Of thy offences be a heavy weight:
> Oh grief! that Earth's best hopes all rest with Thee!

The note of residual radicalism is dominant here. England is charged with numerous 'trespasses' which have prevented its '[fair] seed-time' from ripening into a 'better harvest' – an ominous interruption of the natural order of things. Chief among these seems to be its treatment of foreign and especially non-European countries attempting to liberate themselves; England would 'step between' if any good were intended for these countries in order to preserve its own commercial and financial interests irrespective of the higher claims of morality and justice. The sestet's conclusion that England remains the best hope of the world because France is far worse is given additional force by the unobtrusive word 'freight', which encapsulates Wordsworth's ambivalence towards his own country. It represents the culmination of the motif of ships and seafaring which spans both groups of sonnets, subtly transforming one of the key elements in Wordsworth's symbolic vocabulary and mitigating the force of the poet's condemnation of his own country. In Wordsworth's previous collection, *Lyrical Ballads*, seafaring functions as an emblem of alienation and rootlessness, and is inextricably linked to the largely seaborne war against France. To give just two examples: in 'The Female Vagrant' the 'noisy drum' of the recruiting officer beats round 'to sweep the streets of want and pain', leading directly to the heroine's eventual destitution (ll. 93–4); while in 'The Brothers' the hero Leonard loses his connection to his place of origin and ends up 'a Seaman, a grey-headed Mariner' (l. 449). In the 'Miscellaneous Sonnets', however, Wordsworth begins the process of replacing these negative connotations with more positive ones. The second, 'Where lies the Land to which yon Ship must go?', indicates a certain anxiety at the idea of seafaring, a 'reverential fear', which the poet attempts to counteract by loading the ship with Shakespearean epithets; it is '[as] vigorous as a Lark at break of day', a 'joyous Bark' (ll. 3, 14). In number 8, 'With ships the sea was sprinkled far and nigh', the ships are compared to stars, the highest metaphorical honour in Wordsworth's gift, and the poet's praise of them is not undermined by any reference to fear or trepidation. These sonnets pave the way for the overt identification of the sea with British freedom in the 'Sonnets Dedicated to Liberty'. The 'Thoughts... on the Subjugation of Switzerland', for instance, praise Britain and Switzerland as the voices of freedom emanating from the sea and the mountains respectively; 'London, 1802' describes Milton, the brightest star in Wordsworth's poetic firmament, as having had 'a Voice whose sound was like the sea'; and the sixteenth sonnet, 'It is not to be thought of ', speaks of 'the Flood/ Of British freedom' (ll. 1–2) and of the sea as a 'Road by which all might come and go that would,/ And bear out freights of worth to foreign lands' (ll. 5–6). The reference to the 'freight' of Britain's offences in 'England! the time is come' is, then, very delicately poised between these two opposing senses. The word refers both to the benign process of traffic and commerce, to the carrying of 'freights of worth to foreign lands', and also to the identification of the sea with the misuse of British power for selfish ends.

Wordsworth's rehabilitation of the sonnet in *Poems in Two Volumes* was widely recognised and applauded by his contemporaries. Even Francis Jeffrey, editor of the *Edinburgh Review* and one of Wordsworth's severest critics, exempted the sonnets from his general accusation that the collection was guilty of an 'open violation of the established laws of poetry':

All English writers of sonnets have imitated Milton; and, in this way, Mr. Wordsworth, when he writes sonnets, escapes again from the trammels of his own unfortunate system; and the consequence is, that his sonnets are as much superior to the greater part of his other poems, as Milton's sonnets are superior to his.[48]

Wordsworth himself, moreover, far from finding 'short solace' in the form, was prompted by the success of this venture to make the sonnet one of his most important and enduring modes of expression. Yet he also bequeathed to his successors a legacy of uncertainty about the value of the form itself. The tension between the limitations of the form and the sublimity of the experiences he wishes to record in it leads him occasionally to 'o'erflow the measure', and point towards his own eventual resumption of higher and more ambitious personal and poetic projects.[49] One such moment takes place in the sonnet 'To the River Duddon':

> O mountain Stream! the Shepherd and his Cot
> Are privileg'd Inmates of deep solitude:
> Nor would the nicest Anchorite exclude
> A field or two of brighter green, or Plot
> Of tillage-ground, that seemeth like a spot
> Of stationary sunshine: thou hast view'd
> These only, Duddon! with their paths renew'd
> By fits and starts, yet this contents thee not.
> Thee hath some awful Spirit impell'd to leave,
> Utterly to desert, the haunts of men,
> Though simple thy Companions were and few;
> And through the wilderness a passage cleave,
> Attended but by thy own Voice, save when
> The Clouds and Fowls of the air thy way pursue.

The river here becomes an image of an asceticism so complete that an inversion of values takes place, and what begins as voluntary renunciation becomes heroic self-sacrifice. In the octave we return to the 'scanty plot of ground' of the Prefatory Sonnet, but even this meagre allotment is too opulent for the River Duddon, which is compelled by an 'awful Spirit... Utterly to desert, the haunts of men'. The river becomes a kind of voice crying in the wilderness. This shift is mirrored in the form of the sonnet. There are few Wordsworthian sonnets in which the break between octave and sestet is so complete; the sestet literally 'leaves' the octave behind, adopting a Miltonic cadence and prophetic tone far removed from the latter's homely vocabulary. The approach towards sublimity seems to be putting the sonnet form under some strain; and it is, perhaps, not surprising to find that Wordsworth literally overflowed the boundaries of the sonnet form in this case, eventually making this sonnet the source of an entirely new lyric sequence following the course of the river to the sea.[50]

There is another and perhaps even more significant example of 'overflowing' in a poem which Wordsworth did not feel able to place within either of the two sonnet series in *Poems in Two Volumes*, 'It is no Spirit who from Heaven hath flown':

> It is no Spirit who from Heaven hath flown,
> And is descending on his embassy;
> Nor Traveller gone from Earth the Heavens to espy!
> 'Tis Hesperus – there he stands with glittering crown,
> First admonition that the sun is down!
> For yet it is broad day-light: clouds pass by;
> A few are near him still – and now the sky,
> He hath it to himself – 'tis all his own.
> O most ambitious star! an inquest wrought
> Within me when I recognised thy light;
> A moment I was startled at the sight:
> And, while I gazed, there came to me a thought
> That I might step beyond my natural race
> As thou seem'st now to do; might one day trace
> Some ground not mine; and, strong her strength above,
> My Soul, an Apparition in the place,
> Tread there, with steps that no one shall reprove!

Meditating on the appearance of Hesperus, the 'most ambitious star', Wordsworth feels the urge to 'step beyond' the limits allotted to him; and this thought naturally manifests itself in a transgression of the boundaries of the sonnet. This transgression is, like most of Wordsworth's innovations, sanctioned by Milton, whose sonnet 'On the New Forcers of Conscience under the Long Parliament' represents the most famous example of the 'tailed' or 'caudated' sonnet in English.[51] Wordsworth, however, does not use this form for its traditional satirical purpose, but to announce his intention to leave behind this kind of voluntary self-limitation. The fifteenth line begins with the phrase 'some ground not mine'; the poet has stepped beyond the limits of the 'scanty plot of ground' to which he had previously confined himself, and is ready to resume his highest poetic ambitions. Moreover, in this imagined future, the poet will be free to tread this new ground 'with steps that no one shall reprove'; his transgression of the allotted limits will not be construed as dangerous licence.

2
'Transcripts of the private heart': The Sonnet and Autobiography

Between the publication of *Poems in Two Volumes* in 1807 and Wordsworth's death in 1850, he remained without question the single most important practitioner of the sonnet in the English language. His critical reputation rose steadily throughout the 1820s and 1830s, and the reputation of his sonnets rose along with it. In a review of poems by Alfred and Charles Tennyson in *The Tatler* of March 1831, Leigh Hunt observed *à propos* of the Petrarchan sonnet: 'It has been doubted whether that construction suits the genius of the English language: but the doubt is anterior to the publication of Mr. Wordsworth's sonnets, and after that it would be difficult to repeat it.'[1] By 1833, when his critical reputation was approaching its zenith, many of his contemporaries would have agreed with Alexander Dyce's verdict: 'The success with which [the sonnet] has been recently cultivated by Mr. Wordsworth, would alone have conferred an enduring celebrity on his name, even if he had achieved no other triumphs'.[2] During this period Wordsworth did not simply repeat the gestures of 1807; he continued to experiment and innovate with the form. In 1820 he published a set of sonnets which returned to the 'loco-descriptive' tradition of Bowles, tracing the course and character of the River Duddon, and followed this up with other series recording tours to Scotland and the continent.[3] He produced a series of one hundred and two sonnets on the history of Christianity in England,[4] and a series entitled 'Sonnets upon the Punishment of Death' arguing against the abolition of the death penalty which Leigh Hunt compared to a nightingale encouraging the vigils of a hangman.[5] These innovations, particularly the 'River Duddon' sonnets, helped to facilitate the later nineteenth century's development of the sonnet sequence, but for Wordsworth's contemporaries it was his free-standing Miltonic sonnets which constituted his definitive achievement in the form.

Although it prompted a rash of feeble imitations, Wordsworth's domination of the form seems to have stifled the efforts of many of his more ambitious contemporaries; it is notable that most of the 'second generation' of Romantic poets avoided the sonnet, or ended up abandoning it. One of the few things which prompted Wordsworth's younger contemporaries to take up the sonnet was the coupling, insisted on so stridently by Wordsworth himself, of Wordsworth and Milton. Wordsworth's attempt to portray himself as the legitimate heir of the Miltonic tradition in English poetry was bitterly resented by many in the light of his subsequent political apostasy. Leigh Hunt reflects on Wordsworth's betrayal of this heritage in his sonnet 'To Robert Batty M.D., on his giving me a lock of Milton's hair':

> I'll wear it, not as my inherited due,
> (For there is one, whom had he kept his art
> For freedom still, nor left her for the crew
> Of lucky slaves in his misgiving heart,
> I would have begged thy leave to give it to)
> Yet not without some claims, though far apart (ll. 9–14)

And Shelley tropes on Wordsworth's own resonant description of Milton – 'Thy soul was like a Star and dwelt apart' – in his lament for the lost leader:

> Poet of Nature, thou hast wept to know
> That things depart which never may return:
> Childhood and youth, friendship and love's first glow,
> Have fled like sweet dreams, leaving thee to mourn.
> These common woes I feel. One loss is mine
> Which thou too feel'st, yet I alone deplore.
> Thou wert as a lone star, whose light did shine
> On some frail bark in winter's midnight roar:
> Thou hast like to a rock-built refuge stood
> Above the blind and battling multitude:
> In honoured poverty thy voice did weave
> Songs consecrate to truth and liberty, –
> Deserting these, thou leavest me to grieve,
> Thus having been, that thou shouldst cease to be.[6]

But it was not simply unhappiness with Wordsworth's usurpation of the Miltonic tradition which lay behind this widespread unease with the form. There was also a feeling that it was fascinating but trivial, a mere technical exercise which took the place of more substantial poetic exertion. Coleridge certainly seems to have felt this; as Daniel Robinson has pointed out, the sonnet is a 'source of anxiety and embarrassment' for Coleridge during the 1790s: 'I love Sonnets,' he wrote to John Thelwall in 1796, 'but upon my honour I do not love my Sonnets.'[7] As an atavistic and arbitrary form, it seemed to lie on the wrong side of Coleridge's distinction between 'Form as proceeding' and 'Shape as superinduced': 'the latter either the death or the imprisonment of the Thing; the former its self-witnessing and self-effected sphere of agency.'[8] Wordsworth had, as we have seen, found a resonant and poetically fertile use for this 'imprisoning' shape, but his successors were inclined to be much less sanguine about the benefits of imprisonment. The author of the *Prometheus Unbound* could never, as Leigh Hunt puts it, 'content himself in these sequestered corners of poetry. He was always, so to speak, for making world-wide circuits of humanity'.[9]

It is against this background that Keats' formal experiments with the sonnet, and in particular his rediscovery of the Shakespearean sonnet, should be seen. The story of the stylistic evolution of Keats' sonnets is a familiar one. He begins by adopting the legitimate or Petrarchan form under the aegis of Wordsworth and Leigh Hunt, but from the beginning there are signs of a certain restlessness with its restrictions and limitations. There is little respect for the formal division into octave and sestet, and, as Walter Jackson Bate points out, a systematic failure to observe the line-end caesura.[10] This restlessness eventually produces a number of formal experiments. The sonnet 'To my Brother George', composed in 1816, follows the Petrarchan form but finishes with an epigrammatic couplet in the Shakespearean manner, while one of the sonnets addressed to Benjamin Robert Haydon boldly omits the last five syllables of the penultimate line in order to allow the reader to listen for 'the hum/ Of mighty workings'. This impatience with the Petrarchan form eventually resulted in a decisive switch to the Shakespearean sonnet in January 1818. Keats was engaged at this time in a vigorous and almost frenzied rediscovery of Shakespeare, so it is not surprising that he should have turned to the Shakespearean sonnet as a potential model. He uses a hybrid of the Petrarchan and Shakespearean forms to record his feelings 'On sitting down to read *King Lear* once again', and adopts the fully-fledged Shakespearean form in 'When I have fears that I may cease to be'. In this poem, according to Jonathan Bate, 'the Shakespearean sonnet is actively revived, both formally and tonally, by a major English poet for the first time in two hundred years:'[11]

> When I have fears that I may cease to be
> Before my pen has glean'd my teeming brain,
> Before high-piled books, in charactery,
> Hold like rich garners the full ripen'd grain;
> When I behold, upon the night's starr'd face,
> Huge cloudy symbols of a high romance,
> And think that I may never live to trace
> Their shadows, with the magic hand of chance;
> And when I feel, fair creature of an hour,
> That I shall never look upon thee more,
> Never have relish in the faery power
> Of unreflecting love;---then on the shore
> Of the wide world I stand alone, and think
> Till love and fame to nothingness do sink.

This is not merely reminiscent of Shakespeare in its structure and subject matter, but includes (as Keats' editors and critics have noted) a number of allusions to individual sonnets.[12] Shakespeare's twelfth sonnet – 'When I do count the clock that tells the time' – also begins each quatrain with an adverbial clause of time, and contains in its central quatrain, as Jonathan Bate points out, an image recycled by Keats in the opening four lines of his poem:

> When lofty trees I see barren of leaves,
> Which erst from heat did canopy the herd,
> And summers green all girded up in sheaves
> Borne on the bier with white and bristly beard. (ll. 5–8)

There is, however, a significant difference of emphasis in the use of this metaphor in the two sonnets. Shakespeare's sonnet is directed throughout towards the addressee; it is the effect of the passage of time on his beauty which is lamented. Keats' poem, on the other hand, is directed towards himself, and more specifically towards his own poetic production. Keats' metaphor therefore reverses the polarity of Shakespeare's. For Shakespeare, the harvest is a funeral procession mourning the passing of 'summers green'; for Keats, it is the time in which the 'full-ripen'd grain' of poetry can be safely gathered in. There is a similar desire for an early harvest in the unrhymed sonnet 'O thou whose face

hath felt the winter's wind' with its promise to those who have sur-
vived the harshness of winter: 'To thee the spring will be a harvest-
time' (l. 4). Such a telescoping of spring and autumn, seed-time and
harvest, has an irresistible autobiographical resonance in the light of
Keats' early death, and in this respect renders Keats' sonnets available
for the kind of reading Shakespeare's received later in the century.[13]

Keats' revival of the Shakespearean sonnet was, however, neither prolonged nor consistent. He continued to experiment with unrhymed and
'hybrid' sonnets, and in a well-known letter of May 1819 articulates his
unhappiness both with the 'pouncing rhymes' of the 'legitimate' sonnet, and with the excessively elegiac quality of the Shakespearean
version, adding that 'the couplet at the end of it has seldom a pleasing
effect'.[14] This dissatisfaction led in a number of different directions. An
incomplete translation of a sonnet by Ronsard, along with the late
sonnets addressed to Fanny Brawne, suggests a tentative movement
towards the revival of the amatory sonnet sequence; but the decisive
movement was away from the sonnet form itself:

> If by dull rhymes our English must be chained,
> And, like Andromeda, the sonnet sweet
> Fettered, in spite of painèd loveliness,
> Let us find out, if we must be constrained,
> Sandals more interwoven and complete
> To fit the naked foot of Poesy.
> Let us inspect the lyre, and weigh the stress
> Of every chord, and see what may be gained
> By ear industrious, and attention meet;
> Misers of sound and syllable, no less
> Than Midas of his coinage, let us be
> Jealous of dead leaves in the bay wreath crown;
> So, if we may not let the Muse be free,
> She will be bound with garlands of her own.

This sonnet adopts a more 'interwoven and complete' rhyme scheme
than either the Petrarchan or the Shakespearean. The distance between
rhymes – no two rhymes are closer than three lines apart until the end
– means that the relative proximity of 'crown' and 'own' in the closing
lines succeeds in imparting a sense of closure to the poem without the
need for a final couplet. Even this experimental sonnet, however,
emphasises the pain and constriction which the form inflicts on
Andromeda, and fails to eliminate all the 'dead leaves in the bay

wreath crown'; and Keats eventually abandons the sonnet, or rather subsumes it into the freer and more flexible ten-line stanzas of his great odes.

Like the rest of his poetry, Keats' sonnets made little immediate impact on his contemporaries; 'On First Looking into Chapman's Homer' finds its way into Alexander Dyce's 1833 anthology of English sonnets, but nothing else does. His revival of the Shakespearean sonnet was, however, destined to become important later on in the century, as poets looked for alternatives to the Miltonic-Wordsworthian model. His elaborately metaphorical neo-Elizabethan diction influences the work of the Pre-Raphaelite poets, and by the end of the century he is being ranked alongside Shakespeare, Milton and Wordsworth as one of the pre-eminent masters of the English sonnet form.[15] In the introduction to his 1886 anthology *Sonnets of This Century* William Sharp states that Keats 'has never been and probably never will be a really popular poet', but adds that 'his influence on other poets and on poetic temperaments generally has been quite incalculable'.[16] The aesthetes and decadents of the later part of the century came to see in Keats' isolated rediscovery of the Shakespearean sonnet a poignant anticipation of their own more wide-ranging attempt to revive the values and beliefs of the Renaissance.[17]

An exception to the general rule that the second generation of Romantic poets avoided the sonnet should also be made in the case of John Clare, the Northamptonshire 'peasant-poet' who shared a publisher with Keats.[18] Clare was a prolific sonnet writer who seems to have seen the sonnet as a kind of poetic device for recording immediate and spontaneous impressions: 'I have made up my mind to write one hundred Sonnets as a set of pictures on the scenes of objects that appear in the different seasons & as I shall do it soly for amusement I shall take up wi gentle & simple as they come whatever in my eye finds any interests not merely in the view for publication but for attempts'.[19] The pictorial metaphor used by Clare here has been adopted by many of his critics; Jonathan Bate suggests that 'Clare found in the sonnet the place where he could sketch the glimpses and glancing recollections that meant so much to him', and the editors of the *Northborough Sonnets* note that it has 'become common to draw a comparison between the Northborough sonnets and [Thomas] Bewick's engravings'.[20] This 'pictorial' use of the sonnet anticipates the Pre-Raphaelite and aesthetic sensibility which represented the form as a kind of photographic record of experience, and might have been expected to appeal to a poet like Keats who longed for a life of sensations rather than thoughts.[21] Keats is, however, reported to have said that in Clare's poetry 'Images from Nature are too much introduced without being called for by a particular Sentiment', and this suggestion that Clare's poems make painstaking description of natural objects an end in itself has become commonplace in criticism of his work, and especially of his sonnets.[22] For some critics, the apparent absence of any organising principle or intellectual framework behind his sonnets produces a daring and novel poetry 'almost breathtakingly devoid of overt comment'; but for others it suggests that the sonnet becomes in his work a kind of default setting for poetry which eventually induces an insensibility to the poetic potential of the form.[23]

The sonnets in Clare's early collections repeatedly betray the contradictions between the ideal of rustic life which made the early nineteenth-century public receptive to his poetry and the harsh realities of rural poverty. In *The Village Minstrel*, sonnets praising rural retirement and the pleasures of the poet's 'lowly cot' are juxtaposed with others reminding the reader of Clare's actual position in the world:

> Life, thou art misery, or as such to me;
> One name serves both, or I no difference see;
> Tho' some there live would call thee heaven below,
> But that's a nickname I've not learn'd to know:
> A wretch with poverty and pains replete,
> Where even useless stones beneath his feet
> Cannot be gather'd up to say 'they're mine,'
> Sees little heaven in a life like thine.[24]

Clare was a great admirer of Wordsworth's sonnets – 'his Sonnet on "Westminster Bridge"... owns no equal in the English language' – and in some of these early poems there are suggestions of a Wordsworthian attention to the poetic potential of the form's limitations.[25] As someone who was bound to his 'scanty plot of ground' by social class and grinding poverty rather than choice, Clare seems to have been aware of the sonnet's ability to provide an image of his own predicament. In his reading of one of Clare's many manuscript sonnets – 'I walked with poesy in the sonnets bounds' – John Barrell notes the way in which it establishes an equation between the sonnet form and Clare's own 'imprisonment' within the village of Helpston and its immediate environment, an imprisonment which his brief literary celebrity had not enabled him to escape: 'the form of the sonnet is identified with the "bounds" of a landscape, and it restricts him... to his "knowledge"... to break out of the sonnet form is, precisely, to go out of his knowledge into the freedom of the wilderness'.[26] In making the sonnet an emblem of imprisonment Clare is, of course, following Wordsworth's example; and in referring, as he does in this poem, to the 'sonnets little garden home' he is both appropriating and personalising Wordsworth's governing image from the Prefatory Sonnet. Moreover, like Wordsworth, Clare uses the limitations of the form to articulate his ambivalence about the restrictions to which he is subject. To quote Barrell again, '[the] sense of place... that Clare's sonnets express is closely related to his consciousness of their form: the alternative possibility, the long poem, has the same attractions and arouses the same apprehensions as does the thought of leaving the "crampt circle" of his knowledge.'[27] Helpston appears repeatedly in his poetry as both the enabling condition of Clare's creativity and the limit from which it can never really escape.

It is, in fact, when Clare leaves the 'bounds' of his native village that his consciousness of and ability to exploit the 'bounds' of the sonnet form disappear.[28] The intricate rhyme-scheme of sonnets like 'I walked with poesy', which closely parallels the 'interwoven' form of Keats' 'If by dull rhymes', is replaced by a tendency to use groups of seven rhyming couplets, and to amalgamate these 'sonnets' into straggling narrative series of uncertain size.[29] And there is an increasing sense of alienation from the natural world which had previously been his refuge and delight. The first of the unpublished poems issued by Clare's modern editors as the *Northborough Sonnets* describes the 'hermit nest that lies/ Beneath the old oak in its green disguise', but the third sonnet shows this nest being violated and destroyed. Nature is compared to 'tyrant man' in its merciless cruelty, and the nightingale's carefully constructed nest, deep in the poet's 'weedy orchard hedge', is ransacked by a magpie, which 'like a robber found her home/ & one by one it took away/& murdered musics little heirs'.[30] The nest of the sonnet is clearly no longer a place of safety for Clare, a point brilliantly reinforced by the perplexed and dissonant non-rhyme of these closing lines. Such reflexive moments are, however, very much the exception in the *Northborough Sonnets*. Even the topic of imprisonment – 'Free from the world I would a prisoner be' – fails to produce a gesture towards the limits imposed by the form.[31] Instead we find a poetry in which the boundaries between poems seem to have dissolved altogether; many of the sonnets 'are written in couplets so lacking in connection that they could be arranged in any order in the poem, or exchanged with couplets from other poems on similar subjects without any serious loss'.[32] Clare's later sonnets are, in some senses, not real sonnets at all, but 'only fourteen-line poems' which would be little better or worse 'for being two or three lines shorter or longer': 'There is no inevitableness about them: one feels that the choice of vehicle has been purely arbitrary'.[33]

Wordsworth himself was not immune from a certain amount of unease about the increasing dominance of the sonnet in his own poetic output. In the postscript to the 'River Duddon' sonnets of 1820 he laments 'the restriction which the frame of the Sonnet imposed upon me', arguing that the form '[narrowed] unavoidably the range of thought, and [precluded], though not without its advantages, many graces to which a freer movement of verse would naturally have led'.[34] In a similar vein he complains in a letter to Walter Savage Landor of 1822 that he has 'filled up many a moment in writing Sonnets, which, if I had never fallen into the practice, might easily have been better employed'.[35] And in the 1827 poem with which he closed the second series of 'Miscellaneous Sonnets', the note of apology is clearly dominant:

> If these brief Records, by the Muses' art
> Produced as lonely Nature or the strife
> That animates the scenes of public life
> Inspired, may in thy leisure claim a part;
> And if these Transcripts of the private heart
> Have gained a sanction from thy falling tears;
> Then I repent not. But my soul hath fears
> Breathed from eternity; for as a dart
> Cleaves the blank air, Life flies: now every day
> Is but a glimmering spoke in the swift wheel
> Of the revolving week. Away, away,
> All fitful cares, all transitory zeal!
> So timely Grace the immortal wing may heal,
> And honour rest upon the senseless clay.

The production of sonnets indicates a mind too attuned to the 'revolving week', insufficiently aware of the higher and more arduous claims of eternity. But this apology also indicates a way of justifying the activity of sonnet-writing which was to become increasingly important to Wordsworth and his successors. Wordsworth's initial adoption of the form had, as we saw in the last chapter, been justified as a voluntary renunciation of 'too much liberty', a way of obtaining what the poet describes in 'The Pass of Kirkstone' as 'the rich bounties of constraint' (l. 68); and this justification is still apparent in many of the later sonnets. A sonnet written in 1809 contrasts Swiss resistance to Napoleon with German acquiescence, and praises those who cut through the 'long laborious quest' for absolute moral certainty with the help of 'a few strong instincts and a few plain rules'(l. 11); another written in the character of Mary, Queen of Scots urges heaven to 'contract the compass of my mind/ To fit proportion with my altered state!' (ll. 9–10).[36] But new justifications for the sonnet also begin to emerge as Wordsworth continues to explore the form. 'If these brief records' describes sonnets as '[transcripts] of the private heart', moments in which the poet's private and personal feelings are revealed; and this phrase sums up the attempt in the work of Wordsworth and many of his contemporaries to reposition the sonnet as a site of privileged auto-biographical utterance within the system of poetic genres. This attempt is, as we shall see, inextricably bound up with the rediscovery and revaluation of Shakespeare's sonnets, which are rescued from critical neglect and transformed into the paradigmatic instance of the sonnet-sequence as disguised autobiography.

The tendency to read sonnets as autobiographical utterances is already apparent in the critical response to Charlotte Smith's *Elegiac Sonnets*. Duncan Wu has commented on the 'blend of the confessional and the sentimental' perfected by Smith; her poems seem like heartfelt cries of despair, but withhold from the reader any information about the poet's own circumstances. Smith herself commented enigmatically in the Preface to the sixth edition of the *Elegiac Sonnets* that she wrote 'mournfully' because she was 'unhappy' and had 'unfortunately no reason, though nine years have since elapsed, to change [her] tone'.[37] Such a combination invites speculation, and it is not surprising to find that some early reviewers expressed concern about the poet's mental and emotional well-being.[38] The *Elegiac Sonnets* helped to position the sonnet as a fundamentally autobiographical form, and the kinds of speculations aroused by living writers like Smith were eventually directed towards sonnet writers from previous periods, as Hazlitt's remarks on Milton make clear:

> The great object of the Sonnet seems to be, to express in musical numbers, and as it wore with undivided breath, some occasional thought or personal feeling, 'some fee-grief due to the poet's breast.' It is a sigh uttered from the fulness of the heart, an involuntary aspiration born and dying in the same moment. I have always been fond of Milton's Sonnets for this reason, that they have more of this personal and internal character than any others; and they acquire a double value when we consider that they come from the pen of the loftiest of our poets.[39]

The sonnets are more 'personal and internal' than Milton's more ostentatious public performances; they are sighs 'uttered from the fulness of the heart', the spontaneous overflow of powerful feeling. In a similar vein Thomas Babington Macaulay, writing a decade later, calls Milton's sonnets 'simple but majestic records of the feelings of the poet; as little tricked out for the public eye as his diary would have been'.[40] Even poets regarded as proverbially insincere were reinterpreted as verse-diarists. Petrarch, for instance, had often been taxed with insincerity; in the essay just cited Macaulay refers to 'the hard and brilliant enamel' of Petrarch's style.[41] His elaborate intellectualism, and the way in which he subsumed all events, even the death of his beloved Laura, into his sonnet sequence, had seemed to many, in the words of the Italian exile Ugo Foscolo, evidence that 'his verses were the work less of a lover than of a poet'. But Foscolo goes on to argue that '[in] Petrarch's letters as well as in his poems and treatises, we always identify the author with the man who felt himself irresistibly impelled to develope his own intense feelings', a sentiment echoed by Wordsworth in 'Scorn not the Sonnet': 'the melody/ Of this small lute gave ease to Petrarch's wound' (ll. 3–4).[42]

The most striking example of this autobiographical impulse is, however, to be found in the case of Shakespeare's sonnets. The sonnets were slow to share in the late eighteenth-century resurgence of Shakespeare's critical reputation. According to Nathan Drake's *Literary Hours*, published in 1798, they are 'buried beneath a load of obscurity and quaintness; nor does there issue a single ray of light to quicken, or to warm the heavy mass.'[43] This opinion is implicitly seconded by George Henderson in his *Petrarca: A Selection of Sonnets from Various Authors* (1803), which includes ten sonnets by Sir Brooke Boothby, seven each by Charlotte Smith and Anna Seward, but just two by Shakespeare, and indeed only one by Milton. The charge of 'obscurity and quaintness' against Shakespeare's sonnets was still being repeated by Hazlitt as late as 1815:

> Shakespear's, which some persons better informed in such matters than I can pretend to be, profess to cry up as 'the divine, the matchless, what you will,' – to say nothing of the want of point or a leading, prominent idea in most of them, are I think overcharged and monotonous, and as to their ultimate drift, as for myself, I can make neither head nor tail of it.[44]

Yet, as Hazlitt suggests here in his sarcasm against 'persons better informed in such matters than I can pretend to be', the critical tide was turning in favour of Shakespeare's sonnets. Perhaps the decisive moment in this shift was the translation of August Wilhelm von Schlegel's *Lectures on Dramatic Art and Literature* in 1815, the very year in which Hazlitt made the caustic remarks cited above. Schlegel notes the difficulties involved in obtaining accurate information about Shakespeare's life, but accuses his critics of 'more than ordinary deficiency of critical acumen' for not 'availing themselves of his sonnets for tracing the circumstances of his life': 'These sonnets trace most unequivocally the actual situation and sentiments of the poet; they make us acquainted with the passions of the man; they even contain remarkable confessions of his youthful errors'.[45] This sentiment is echoed by Wordsworth in the Essay he appended to the Preface to his *Poems of 1815*, in which he describes the whole volume of 'miscellaneous poems' or lyrics of Shakespeare as 'Poems in which Shakespeare expresses his own feelings in his own Person'.[46] The lyrics in general, and the sonnets in particular, constitute an encrypted biography, a 'key' (to use the phrase Wordsworth made famous a few years later in 'Scorn not the Sonnet') with which the heart of this most elusive and 'objective' of poets might be unlocked.

The invitation to decode this sequence and shine light into the dark corners of Shakespeare's life was taken up with enthusiasm by some of Wordsworth's contemporaries. Charles Armitage Brown, for instance, in his 1838 monograph *Shakespeare's Autobiographical Poems*, credits A.W. Schlegel with having 'directed our particular attention' to the sonnets, but adds: 'Since that time few have attempted to unfold their meaning; none with success'.[47] Brown's hypothesis is that the sonnets are not really sonnets, but 'POEMS in the *sonnet-stanza*. These poems are six in number; the first five are addressed to his friend, and the sixth to his mistress. This key, simple as it may appear, unlocks every difficulty, and we have nothing but pure uninterrupted biography'[48] Oddly, in view of the self-evidently Wordsworthian phrasing of this passage, Brown makes no mention of 'Scorn not the Sonnet'; even more remarkably, he does not seem to like Shakespeare's sonnets, and doubts if his discoveries will make them any more popular: 'The conceits and forced metaphors, which in his day seem to have been admired, may be forgiven by us; but the languid prolixity and monotony of cadence, pervading almost all the stanzas, are wearisome to modern readers'[49] But his remarks indicate the strength of the biographical impulse behind this reading of Shakespeare's sonnets. In an age increasingly preoccupied with biography – which followed Wordsworth in making 'What is a Poet?' the centre of its critical preoccupations rather than 'What is Poetry?' – Shakespeare's sonnets seemed to provide vital biographical information about Shakespeare the man, evidence necessary for a proper understanding of his work. Indeed, by the time Thomas Carlyle delivered his lectures on 'The Poet as Hero' in 1840, the sonnets had become the more important part of Shakespeare's work; the plays illustrate the fact that he 'had to write for the Globe Playhouse; his great soul had to crush itself, as it could, into that and no other mould', while the sonnets are his personal testimony: 'Doubt it not, he had his own sorrows; those *Sonnets* of his will even testify expressly in what deep waters he had waded, and swum struggling for his life'.[50]

There is an incipient contradiction between the emphasis on the sonnet as a 'transcript of the private heart', a spontaneous and irrepressible overflow of feeling, and the arbitrary and rule-governed nature of the form itself. This contradiction is apparent in Leigh Hunt's remarks on Shakespeare's sonnets in the review of the Tennysons mentioned earlier. Hunt excuses Shakespeare's failure to write 'legitimate' Petrarchan sonnets by arguing that 'Shakespeare's sonnets... are in one respect of the most legitimate kind. They are evidently written under the impulses of the moment: which is probably one of the reasons why he would not stoop to consider the arbitrary construction.' But he also suggests that a stricter adherence to Petrarchan form would have produced even greater poetry: 'the greater the difficulty, the greater the mastery, provided the current of the poet's words be unimpeded'.[51] This seems to imply that it is the very arbitrary and artificial quality of the sonnet that makes it an appropriate vehicle for the expression of emotion. The rules of the sonnet constitute, in the terms used by the Tractarian poet John Keble, a kind of 'safety-valve', regulating and to a certain extent disguising emotions which demand expression:

> Emotions which in their unrestrained expression would appear too keen and outrageous to kindle fellow feeling in any one, are mitigated, and become comparatively tolerable, not to say interesting to us, when we find them so far under control, as to leave those who feel them at liberty to pay attention to measure, and rhyme, and the other expedients of metrical composition.[52]

Hence the idea of the sonnet as a site of privileged autobiographical utterance can also include the idea that such utterance should be, to a certain extent at least, disguised or encrypted.

This ability to combine expressiveness and decorum – sincere personal utterance and what Keble calls 'modest reserve' – is one of the features that makes the sonnet form so attractive to Wordsworth's immediate successors, and in particular to the women poets of the early nineteenth century. The place of the sonnet within the 'express-ive' poetics underlying the practice of the 'poetesses' has not yet been noted.[53] What Isobel Armstrong calls the 'aesthetics of the *secret*' which dominates women's poetry during the early nineteenth century gives rise not only to various forms of masking and displacement (such as the dramatic monologue), but also to the retention of a privileged site of encoded personal utterance in the sonnet.[54] This heavily rule-governed yet apparently spontaneous form allowed women poets to articulate what Dora Greenwell, in revealingly Wordsworthian lan-guage, calls the 'Open Secret, free to all who could find its key – the secret of a woman's heart, with all its needs, its struggles, and its aspirations'.[55] Moreover, this emphasis on the 'confessional' dimension of the sonnet enabled women writers of the early nineteenth century to revive and amplify the distinctively female tradition of the elegiac sonnet. In writing sonnet sequences obliquely expressing their secret sufferings, both Felicia Hemans and Elizabeth Barrett were following in the footsteps of Charlotte Smith as much as those of Wordsworth.

The three groups of sonnets Felicia Hemans wrote during 1834–5 – 'Records of the Spring of 1834', 'Records of the Autumn of 1834', and 'Thoughts during Sickness'[56] – form a loosely connected autobiographi-cal series taking the reader through the closing stages of the poet's life; the last poem, 'Sabbath Sonnet', is described in a note as 'composed... a few days before [Mrs Hemans's] death, and dictated to her brother'. There is little overt reference to the poet's personal situation, although titles like 'Recovery' (poignantly the penultimate poem of the sequence) allow the reader to construct a vestigial narrative; but there is a contin-ual emphasis on the loss of youth and childhood, the fading glories of this world, and the steadfast consolations of religion and home. (The Mrs Hemans who undermines the domestic pieties of her readers while appearing to endorse them is not to be found in these sonnets.)[57] Moreover, like both Charlotte Smith in the *Elegiac Sonnets* and Words-worth in the 'Miscellaneous Sonnets', Mrs Hemans binds her poems together through the repetition of key phrases and images, the iteration of which allows the later poems to resonate with additional signific-ance. There is, for instance, a chain of imagery introduced in the very first poem of 'Spring', entitled 'A Vernal Thought', connecting the unfrozen streams of spring with the kind of imaginative and personal liberation no longer available to the poet herself. In the next poem, 'To the Sky', Hemans contrasts the 'flashing streams' of the landscapes of her childhood with the 'sounding flow/ Of restless life' in the 'dim city' she currently inhabits (ll. 4, 5–6); and in 'Autumn' she asks the recently released political prisoner Silvio Pellico '[how] flows thy being now?', implicitly contrasting his liberation with her continuing imprisonment (l. 1).[58] This iteration of the image gives added poignancy to the metaphor chosen by the poet to represent the revival of a simple, child-like faith during the most dangerous phase of her illness:

> Ye childlike thoughts! the holy and the true –
> Ye that came bearing, while subdued I lay,
> The faith, the insight of life's vernal morn
> Back on my soul, a clear, bright sense, new-born,
> Now leave me not! but as, profoundly pure,
> A blue stream rushes through a darker lake
> Unchanged, e'en thus with me your journey take,
> Wafting sweet airs of heaven thro' this low world obscure.
>
> ('Recovery', ll. 7–14)

The poet's (temporary) recovery from sickness is also the more permanent recovery of a straightforward faith. The rather ungainly religious vocabulary of the earlier sonnets, which often strains unconvincingly to contain the nostalgia or disenchantment articulated within the poem, gains added strength here from its association with the metaphor of the 'blue stream' which seems to have grown organically from the series itself; and this new-found reaffirmation of faith is triumphantly reiterated in the last, death-bed poem, 'Sabbath Sonnet'. As the 'blessed groups' of pious families are wending their way through 'England's primrose meadow-paths' to church, the 'hamlets low' are seen to 'Send out their inmates in a happy flow,/ Like a freed vernal stream.' (ll. 8–9) The poet herself is still 'to the bed/ Of sickness bound' (ll. 10–11), but this reassignment of the image which had earlier encapsulated her longing for the lost paradise of childhood and youth indicates the progress that has been made within the series towards acceptance of and even thankfulness for the fading of life and strength.

The similarities between Hemans' sonnets and those published by Elizabeth Barrett in *Poems* (1844) are striking. Barrett adopts her precursor's habit of giving each of the sonnets a brief and often enigmatic title; where Hemans has 'Foliage', 'Sickness like Night', 'Flowers', and 'Thoughts Connected with Trees', Barrett has 'Irreparableness', 'Perplexed Music' and 'Patience Taught by Nature'. Hemans' ostentatiously humble and submissive vocabulary – her favourite word is 'low' – seeps into Barrett's: 'Speak low to me, my Saviour, low and sweet' (ll. 1–2). Most significantly, both chart the course of a deeply felt but largely unexplained personal experience, tracking it from its initial stages through to its final resolution in a strengthened and purified Christian faith. But Barrett's adoption of the sonnet form at this late stage in her career is not only due to the example of the 'poetesses', towards whom she had a markedly ambivalent attitude; she thought Hemans 'too ladylike in proportion to [her] humanity', for instance, and suggested, in a significant metaphor, that 'her refinement, like the prisoner's iron... enters into her soul.'[59] This turn towards the sonnet is also connected to her rediscovery of Wordsworth and consequent recognition of the iconic potential of the form. The sonnets of 1844 exhibit a tortured fascination with the Wordsworthian dialectic of freedom and limitation, with the pains and benefits of imprisonment, and inaugurate a six-year-long engagement with the form which eventually leads to its repudiation.

One of Elizabeth Barrett's earliest efforts in the sonnet form was prompted by Benjamin Robert Haydon's portrait 'Wordsworth on Helvellyn',[60] and her revaluation of a form she had previously disdained or ignored is bound up with her renewed admiration for Wordsworth at this stage of her career.[61] Her letters of this period are full of references to him as a kind of 'king' or ruler, as is 'The Book of the Poets', the survey of the history of English poetry she published in *The Athenaeum* in 1842: '[Of] all poets... who have been kings in England, not one has swept the purple with more majesty than this poet, when it hath pleased him to be majestic. *Vivat rex*'.[62] She singles out his sonnets for particular praise, stating that he has surpassed all of his great precursors in his use of the form: '[The] greatest poets of our country, – the Shakespeares, Spensers, Miltons, – worked upon high sonnet-ground, [but] not one opened over it such broad and pouring sluices of various thought, imagery, and emphatic eloquence as he has done.'[63] Barrett was, moreover, at this time wrestling with problems similar to those which had produced Wordsworth's own turn towards the sonnet forty years earlier. There are signs in her work around this time of an increasing ambivalence towards the large-scale poetic projects into which she had previously poured most of her energies. Marjorie Stone emphasises the transgressive nature of the 'Romantic Prometheanism' of much of Barrett's early work, her determination to write herself into the male tradition of epic poetry.[64] But this ambition was clearly waning by the early 1840s. The title poem of her 1838 volume, *The Seraphim and other poems*, is an ambitious and overwrought attempt to describe Christ's passion and death from the point of view of two watching angels, but by 1842 Barrett was seeking to distance herself from it, describing it in a letter to Benjamin Robert Haydon as 'almost the worst poem' in the collection.[65] The decision to lead the 1844 volume with 'A Drama of Exile' indicates a similar ambivalence about her own epic ambitions. On the one hand the poem, which continues the story of the Fall after the expulsion from Paradise, seems to challenge comparison with Milton's epic; but on the other hand it highlights the extent to which Barrett is herself an 'exile' from this epic tradition. This conflict is articulated in the impassioned Preface to the collection:

> I had promised my own prudence to shut close the gates of Eden between Milton and myself, so that none might say I dared to walk in his footsteps. He should be within, I thought, with his Adam and Eve unfallen or falling, – and I, without, with my EXILES, – I also an exile! It would not do. The subject, and his glory covering it, swept through the gates, and I stood full in it, against my will, and contrary to my vow, – till I shrank back fearing, almost desponding; hesitating to venture even a passing association with our great poet before the face of the public.[66]

The Promethean attempt to steal Milton's fire is here transformed into a stereotypically feminine gesture of passivity and weakness; she is literally overpowered by the force of Milton's genius, and tackles the subject 'against her will' and 'contrary to [her] vow'. This note of apology continues throughout the remainder of the Preface; she is 'too low' and too weak – 'the weakest', in fact – to be suspected of a genuine challenge to Milton's poetic authority.

This adoption of a stereotypically, almost exaggeratedly feminine subject position in the defence of her work points to some of the reasons for Barrett's decision to scale down her poetic ambitions at this stage of her career. Like Wordsworth during the first decade of the nineteenth century, she was faced with a set of profoundly uncongenial external circumstances; but in her case these circumstances derived almost entirely from the fact of her gender. Biographical accounts of Barrett's life stress the extent to which her early life was characterised by a refusal to accept the limitations placed on the lives of girls and women; but following the death of her brother in 1840, and her father's increasingly tyrannical and irrational behaviour towards his children thereafter, she seems to have decided to become the very embodiment of the passive, suffering femininity fetishised by Victorian society. She had, as she puts it in some of her earliest letters to Robert Browning, decided to 'stand still in her stall', confining herself to her room 'like Mariana in the moated grange'.[67] This gesture was not a simple retreat into femininity, however; it was both retreat and defiance, and like Wordsworth's withdrawal from his society found its perfect poetic embodiment in the sonnet's paradoxical combination of freedom and self-imposed restriction. Her attention may have been drawn to this dimension of Wordsworth's sonnets by Sir Henry Taylor's remarkable review-essay on 'The Sonnets of William Wordsworth' in the *Quarterly Review* for 1842, discussed in the first chapter.[68] Barrett must have read this review; it includes the first publication of the notorious 'Sonnets upon the Punishment of Death', which she refers to in 'The Book of the Poets' (also published in 1842) as 'a misplaced "Benedicite" over the hangman and his victim'.[69] Picking up on Wordsworth's 'comparison mutually illustrative' between the sonnet form and voluntary self-restraint, Barrett presents herself in the 1844 sonnets as a kind of prisoner, accepting the limitations of her position and seeking in them the raw material for her imaginative life. Chastening her 'exuberant and discursive imagination' she takes up the mantle of the 'poetess' left vacant by her recently deceased contemporaries Felicia Hemans and L.E.L., inviting the reader to see her sonnets as a record of profound and imperfectly articulated personal suffering; in the Preface she states that her poems have her 'heart and life' in them, and represent 'the completest expression' of her personal being 'to which [she] could attain'.[70] But the narrative trajectory of the series also suggests a residual dissatisfaction with this role, and points to the desire to regain the possibility of fuller and freer utterance.

The first poem of the sequence, 'The Soul's Expression', takes up and intensifies the Wordsworthian apprehension of the paradoxical relation between freedom and limitation in the sonnet's form:

> With stammering lips and insufficient sound
> I strive and struggle to deliver right
> That music of my nature, day and night
> With dream and thought and feeling interwound,
> And inly answering all the senses round
> With octaves of a mystic depth and height
> Which step out grandly to the infinite
> From the dark edges of the sensual ground.

This song of soul I struggle to outbear
Through portals of the sense, sublime and whole,
And utter all myself into the air:
But if I did it, – as the thunder-roll
Breaks its own cloud, my flesh would perish there,
Before that dread apocalypse of soul.

Barrett here transforms the sonnet into something like a Romantic or even prophetic fragment, pointing beyond itself to the inarticulable sublime. The first eight lines exploit the latent musical pun in the term octave to produce a syntactically complex and disorientating conceit. The poet 'strives and struggles' – a telling redundancy – to deliver the 'music' of her nature. This music 'inly' answers 'all the senses round'; this could mean either that it answers all the senses which surround it; or it could be a continuation of the underlying musical metaphor, suggesting that the senses are singing a 'round' which is answered by the poet's inmost nature. Similarly, the 'octaves of a mystic depth and height' intoned by the poet's soul step out towards the infinite '[from] the dark edges of the sensual ground'. This last word combines the musical metaphor – the senses are a 'ground' or *basso continuo* against which the soul's music defines itself – with the traditional notion that the soul has the ability to escape from the earthbound senses. These ambiguities, and indeed the syntactic complexity of the octave, reinforce the notion articulated more simply and clearly in the sestet; that the attempt to 'outbear' the soul's music in its pristine completeness would produce a 'dread apocalypse of soul', destroying both poet and poem. Like the prophet Isaiah, she can only speak to 'this people' with 'stammering lips' and with 'another tongue'.[71] Human beings must accept the limitations of their condition; their work can point towards the 'infinite', but cannot hope to embody it adequately. The sonnet form is an emblem of the inescapability of this condition.

It is, as the remainder of the series makes clear, the poet's 'suffering' which gives her access to the boundless depths of the sublime. This use of suffering as a source of the sublime has a considerable Romantic heritage, and is explicitly alluded to in the Preface to 1844, where Barrett states that 'A Vision of Poets' is intended 'to indicate the necessary relations of genius to suffering and self-sacrifice', and that 'if knowledge is power, suffering should be acceptable as a part of knowledge'.[72] Burke asserts that he knows of 'nothing sublime which is not some modification of power', and the sublimity in this case comes from the poet's powerlessness to resist the grief and suffering which have been inflicted on her by a higher power.[73] A number of the sonnets illustrate the 'depth and height' of this suffering by emphasising their inability to articulate it fully within the confines of the sonnet form. In 'Grief', for instance, the poet highlights the peculiar fitness of 'artificial' and inorganic forms for the representation of the deepest kinds of suffering. A grief that can express itself in tears is one which holds out hope of recovery; a tearless grief, on the other hand, is silent and changeless:

> I tell you, hopeless grief is passionless;
> That only men incredulous of despair,
> Half-taught in anguish, through the midnight air
> Beat upward to God's throne in loud access
> Of shrieking and reproach. Full desertness,
> In souls as countries, lieth silent-bare
> Under the blanching, vertical eye-glare
> Of the absolute Heavens. Deep-hearted man, express
> Grief for thy Dead in silence like to death –
> Most like a monumental statue set
> In everlasting watch and moveless woe
> Till itself crumble to the dust beneath.
> Touch it; the marble eyelids are not wet:
> If it could weep, it could arise and go.

A form which was able to mimic the progress of the poet's grief, and so hold out the possibility of change and recovery, would be false to the absolute and inconsolable suffering that the poet is trying to represent. The sonnet, in contrast, is a form which advertises its own artificial and inorganic status, like the 'monumental statue' which crumbles slowly into dust under the 'vertical eye-glare/ Of the absolute Heavens', and so paradoxically becomes the ideal medium for the representation of 'hopeless grief'.[74]

This emphasis on the inadequacy of the form that Rossetti later called a 'moment's monument' is, however, in tension with the tendency of the sonnets to form themselves into a biographical sequence. There is in the collection a kind of progress away from suffering and towards consolation; and this progress, in turn, calls into question the appropriateness of the sonnet form and the limitations and restrictions implied by it. The poem cited above, for instance, is followed immediately by one in which the poet invokes the possibility of a specifically religious consolation – 'Speak THOU, availing Christ! – and fill this pause' (l. 14) – and in the next poem, 'Comfort', this religious consolation offers the possibility of the redemptive 'tears' that had previously been deemed impossible:

> Speak to me as to Mary at Thy feet!
> And if no precious gums my hands bestow,
> Let my tears drop like amber while I go
> In reach of Thy divinest voice complete
> In humanest affection – thus, in sooth,
> To lose the sense of losing. (ll. 5–10)

This theme of religious redemption continues with the mini-sequence of poems on Peter's denial of Christ, which again focus on the healing power of tears and imply that the poet's earlier 'hopeless grief' was itself a kind of impious denial of Christ's mercy; and in 'Fururity' the unnamed cause of the poet's grief becomes an 'idol' that God has deliberately broken in order to prevent earthly love from usurping the place of its heavenly counterpart. This religious consolation is accompanied by a restatement and revaluation of some of the images used in the earlier poems. In 'Substitution' the song of the nightingale is one of the many things that cannot give comfort to the grieving poet, but in 'Exaggeration' it is the poet's excessive emphasis on 'the ills of life' that prevents her from hearing its song:

> … near the alder brake
> We sigh so loud, the nightingale within
> Refuses to sing loud, as else she would.
> O brothers, let us leave the shame and sin
> Of taking vainly, in a plaintive mood,
> The holy name of GRIEF! – holy herein,
> That by the grief of ONE came all our good. (ll. 8–14)

The monumental and artificial aspects of the sonnet, so appropriate for highlighting the inexpressibility of 'hopeless grief', become an impediment when that grief has been superseded. The form now begins to signify a kind of imprisonment, the endless repetition of a gesture which has lost its basis in experience. This sense of frustration is indicated merely by the titles of some of the later sonnets: 'Discontent', 'Patience taught by Nature', 'Exaggeration', and, most strikingly, 'The Prisoner'. The last of these poems 'answers' in some respects the earlier sonnet 'Irreparableness', in which the poet explains the reasons behind her renunciation of the world. The 'nosegays' she had gathered in her wandering have decayed in her over-eager hands, and she cannot go '[back] straightway to the fields to gather more' (l. 10). This voluntary renunciation has now been transformed into an involuntary imprisonment which exiles the poet from life and nature:

I count the dismal time by months and years
Since last I felt the green sward under foot,
And the great breath of all things summer-mute
Met mine upon my lips. Now earth appears
As strange to me as dreams of distant spheres
Or thoughts of heaven we weep at. Nature's lute
Sounds on, behind his door so closely shut,
A strange wild music to the prisoner's ears,
Dilated by the distance, till the brain
Grows dim with fancies which it feels too fine:
While ever, with a visionary pain,
Past the precluded senses, sweep and shine
Streams, forests, glades, and many a golden train
Of sunlit hills transfigured to divine.

In its context, this can be seen as a rewriting of the Prefatory Sonnet's assertion that 'the prison unto which we doom/ Ourselves, no prison is'. There is no suggestion here of the benefits of voluntary confinement; the poet's incarceration gives rise only to a passionate longing for life outside the prison. This sense of unease finds a formal echo in the mid-line endings of the first two sentences, which make the poem as a whole sit uncomfortably across the Petrarchan schema.

The later poems of the series, including 'The Prisoner', manifest a profound dissatisfaction with the passive and exaggeratedly 'feminine' subject position into which the poet has written herself. There are repeated attempts to transform the poet's own experiences into the material for more general reflections; the curious and awkward 'Work and Contemplation', for example, begins with the Wordsworthian image of the 'maid at the wheel', but ends with a tentative and apologetic movement towards the Miltonic public sonnet; and the pair of poems on George Sand both illustrate and attempt to move beyond the identification of femininity with passivity and suffering. This dissatisfaction becomes a more overt and fully narrativised struggle in Barrett's next (and last) series of sonnets, *Sonnets from the Portuguese* (1850). The cultural affiliations of this series indicate Barrett's determination to recover or rather create a distinctively female tradition. In assuming the traditionally masculine role of the unworthy and hopeless lover and in writing poems of 'conjugal' rather than illicit love Barrett is following the lead of the Italian female sonnet writers of the sixteenth century, in particular Vittoria Colonna;[75] and in using the idea of translation from the Portuguese as a disguise she is again paying homage to Felicia Hemans, who translated a number of Camoens' sonnets.[76] The connection between the two writers is made clear in one of her letters to the man who was to become her husband during the six years between these two groups of sonnets, Robert Browning:

> [Talking] of poetesses, I had a note yesterday (again) which quite touched me... from Mr. Hemans – Charles, the son of Felicia... Do you not like to hear such things said? and is it not better than your tradition about Shelley's son? and is it not pleasant to know that that poor noble pure-hearted woman, the Vittoria Colonna of our country, should be so loved and comprehended by some... by one at least... of her own house? Not that, in naming Shelley, I meant for a moment to make a comparison – there is not equal ground for it. Vittoria Colonna does not walk near Dante – no. And if you promised never to tell Mrs Jameson... nor Miss Martineau... I would confide to you perhaps my secret profession of faith – which is... which is... that let us say and do what we please and can... there *is* a natural inferiority of mind in women – of the intellect... not by any means, of the moral nature – and that the history of Art and of genius testifies to this fact openly.[77]

Using Hemans-Colonna as the model for the *Sonnets from the Portuguese* is, however, still a profoundly ambivalent gesture, as this letter indicates. After making grand if implicit claims for Felicia Hemans as the equivalent of Shelley, Barrett quickly resumes her more usual posture of humility and ends up confessing to her future husband her conviction that there is a 'natural inferiority of mind in women' which the history of the arts makes abundantly clear. This combination of assertive appropriation of traditionally male subject positions and reinforcement of traditionally feminine roles is also enacted in the *Sonnets from the Portuguese* themselves. The abject self-abasement of the 1844 sonnets has gone, but it has not been replaced by a straightforward rejection of the passive, imprisoned, suffering model of femininity.

A number of recent critics have described the *Sonnets from the Portuguese* as a narrative of self-emancipation; the poet begins by portraying herself as 'the object of man's love', wavers for most of the series 'between objectifying herself and claiming her own creative and sexual subjectivity', and ends up substituting her own distinctively female voice for 'the conventions of the male tradition'.[78] By the end of the series this inversion of gender roles allows her to depict her husband in the traditionally female guise of the protecting angel: 'New angel mine, unhoped for in the world' (42, l. 14). The thematic and metaphorical continuities between these poems and the 1844 sonnets have, however, been largely overlooked;[79] and these continuities complicate this narrative of emancipation, highlighting the extent to which Barrett's new female persona retains important features of her old one. The very first poem of the *Sonnets from the Portuguese* alludes to the 1844 sonnets on George Sand, the figure who was for Elizabeth Barrett a fascinating and horrifying illustration of the consequences of a complete rejection of conventional femininity. Her attempt to 'break away the gauds and armlets worn/ By weaker women in captivity' is, for Barrett, a 'vain denial':

> ... that revolted cry
> Is sobbed in by a woman's voice forlorn, –
> Thy woman's hair, my sister, all unshorn
> Floats back dishevelled strength in agony.
> ('To George Sand: A Recognition', ll. 5–8)

The same trope of women's hair as the visible embodiment of their femininity – both their 'dishevelled strength' and their weakness – recurs in the first of the *Sonnets from the Portuguese*; here it is the 'mystic Shape' of Love which draws the poet 'backward by the hair' away from her grief-obsessed fixation with death and towards renewed life. There is, then, no possibility of self-emancipation. The poet's liberation from her prison has to be achieved, in a by now familiar paradox, through total submission to the 'mastery' of another, and in particular that of her future husband. He is represented throughout as a prince and a king, but he also becomes, in a potentially blasphemous appropriation of the language of Protestant theology, a kind of God, redeeming her from her own profound unworthiness with his freely given and unmerited love. She continually describes herself, in a return to the language of Hemans, as 'low' – 'There's nothing low/ In love, when love the lowest' (10, ll. 9–10) – and this sense of her own unworthiness sometimes takes extreme forms. After having accepted the love of her Beloved, she asks what shape he would like her to assume:

> A hope, to sing by gladly? or a fine
> Sad memory, with thy songs to interfuse?
> A shade, in which to sing – of palm or pine?
> A grave, on which to rest from singing? Choose. (17, ll. 11–14)

Dorothy Mermin has suggested that these lines function as 'an incisive commentary on male love poems... since the alternatives require not only the woman's passivity and silence but her absence and finally her death'.[80] But there is little support for such an overtly satirical reading in the context of this sonnet. A number of the surrounding poems make the point that the poet has '[yielded] the grave' for the sake of her new love, and given up her 'near sweet view of Heaven, for earth with thee!' (23, ll. 13–14). The self-abnegation of sonnet 17 is earnest and straightforward; like the redeemed sinner, the poet is perfectly willing to sacrifice her life for her redeemer's sake.

In the most famous of these sonnets – 'How do I love thee?' – Barrett asserts the continuity between her old and new selves: 'I love thee with the passion put to use/ In my old griefs, and with my childhood's faith' (43, ll. 9–10). Such continuity means that the narrative of emancipation staged by the *Sonnets from the Portuguese* does not only represent 'the transformation of woman from muse/helpmeet/object into poet/creator/subject', but also something much closer to the myth of rescue developed and sustained by Elizabeth Barrett and Robert Browning during their courtship.[81] It is, moreover, only in the light of this continuity that the rhetorical gestures of the closing sonnets acquire their full resonance. In thanking those who have 'paused a little near the prison-wall/ To hear my music in its louder parts' (41, ll. 3–4) the poet is troping on the image of herself as a prisoner, and of the sonnet as a kind of imprisonment, developed in the earlier series. The last poem similarly recalls the language of 'Irreparableness', in which the poet had described how 'the nosegay' she plucked decayed in her hands because too 'warmly clasped':

> My heart is very tired, my strength is low,
> My hands are full of blossoms plucked before,
> Held dead within them till myself shall die. (ll. 12–14)

Now it is her 'Beloved' who brings flowers to her 'close room'; and her own sonnets, withdrawn from her 'heart's ground', become in turn her flowers:

> ... take them, as I used to do
> Thy flowers, and keep them where they shall not pine.
> Instruct thine eyes to keep their colours true,
> And tell thy soul their roots are left in mine. (44, ll. 11–14)

This metaphor embodies the sonnet's status for Barrett and her contemporaries; it has its 'roots' in the poet's real life, but like a cut flower it is 'withdrawn' from that living process to serve as a lifeless but poignant memento. The *Sonnets from the Portuguese* are retrospectively organised by this metaphor into the record of a superseded stage of the poet's life; the form associated with imprisonment, limitation and confinement is being left behind for ever; and the echoes of the earlier sequence reinforce the message that her future will not simply 'copy fair' her past. Barrett – by now Barrett Browning – in fact abandoned the sonnet form after *Sonnets from the Portuguese* in favour of freer and more expansive forms of utterance.[82]

In leaving the 'close room' of the sonnet behind, however, Elizabeth Barrett left a legacy which can be compared in importance to Wordsworth's. The *Sonnets from the Portuguese* are one of the nodal points of the form during the century, a moment at which a number of different features come together to produce a new orientation. They highlight the extent to which sonnet writers were beginning to become self-conscious about the biographical readings their work would attract, and indeed to conform to the 'confessional' model retrospectively imputed to Shakespeare, Milton and the other masters of the form. Natalie Houston has pointed out the way in which these sonnets construct an 'effect of authenticity' through their rhetoric of intimacy, detailed private allusion and direct personal address: 'Whether or not the poems were intended for publication, their rhetoric presents them as part of a private conversation'.[83] This self-consciousness also manifests itself in the establishment of defensive strategies against the prying eyes of the critic, though the flimsiness of Barrett's pretence that she was merely the translator of her sonnets was seen through more or less instantly.[84] Both these features – the rhetoric of authenticity and the establishment of ever more sophisticated defence mechanisms – will become important later in the century. In addition, the explicit narrativisation of the *Sonnets from the Portuguese* indicates the growing recognition of the potential affinities between serial lyric utterances and the hegemonic literary form of the period, the novel. In making her sonnets tell the archetypal romance story, with herself as Cinderella and Robert as Prince Charming,[85] Barrett was giving her readers a ready-made narrative into which her individual experience could be inserted, and paving the way for the various experiments with lyric sequences which she and her contemporaries and successors would carry out during the middle years of the century. Finally, and perhaps most importantly, the *Sonnets from the Portuguese* represent the first sustained attempt to revive the Petrarchan amatory sonnet sequence in the nineteenth century. Such sequences were commonplace during the Elizabethan period, and there is an element of self-conscious literary antiquarianism about the *Sonnets from the Portuguese* which manifests itself in the sequence's occasionally Spenserian vocabulary ('enow', 'certes') and parallels the kind of antiquarianism which gave rise to the sonnet revival in the eighteenth century. This superimposition of nineteenth-century life and morals onto the early Renaissance template of the amatory sonnet sequence provided Barrett's successors in the final quarter of the nineteenth century with a powerful and resonant model for the exploration of contemporary beliefs and illusions about love and marriage.

3
The Political Sonnet

Matthew Arnold's response to the French Revolution of 1848 was articulated in part through a pair of sonnets addressed 'To a Republican Friend', the friend in question being his close confidant and poetic rival Arthur Hugh Clough. The first of these sonnets expresses a mild if not entirely convincing enthusiasm for the general aims of the revolution, while the second voices an altogether more detached and sceptical view of events:

> Yet, when I muse on what life is, I seem
> Rather to patience prompted, than that proud
> Prospect of hope which France proclaims so loud –
> France, famed in all great arts, in none supreme;
> Seeing this vale, this earth, whereon we dream,
> Is on all sides o'ershadowed by the high
> Uno'erleaped Mountains of Necessity,
> Sparing us narrower margin than we deem.
> Nor will that day dawn at a human nod,
> When, bursting through the network superposed
> By selfish occupation – plot and plan,
> Lust, avarice, envy – liberated man,
> All difference with his fellow-mortal closed,
> Shall be left standing face to face with God.

In suggesting that France is 'famed in all great arts, in none supreme' Arnold is echoing Wordsworth's assertion that France has '[no] master spirit, no determined road' ('Great men have been among us'; 'Sonnets Dedicated to Liberty', XV, l. 13); and Arnold's attitude towards events in France clearly finds an example and a sanction in Wordsworth's ultimate hostility to the Revolution of 1789. But Wordsworth's journey from enthusiasm to hostility took, as we have seen, many years, indeed the whole of his career according to some recent critics, and involved a continual revision and rewriting of earlier poems and selves. Arnold's about-face, in contrast, appears instantaneous. He uses the sonnet not as a way of working out his political position, but as a way of inscribing or memorialising it; and in this respect his poems illustrate something of the fate of the public or political sonnet during the nineteenth century. Wordsworth helped to popularise the Miltonic sonnet as a vehicle for the articulation of political sentiment; but his consciousness of the political resonances and ironies of the form, as well as the never-resolved tension in his work between the individual sonnet and the series, prevented his sonnets from ossifying into the articulation of stock attitudes and beliefs. The interdependence of the individual sonnets in these larger series means, as we have seen, that their key terms and tropes – 'majesty', 'liberty' – are always open to revision and reinterpretation. It is in the poetry of Wordsworth's successors rather than Wordsworth himself that the Miltonic sonnet becomes, in Alan Liu's words, 'a form especially suited to reifying turns of mind'.[1] In 'Great Men have been among us' Wordsworth contrasts two revolutions, the English and the French, and suggests that the kind of 'great men' who acted as moral guardians during the former have failed to emerge in the latter; Arnold's poem, in contrast, dehistoricises the differences between England and France in its suggestion that a nation's art is the exponent of its moral and social character. Disillusionment with the progress of events in France is generalised by Arnold into a gesture of vaguely religious humility; the 'uno'erleaped Mountains of Necessity' mean that our human schemes of liberation will never be achieved without divine intervention. Even the diction of the poem, with its stilted poeticisms and archaic use of syncope, seems to translate the experience it is claiming to record into a register remote from any contact with the languages of liberation being deployed for and against the events of 1848.

It was Arnold, in a letter to Clough written around this time, who suggested that 'one of the signs of the Decadence of a literature... is this – that new authors attach themselves to the poetic expression the founders of a literature have flowered into, which may be *learned* by a sensitive person, to the neglect of an inward poetic life';[2] and, according to his own definition, Arnold might be said to belong to this 'Decadence'. Like many of Wordsworth's successors, he treats the Miltonic-Wordsworthian political sonnet as a fundamentally declamatory or rhetorical form of verse whose qualitative inferiority is marked by its adherence to an 'inorganic' or inert form. The free-standing and occasional political sonnet becomes the refuge of the aesthetically conservative or non-professional poet. For this very reason it also becomes one of the forms most readily available to radical and working-class poets, who tended to be both non-professional and aesthetically conservative. Only rarely, and usually where it remains part of a sequence or group of connected poems, does what Liu (again) calls 'the rhetorical ambition and hardened ideology of the sonnet' soften into something more responsive to the texture of experience.[3]

Some of Wordsworth's occasional sonnets, such as this one inspired by the Reform agitation of the early 1830s, seem to succumb to this 'rhetorical ambition', and to exhibit an ideology which might reasonably be described as 'hardened':

Composed after Reading a Newspaper of the Day

'People! your chains are severing link by link;
Soon shall the Rich be levelled down – the Poor
Meet them half way.' Vain boast! For These, the more
They thus would rise, must low and lower sink
Till, by repentance stung, they fear to think;
While all lie prostrate, save the tyrant few
Bent in quick turns each other to undo,
And mix the poison, they themselves must drink.
Mistrust thyself, vain Country! cease to cry,
'Knowledge will save me from the threatened woe.'
For, if than other rash ones more thou know
Yet on presumptuous wing as far would fly
Above thy knowledge as they dared to go,
Thou wilt provoke a heavier penalty.

The language of 'levelling' is the starting point here for a confusing play on the ideas of height and depth, transgression and punishment. In order to 'rise', the 'Poor' – already reified into a single, menacing entity – must first 'sink lower', at which point the consciousness of their sins will leave them afraid to think. The adverbial clause of time beginning at line 6 describes something that happens while the 'Poor' are sinking lower, and so seems to refer not (as might at first be thought) to the 'Poor' themselves, but to the whole country ('all') lying 'prostrate' while the 'tyrants' plot against one another. There is, moreover, additional confusion over the identity and actions of these 'tyrants'. Are they part of 'the Poor', or an existing social force taking advantage of the confusion caused by the uprising of 'the Poor'? Are they mixing the poison which will eventually be used against themselves – as implied by the reference to their mutual loathing – or are the prostrate people mixing a poison which the 'tyrants' will force them to take? This blurring of conceptual and linguistic boundaries is continued into the sestet. Now it is the 'Country' as a whole which is 'vain' (in the sense of proud or conceited) because it relies on its 'knowledge' to save it from the threat of anarchy; but this country is also (like the Poor) imagined as wanting to rise, ignorant of the penalty awaiting its rashness and conceit. The implicit parallel between the '[vain] boast' of the newspaper and the 'vain Country' indicates the extent to which the 'Country' is complicit with the aims of the leaders of the 'Poor'. The proponents of 'Knowledge' – the kind of useful knowledge being taught at the newly founded London University – are the Benthamite ideologues behind the reform movement and their Whig allies in Parliament. Like Icarus they are guilty of *hybris*, of not respecting the limits of human knowledge; and it is this pride that will lead to their eventual fall.

Part of the reason for the confusion of this sonnet arises from its employment of an excessively abstract and inflexible language; having refined the social conflict into one between 'the Poor' and 'the Rich', with 'the Country' operating somewhere between the two, it is the victim of its own unwieldy machinery. The poem's use of these terms derives from the language of the 'Newspaper of the Day', and may be designed in part to illustrate the futility of attempting to think about complex social questions using abstractions like 'the Rich' and 'the Poor'; but it does not develop an alternative vocabulary against which the shortcomings of this language can be measured. Wordsworth's lyric sequences, in contrast, exhibit a complex intertwining of personal and public histories which prevents them on the whole from lapsing into mere sloganising. The *River Duddon* sonnets are typical in this respect. Wordsworth described them as 'the growth of many years',[4] and they have their source (as mentioned earlier) in one of the *Miscellaneous Sonnets* of 1807. In dedicating the poem to his brother Christopher, then Rector of St. Mary's Lambeth, Wordsworth introduces a comparison which continues throughout the entire sequence between the retirement and leisure imaged in the course of the River Duddon and the 'imperial City's din' (Preface, l. 72). The river is 'remote from every taint/ Of sordid industry' (II, ll. 1–2); its function is 'to heal and to restore,/ To soothe and cleanse, not madden and pollute!' (VIII, ll. 3–14). Yet the poems also establish a link between the course of the river and the course of individual and national life; and as they trace its way from its remote source towards the ocean, they increasingly hint at the connections between the virtues nursed by the River Duddon and the virtues which have allowed London to become an 'imperial City', the centre of a mighty empire. The opening sonnet, perhaps picking up on the connotations of that strikingly political word 'imperial' in the dedication, finds in Horace's *Odes* an analogue to the sequence; just like Horace praising the Bandusian spring, Wordsworth patriotically seeks 'the birthplace of a native stream' (I, l. 9). This 'native stream' is the parent of many native virtues, and these virtues are represented through the typically Wordsworthian sonnet-trope of benevolent imprisonment. Those who 'wear the chain/ That binds them' to the river's side (XXX, ll. 9–10) remain in a state of 'innocence', unlike those who '[make] divorce/ Of that serene companion', and '[walk] with shame,/ With doubt, with fear, and haply with remorse' (XXX, ll. 1–4). Yet this primitive retirement and isolation cannot last; a resting place along the way 'proffers to enclose/ Body and mind, from molestation freed,/ In narrow compass–narrow as itself' (XXIV, ll. 7–9), but the '[maturer] Fancy' finds in the river a source of '[impetuous] thoughts that brook not servile sway' (XXVI, l. 14). And just as the river must continue its determined course to the sea, so the virtues that it both images and nurses must break out of their narrow confines and make themselves known to the world at large. During the early part of the sequence there are metaphorical suggestions of Britain's overseas expansion, such as the comparison between a wintry landscape and '[the] matted forests of Ontario's shore' (XIII, ll. 8–9), and these suggestions are brought to fruition in the penultimate poem of the sequence when the River Duddon fulfils its destiny and becomes part of the main:

> Not hurled precipitous from steep to steep;
> Lingering no more 'mid flower-enamelled lands
> And blooming thickets; nor by rocky bands
> Held; but in radiant progress toward the Deep
> Where mightiest rivers into powerless sleep
> Sink, and forget their nature – *now* expands
> Majestic Duddon, over smooth flat sands
> Gliding in silence with unfettered sweep!
> Beneath an ampler sky a region wide

Is opened round him: – hamlets, towers, and towns,
And blue-topped hills, behold him from afar;
In stately mien to sovereign Thames allied
Spreading his bosom under Kentish downs,
With commerce freighted, or triumphant war.

Duddon joins what Wordsworth in the 1807 sonnets called 'the Flood/ Of British freedom', expanding out of its narrow channels and self-abnegating retirement to become an integral part of the sea which is the source of British wealth and military prestige. The antithesis between rural retirement and the 'imperial City' outlined in the dedication has been shown to be a false one; rightly understood, Britain's imperial status as the centre of a world empire depends on and derives from the very isolation that enabled its children to grow up pure and virtuous.

Like Wordsworth, Shelley uses the sonnet as a vehicle for occasional reflection on public questions, and perhaps surprisingly, given his political orientation, he seems to be beguiled by his great precursor at such moments into adopting a very Wordsworthian-Miltonic language; the execration of the 'fallen tyrant' Buonaparte is carried out in the name of 'virtue', and 'political greatness' is to be found in the man who can 'rule the empire of himself' and 'quell the anarchy/ Of hopes and fears, being himself alone'.[5] There is, however, one political poem in which Shelley makes what we might call both formally and politically radical use of the sonnet form: 'Ode to the West Wind'.[6] Each of the five sections of this poem consists of fourteen lines with various interlocking rhyming patterns, and closes with a rhyming couplet. The sections are not, however, divided into quatrains, but into tercets, producing a kind of formal syncopation which both disguises and exploits the underlying sonnet pattern. While the first three sections drive forward in imitation of the wind to the imprecation 'O, hear!', each developing a different aspect of the power of the west wind, the fourth section constitutes a kind of 'volta' in the sequence as a whole:

If I were a dead leaf thou mightest bear;
If I were a swift cloud to fly with thee;
A wave to pant beneath thy power, and share

The impulse of thy strength, only less free
Than thou, O uncontrollable! If even
I were as in my boyhood, and could be

The comrade of thy wanderings over heaven,
As then, when to outstrip thy skiey speed
Scarce seemed a vision ; I would ne'er have striven

As thus with thee in prayer in my sore need.
Oh! lift me as a wave, a leaf, a cloud!
I fall upon the thorns of life! I bleed!

A heavy weight of hours has chained and bowed
One too like thee: tameless, and swift, and proud.

For Wordsworth, the kind of communion with nature represented here lifted the 'heavy and the weary weight/ Of all this unintelligible world' ('Tintern Abbey', ll. 40–41). For Shelley, in contrast, the freedom of the wind merely serves as a reminder of the extent to which he is 'chained' and 'bowed'; and this message is reinforced by the way in which the closing couplet reveals the sonnet form underlying what had looked like an impassioned and extemporised evocation of freedom. It is this mismatch between the form of his own poetry and the freedom of the wind which leads Shelley, in the closing section, to compare his verse to 'withered leaves' and 'ashes and sparks'; the sections are the inorganic remnants of an extinguished life, but as such capable, with assistance and inspiration, of becoming the harbingers of a new birth.

There is a similarly ambivalent use of the sonnet form in the work of Shelley's heirs, the working-class and radical poets of the Chartist movement. Part of the reason for this may be suggested in Samuel Smiles' biographical introduction to Gerald Massey's *Poems* (1861). After having detailed Massey's extremely difficult childhood as the child of poor agricultural workers in Hertfordshire, Smiles goes on to explain, and to a certain extent justify, the radical tone and temper of much of Massey's early poetry: '[When] such a man does find a voice, surely "rose-water" verses and "hot-pressed" sonnets are not to be expected of him; such things are not by any means the natural products of a life of desperate struggling with poverty'.[7] In suggesting that the sonnet is not a natural outlet for a working-class poet, Smiles is drawing attention to its formal and even courtly quality; it is associated with a self-conscious literary tradition, and indeed with a feudal and aristocratic past, alien to the beliefs and experiences of most radical and working-class writers. The use of the form by such writers often seems, in consequence, to exhibit a certain self-consciousness and even self-division. The sonnet tends to be employed not for political invective – the 'popular' modes of song and ballad are generally found to be more appropriate for this purpose – but for dedications and acts of homage which implicitly remind the poet of the very social conditions against which he is in revolt. Thomas Cooper, described by Miles Taylor in his recent biography of Ernest Jones as 'the undisputed "poet laureate" of Chartism',[8] exemplifies this tendency in the dedication of his 1846 collection *The Baron's Yule Feast* (1846) to Lady Blessington:

> Lady, receive a tributary lay
> From one who cringeth not to titled state
> Conventional, and lacketh will to prate
> Of comeliness – though thine, to which did pay
> The haughty Childe his tuneful homage, may
> No minstrel deem a harp-theme derogate.
> I reckon thee among the truly great
> And fair, because with genius thou dost sway
> The thought of thousands, while thy noble heart
> With pity glows for Suffering, and with zeal
> Cordial relief and solace to impart.
> Thou didst, while I rehearsed Toil's wrongs, reveal
> Such yearnings! Plead! let England hear thee plead
> With eloquent tongue, – that Toil from wrong be freed![9]

The studied archaism of Cooper's language of 'lays', 'minstrels' and 'harp-themes', which serves as a reminder of the medieval origins of the sonnet form, acquires additional resonance in this context. It seems at first sight paradoxical for a radical poet to be writing himself into the traditionally subservient role of the 'minstrel' seeking the patronage of the great and powerful, but Cooper attempts to overcome this difficulty by employing the Carlylean distinction between 'titled state/ Conventional' on the one hand, and the genuine aristocracy of the 'truly great' on the other. This distinction derives in its turn from a medievalist political programme, which sees the solution to 'Toil's wrongs' not in the eradication of class difference but in the revival of a sense of social responsibility on the part of the aristocracy and the church, and a corresponding sense of loyalty and devotion on the part of the poor. Hence his sonnet both echoes and attempts to revive the kind of relationship that supposedly existed between poor 'minstrels' and aristocrats in the medieval period. A form that would seem out of place at a Chartist meeting becomes the obvious vehicle for the expression of the idealised Feudalism which formed an integral part of the radicalism of the 1840s.

If the sonnet's formal and conventional links with a feudal and aristocratic past limited its usefulness for working-class and radical writers,
however, its formal limitations presented self-educated and aesthetically conservative writers with a ready-made device for transforming
their experiences and desires into poetry. In her influential study of the
interaction of literary and popular traditions in the early nineteenth
century, Anne Janowitz draws attention to a series of sonnets published during 1840 in the Chartist journal *The Northern Star* 'by one of
the Newport Chartists under the pseudonym of "Iota"' which com-
memorates the Chartist heroes John Frost and George Shell by the
incongruous but Wordsworthian means of 'a sequence of landscape
meditations.'[10] Self-educated poets using the form often feel con-
strained (as Cooper illustrates) to adopt a 'poetic' dialect remote from
ordinary speech, and to translate their thoughts and feelings into a
suitably abstract register. The anonymous poet who commemorated
the death of the great Chartist leader and radical activist Ernest Jones
in *The Freelance* in 1869 offers a cosmic perspective on Jones' life in
keeping with the memorialising tendencies of the form:

> How futile are man's purposes! In vain
> He struggles onward, and with patient soul
> Strains to the landmark of some distant goal,
> In steadfastness of mind, and heart, and brain
> That know no daunting: for one darling Hope –
> Whate'er it be – Ambition, Riches, Fame –
> That aery phantom of a lofty name –
> He all things dares, defies.[11]

Such uses of the sonnet render it the visible symbol of the 'middle-class
cultural hegemony' to which all aspirant self-taught writers were subject; it seems to import alien norms, values and beliefs into the heart of
working-class writing. But by virtue of its very availability as a universal vehicle of poetic expression the sonnet also becomes the site of
some more complex transactions between writers from different classes
and traditions, as illustrated in the case of the Crimean War. This event
lent itself naturally to outpourings of patriotic sentiment (and also
national self-chastisement) along the lines set down by Milton and
Wordsworth in their public sonnets; one such offering is the *Sonnets on
the War* (1855) jointly authored by Alexander Smith and Sydney
Dobell.[12] Both Smith and Dobell had achieved a certain amount of
fame, and indeed notoriety, by the time this collection appeared. Their
early performances – Smith's *A Life Drama* (1852), Dobell's *Balder*

(1853) – had been enthusiastically received by the literary elite; the work of the 'Glasgow mechanic' Smith, in particular, seemed to indicate the promise of vibrant cultural life amongst the working classes.[13] But during 1853 and 1854 the critical tide turned strongly against them, with Charles Kingsley ridiculing the 'spasmodic, vague, extravagant, effeminate school of poetry' to which they seemed to belong, and William Edmonstone Aytoun satirising them in *Firmilian* (1854).[14] Under these circumstances their decision to publish a set of poems documenting the events of the war and the range of responses to it looks like a shift (in the critical jargon of the time) from the 'subjective' to the 'objective', from a diseased and counter-productive obsession with self to a healthy and balanced interest in and response to the external world. This shift is underlined by the refusal to ascribe individual poems to either of the authors; what they are attempting to provide is a response which echoes and articulates the varied feelings of the nation, not the idiosyncratic responses of self-absorbed individuals. In her recent discussion of this collection Natalie Houston highlights the dialogical quality of the resulting poems, which (as in this poem on the charge of the Light Brigade) give space to competing and discordant voices in the service of national commemoration:

> We mourn them with remorseful tenderness,
> And yet, methinks, our tears should be denied
> By a proud effort. When they *so* have died,
> What is a little breathing more or less?
> 'Woe's me! each bosom was a Russian targe.'
> 'Who would not pay that priceless price to feel
> The trampling thunder and the blaze of steel –
> The terror and the splendour of the charge?'
> 'In vain that human thunderbolt was flung –
> In vain 'twas shivered.' 'At the word they sprung
> In one wild light of sword and gleaming corse,
> And at the terrible beauty of their look
> Death stood dismayed. Jove! how the cowards shook
> When on them burst that hurricane of horse!'[15]

There is a range of responses to the event here, from the third speaker's recognition of its futility to the fourth's glorification of its 'terrible beauty' and sublime recklessness, but little or no attempt at synthesis; the personality of the poet is more or less completely excluded, and the poem becomes a medium for the transcription of public sentiment.

Indeed, this poem and many others like it are so determinedly impersonal that Houston compares them to the official photographic record of the war, suggesting that the sonnet and the photograph represent 'analogous technologies of representation'.[16]

This movement from 'spasmodic' self-indulgence to patriotic self-abnegation on the part of Smith and Dobell parallels the career of the hero of Tennyson's *Maud*, also published in 1855; in the notorious closing section of the poem, the hero sees the outbreak of the Crimean War as a way of escaping his own diseased subjectivity.[17] Moreover, Tennyson imitates Smith and Dobell's formal progress by making the last section of *Maud* a kind of sonnet sequence; of the five parts in this section the first two are very similar to sonnets, although irregular in metre and rhyme-scheme, and the last three read like sonnets hacked into irregular lengths. The second poem, in particular, has a classic octave/sestet division, and even invokes Milton ('all in all') in its closing lines about the effects of Peace:

And it was but a dream, yet it yielded a dear delight
To have looked, though but in a dream, upon eyes so fair,
That had been, in a weary world, my one thing bright;
And it was but a dream, yet it lightened my despair
When I thought that a war would arise in defence of the right,
That an iron tyranny now should bend or cease,
The glory of manhood stand on his ancient height,
Nor Britain's one sole God be the millionaire:
No more shall commerce be all in all, and Peace
Pipe on her pastoral hillock a languid note,
And watch her harvest ripen, her herd increase,
Nor the cannon-bullet rust on a slothful shore,
And the cobweb woven across the cannon's throat
Shall shake its threaded tears in the wind no more.

(*Maud*, III, vi, ll. 15–28)

This part of the closing section of *Maud* helps to explain the appeal of the Crimean War to former radicals and working-class poets like Smith and Dobell. In promising to replace 'sloth', decay and the worship of money with the 'glory of manhood' and the 'defence of the right', the war seems to promise an end to precisely those divisions of wealth and rank which radicals found most oppressive. The impersonality promised by the war is also a forgetting of merely selfish concerns and interests in a great national undertaking. This sentiment certainly forms part of Smith and Dobell's response; they eulogise those 'who fall that Liberty may stand' as martyrs to a 'holy' cause (19, ll. 7, 13). And it can also be seen in the work of their contemporary Gerald Massey, whose extraordinarily bloodthirsty collection *War Waits* (1855) has striking similarities to the ending of *Maud*.[18] Massey's description of the condition of England before the war in the title poem could, indeed, have come from the ending of *Maud*:

> ... England swooned beneath the kiss of Peace,
> And languished in her long voluptuous dream,
> While weed-like creatures crept along her path.
> Where leapt of old proud waves of glorious life,
> The sluggish channels choked with golden sand. (ll. 10–14).

The final section of *Maud* seems, then, to allude to a structure of feeling prevalent amongst working-class, radical and self-educated poets, and to do so by means of a form – the sonnet – adopted by a number of those poets as a way of announcing their 'conversion' from self-absorption to collective purpose. Recognition of this intertextual dimension lends credibility to the idea (which Tennyson was keen to stress) that *Maud* is essentially a dramatic utterance: 'I took a man constitutionally diseased and dipt him into the circumstances of the time and took him out on fire'.[19] In the work of Smith, Dobell and Massey, Tennyson seems to have discovered precisely the kind of hysterical response to social inequality called for by the dramatic situation of his poem; and in their use of a form that he himself had largely disavowed he may have seen an indication of the sonnet's suitability for articulating limited and incomplete but nonetheless poignant responses to experience on the part of those excluded from the higher reaches of culture.

Tennyson's own abandonment of the political sonnet is, in fact, typical of a more general retreat from the form on the part of established or professional writers for much of the remainder of the nineteenth century. Great public events of the mid-century are rarely commemorated in sonnet form, and even the most politically committed poets – Elizabeth Barrett Browning, Algernon Charles Swinburne – tend to prefer other forms in their writings about slavery and the Italian struggle for national liberation. Sonnets are used as a means of commemorating, reflecting or moralising, but rarely as a way of engaging with ongoing political debate. Matthew Arnold's 1867 sonnets graphically illustrate this lack of engagement, even while attempting to tackle social and political questions.[20] The 1860s saw a period of renewed reform agitation, to which Arnold responded in prose with *Culture and Anarchy*, and in poetry with his paired sonnets 'East London' and 'West London'. Both poems deal with the interaction of the 'two nations' of Victorian Britain. In the first, the poet meets a preacher amongst 'the squalid streets of Bethnal Green', and finds him not downcast by the misery and poverty he encounters there, but '"much cheered with thoughts of Christ, *the living bread*."' (ll. 2, 8) In the second, in contrast, a charmless female beggar – 'ill, moody, and tongue-tied' (l. 2) – finds herself near affluent Belgrave Square but ignores the rich, waiting until she sees '[some] labouring men' before sending her child to ask for money. These class interactions are used as the basis for some conventional moralising, but also for some reflections on the overriding value of labour. In both instances it is the labourers who are the agents of charity; the preacher '[labours] through the night' in the hope of attaining 'heaven' for himself and his congregation, while the labourers who give alms to the West-End beggar are implicitly contrasted with 'the rich', 'aliens' who offer nothing more than 'cold succour' to the beggar because of their inability to sympathise with 'common human fate'. Similarly, both end with a vision of 'heaven'; a conventional religious vision in the case of the preacher, and a more secular vision of a world of greater fellowship and equality in the case of the beggar; her actions '[point] us to a better time than ours'. There are obvious continuities between the structure of feeling apparent in these poems and the Christian Socialist movement of Maurice and Kingsley, but the incidents depicted in the poems highlight the lack of any vital connection between the poet and the social world he describes. In the first poem the 'thrice dispirited' Spitalfields weaver is glimpsed 'through a window', and the poet only interacts with the representative of his own class; in the second the characters are merely the prelude to the moralising and abstracting voice of the sestet:

> Thought I: 'Above her state this spirit towers;
> She will not ask of aliens, but of friends,
> Of sharers in a common human fate.
>
> She turns from that cold succour, which attends
> The unknown little from the unknowing great,
> And points us to a better time than ours.' (ll. 9–14)

There is no possibility of interaction between the representatives of suffering humanity and the subtle, reflective consciousness which transforms their actions into platitudes on the human condition. The poet's urgent moral concerns are undermined by his status as a *flâneur* or wanderer in the city, regarding human life as a spectacle for contemplation rather than a field for purposeful activity. Here, as elsewhere in his work, Arnold seems almost unwittingly to anticipate the writers of the Decadence, who complete this process of disengagement by detaching the *flâneur* completely from questions of morality and politics and aestheticising the objects of his gaze.[21]

The last years of the century did, however, see the emergence of what we might call the sonnet of Imperialism. William Michael Rossetti's much-anthologised 'Emigration' is a good specimen of this new type of poetry, which picks up the strain of patriotism in Milton and Wordsworth to glorify England's imperial heroes and national destiny:

> Weave o'er the world your weft, yea weave yourselves,
>   Imperial races weave the warp thereof.
>   Swift like your shuttle speed the ships, and scoff
> At wind and wave. And, as a miner delves
> For hidden treasure bedded deep in stone,
>   So seek ye and find the treasure patriotism
>   In lands remote and dipped with alien chrism,
> And make those new lands heart-dear and your own.
> Weave o'er the world yourselves. Half-human man
>   Wanes from before your faces like a cloud
>   Sun-stricken, and his soil becomes his shroud.
>   But of your souls and bodies ye shall make
> The sov'reign vesture of its leagueless span,
>   Clothing with history cliff and wild and lake.[22]

The nadir of this uniquely bad poem comes in the sestet's glorification of the extinction of the 'half-human' people who stand in the way of England's emigrants. It illustrates the odd combination of imperial sentiment and aesthetic delicacy that characterises a good deal of the political poetry of the late nineteenth century. Theodore Watts-Dunton, friend of Swinburne and composer of a number of distinguished sonnets in the aesthetic mould, finished his career (in both senses) with a sonnet sequence on the death of Rhodes; and William Watson moved from the Pre-Raphaelitism of *The Prince's Quest* to his sonnets on the death of the greatest of all imperial heroes, Gordon.[23] This combination finds its most complex expression, however, in the work of a poet who had voluntarily cut himself off from the outside world and saw the great social and political events of his time (as he put it) 'in a bat-light'.[24] In late 1887, Gerard Manley Hopkins, Jesuit priest and Professor of Greek at University College Dublin, composed a pair of sonnets – 'Harry Ploughman' and 'Tom's Garland' – in which he attempts to encapsulate both his own vision of the ideal society and his anxieties about the turbulent political events of the decade. These poems have only occasionally been studied as a pair; this is slightly surprising, as Hopkins clearly thought about them in this way. Apologising to his friend (and part of his extremely small and select audience) Robert Bridges for the similarities between them, he wrote: 'They were conceived at the same time: that is how it is'.[25] Moreover, as a number of critics have pointed out, the characters in the poems are given the names Tom, Dick and Harry, suggesting a desire on Hopkins' part to provide a portrait of the labouring classes of town and country, both as they are and as they might become in some future state of society. Once seen as a pair, these poems acquire a heavily and even grotesquely emblematic quality; they admit, as we shall see, a bewildering variety of political discourses into what Hopkins calls their 'underthoughts', and activate the latent resonances of the sonnet as a form more thoroughly than any sonnets since Wordsworth's.[26]

The first of the pair, 'Harry Ploughman', alludes in its title to one of the iconic figures of British social and political debate. From *Piers Plowman* to Shelley's 'Song to the Men of England' the ploughman figures as the very type of honest and productive labour, and Hopkins continues this tradition in his idealised portrait:

Hard as hurdle arms, with a broth of goldish flue
Breathed round; the rack of ribs; the scooped flank; lank
Rope-over thigh; knee-nave; and barrelled shank –
        Head and foot, shoulder and shank –
By a grey eye's heed steered well, one crew, fall to;
Stand at stress. Each limb's barrowy brawn, his thew
That onewhere curded, onewhere sucked or sank –
        Soared or sank –,
Though as a beechbole firm, finds his, as at a rollcall, rank
And features, in flesh, what deed he each must do –
        His sinew-service where do.
He leans to it, Harry bends, look. Back, elbow, and liquid waist

In him, all quail to the wallowing o' the plough. 'S cheek crimsons; curls
Wag or crossbridle, in a wind lifted, windlaced –
    Wind-lilylocks-laced;
Churlsgrace, too, child of Amansstrength, how it hangs or hurls
Them – broad in bluff hide his frowning feet lashed! raced
With, along them, cragiron under and cold furls –
    With-a-fountain's shining-shot furls.

In depriving the reader, to a large extent, of the usual resources of syntax, Hopkins forces our attention onto the poem's metaphorical clusters, and these therefore become the bearers of its 'underthought'. One such cluster gives Harry an architectural quality; the 'ribs', the 'scooped' flank, the 'knee nave', and even the ornamental-sounding 'rope-over' imply an analogy between his sturdiness and the massive solidity of a Gothic cathedral. This, in turn, establishes a broadly medieval, or perhaps more accurately medieval-revival framework for the poem. Looking to the Middle Ages for a stable, hierarchical, organic political community was (as we have already seen in the case of Thomas Cooper) an integral part of Victorian political discourse. This medievalism was, moreover, almost always ruralist in orientation; indeed, much of its motivation was based on an outright rejection of the urbanisation and industrialisation of the modern world. Hence Ruskin, for instance, established his 'Guild of St. George' in an attempt to restore 'lost values' 'through a return to a form of economy based on agriculture and crafts'.[27] Hopkins knew and valued the work of Ruskin, and of his disciple Morris. He was, indeed, a more thoroughgoing medievalist than either; as a convert to Roman Catholicism, he looked forward to the day when England would again be part of the Roman Catholic communion. Harry Ploughman is, then, an emblematic figure, an idealised rural labourer of a renewed middle ages; this is why his actions, in their sinewy strength, are said to have a 'Churlsgrace'. As Sjaak Zonneveld points out, '[in] Anglo-Saxon times, a churl, or "ceorl", was a member of the third or lowest rank of freemen', so to have a 'churlsgrace' is to have the kind of dignity and honour appropriate to his station in life.[28]

This sense of a hierarchical social organisation is also present in another of the poem's metaphorical clusters which links Harry to the organisation and discipline of the military. He is said to 'steer' well both his own limbs and the horse he is controlling; they are 'one crew' who stand, not at ease, but 'at stress'. When called upon each limb 'finds his, as at a rollcall, rank', and is sent where he must do his 'sinew-service'. These military connotations have a number of valences. On the one hand they bond with Ruskin's suggestion in *Unto this Last* (and elsewhere in his work) that the armed forces provide a paradigm of the harmonious hierarchical society:

> Whether socialism has made more progress among the army and navy (where payment is made on my principles), or among the manufacturing operatives (who are paid on my opponents' principles), I leave it to those opponents to ascertain and declare... if there be any one point insisted on throughout my works more frequently than another, that one point is the impossibility of Equality... My principles of Political Economy were all involved in a single phrase spoken three years ago at Manchester: 'Soldiers of the Ploughshare as well as Soldiers of the Sword:' and they were all summed in a single sentence in the last volume of 'Modern Painters' – 'Government and co-operation are in all things the Laws of Life; Anarchy and competition the Laws of Death.'[29]

Harry is literally a soldier or (given the presence of so many aquatic metaphors in the poem) a sailor of the ploughshare, and both emblematises and participates in a social order made up of appropriate gradations of 'rank'. But these military implications also bond with a language of racial degeneration and decay which will become important in the partner-poem 'Tom's Garland'. John Lucas cites a letter of Hopkins to Alexander Baillie (written in May 1888) in which he links the physical degeneration of urban living to the military fiasco of Majuba Hill:

> What I most dislike in towns and in London in particular is the misery of the poor; the dirt, squalor, and the illshapen degraded physical (put aside moral) type of so many of the people, with the deeply dejecting, unbearable thought that by degrees almost all our population will become a town population and a puny unhealthy and cowardly one. Yes, cowardly. Do you know and realise what happened at Majuba Hill? 500 British troops after 8 hours firing, on the Dutch reaching the top, ran without offering resistance before, it is said, 80 men. Such a thing was never heard in history.[30]

Like many of his contemporaries, Hopkins was a fiercely patriotic poet; some of his efforts, like 'What shall I do for the land that bred me?', anticipate Kipling's *Barrack-Room Ballads* in their attempt to provide the ordinary soldier with a language of service and patriotism. Seen against this background, 'Harry Ploughman' implies that an agrarian society of the kind envisaged by the Guild of St. George will also restore England's martial prowess and prestige; Harry's 'hard as hurdle arms' and 'barrowy brawn' can, the 'underthought' implies, quickly be pressed into military service if needed.

Finally, the poem as a whole reinforces these implications by reactivating the dormant medieval connotations of the sonnet form. Hopkins' experiments with 'sprung rhythm'[31] were prompted by a desire to develop a form of poetry linked as closely as possible with the 'native and natural rhythm of speech', and found their model in the alliterative poetry of Old and Middle English – in texts such as *Piers Plowman*, which Hopkins read in 1882.[32] In a similar vein, he attempted to 'naturalise' the sonnet in the English language by adding the 'outriding feet' and 'burden lines' which punctuate 'Harry Ploughman'. Hopkins suggests in a letter of October 1881 that the English sonnet is deficient in length when compared to its Italian counterpart, because the lines of the Italian sonnet are typically twelve or thirteen syllables long, and that it is as a result 'short, light, tripping, and trifling'. The best English sonnet writers, such as Wordsworth, have intuitively attempted to overcome this deficiency in various ways, but Hopkins suggests that 'for a mechanical difficulty the most mechanical remedy is the best', and adds to his sonnets what he calls 'outriding feet' or extra-metrical syllables designed to make the English line as long as or even longer than its Italian counterpart.[33] In 'Harry Ploughman' Hopkins' idiosyncratic metrical notation suggests that the last long syllable of 'Amansstrength' is meant to be read in this way, as a kind of additional foot which does not disrupt the fundamental rhythm.[34] Moreover, in 'Harry Ploughman', Hopkins uses the additional device of 'burden lines', the five indented or half-lines which might, as he puts it, 'be recited by a chorus'.[35] It is very difficult to weld Hopkins' various devices into a single coherent structure – there is no reliable record of the imaginary orchestration which might have brought his metrical marks to life – but the intention behind them is clear; Hopkins is trying to revive and improve a medieval structure to make it usable in the nineteenth century. Like the great Victorian architects and engineers, he is happy to use 'mechanical' devices to achieve his aims, and the result in 'Harry Ploughman' is a kind of Gothic revival masterpiece, a pastiche of what an English sonnet might have looked like in the days of Langland and Chaucer.

The symmetry of 'Harry Ploughman' and 'Tom's Garland: Upon the Unemployed' has been slightly obscured by the fact that the second of the poems was revised in response to contemporary political events. Hopkins seems to have begun it in September 1887, and at that time it consisted of just the first ten lines; he then badgered his friend Bridges for information on how to write a 'caudated' or tailed sonnet, perhaps recognising in that form what Michael Spiller calls 'a generic signal of satirical intent', and added the extra lines around December of that year, closely following the model of Milton's sonnet 'On the New Forcers of Conscience'.[36] Between the first draft of the poem and its completion, a number of demonstrations of 'the unemployed' had taken place in England, culminating in what came to be known as 'Bloody Sunday' (13 November 1887) when the police forcibly broke up a rally of the unemployed in Trafalgar Square, injuring a number of demonstrators and killing two.[37] The impact of this event and others like it is clearly inscribed in both the title and the form of the poem. The second section of the sonnet switches attention from an idealised portrait of the urban labourer to the condition of 'the unemployed', but Hopkins struggles, both thematically and formally, to bring these two subjects together, and the result is a spectacularly compressed display of strong but unfocussed feeling. The colon in the title of the poem marks a separation as much as a conjunction; the poem is both 'Tom's Garland' and a meditation 'upon the unemployed', but finds no language in which both can be accommodated.

In presenting an idealised image of urban labour to go alongside 'Harry Ploughman', Hopkins is writing in a long-established and indeed rather old-fashioned Carlylean idiom; the idiom that inspired, for instance, Ford Madox Brown's iconic painting 'Work':

Tom – garlanded with squat and surly steel
Tom; then Tom's fallowbootfellow piles pick
By him and rips out rockfire homeforth – sturdy Dick;
Tom Heart-at-ease, Tom Navvy: he is all for his meal
Sure, 's bed now. Low be it: lustily he his low lot (feel
That ne'er need hunger, Tom; Tom seldom sick,
Seldomer heartsore; that treads through, prickproof, thick
Thousands of thorns, thoughts) swings through. Commonweal
Little I reck ho! lacklevel in, if all had bread:
What! Country is honour enough in all us – lordly head,
With heaven's lights high hung round, or, mother-ground
That mammocks, mighty foot. But no way sped,

> Nor mind nor mainstrength; gold go garlanded
> With, perilous, O nó; nor yet plod safe shod sound;
>   Undenizened, beyond bound
> Of earth's glory, earth's ease, all; no one, nowhere,
> In wide the world's weal; rare gold, bold steel, bare
>   In both; care, but share care –
> This, by Despair, bred Hangdog dull; by Rage,
> Manwolf, worse; and their packs infest the age.

As a number of critics have pointed out, Hopkins' 'Tom Navvy', weary but happy after his hard day's work, would fit easily into Madox Brown's famous painting. As in 'Harry Ploughman', moreover, Hopkins includes in the 'underthought' various suggestions about Tom's place within the national hierarchy. In calling the steel nails in the soles of his boots his 'garland', Hopkins is implying that Tom too is a kind of monarch of his realm; if he lacks power and influence, he gains the peace of mind that comes from little responsibility and the bodily strength that comes from physical labour. As Zonneveld points out, there are numerous allusions to and reminiscences of Shakespeare's history plays in this sonnet, especially *Henry IV* and *Henry V*; and the general feeling of it is summed up in *Henry V*, IV, i, 232–3: 'What infinite heart's ease/ Must kings neglect that private men enjoy!' Like 'Harry Ploughman', moreover, Tom is an emblematic figure, literally the foot of the 'commonweal'. In a letter explaining the meaning of the poem (written in despair at the inability of even his close friends and supporters to make out his meaning), Hopkins states that it is based on the venerable analogy of the 'body politic':

> [The] commonwealth or well ordered human society is like one man; a body with many members and each its function; some higher, some lower, but all honourable, from the honour which belongs to the whole... The foot is the daylabourer, and this is armed with hobnail boots, because it has to wear and be worn by the ground... the 'garlands' of nails they wear are therefore the visible badge of the place they fill, the lowest in the commonwealth.[38]

Tom and Dick are, then, 'fallowbootfellows' in a literal sense, the feet upon which the whole of the commonwealth rests. There are, however, 'underthoughts' of tension and violence which run counter to this idea of a peaceful and harmonious hierarchy. Tom and Dick seem to possess an elemental capacity for violence; even their contented walk home 'rips out rockfire' from the earth. And the nexus of Shake-spearean allusions in the poem clusters around the motif of usurpa-tion; Zonneveld, again, notes that the vocabulary of 'mammocking' their 'mother-ground' comes from *Coriolanus*, and that Volumnia attempts to dissuade her son from marching on Rome by comparing the act to treading 'on thy mother's womb/ That brought thee to this world' (V, iii, 124–5).[39] There is, then, a suggestion that the great phys-ical strength and destructive capacity of Tom and his like might even-tually be turned against the very 'body' of which they form a valuable (though perhaps neglected) part; and it is this suggestion which produces the barely coherent and almost unsayable exclamation of lines 8–9: 'Commonweal/ Little I reck ho! lacklevel in, if all had bread'. Hopkins' own gloss on these lines is that '[the] witnessing of [the labourers'] lightheartedness makes me indignant with the fools of Radical Levellers'. The 'Radical Levellers', such as William Morris' Socialist League, which established a journal called *Commonweal* in 1885, are, the poem suggests, wrong to make Tom dissatisfied with his place in the hierarchy; there is no problem with a 'lacklevel' society as long as everyone has enough to eat.[40] This exclamation exposes the undercurrents of violence in the poem as potentially revolutionary, and represents a symptom of the poet's anxiety about the condition and restlessness of the urban poor during a turbulent decade.

It is at this point, according to the poet's summary, that he remem-bers that his observations on a 'lacklevel' society are 'all very well for those who are in, however low in, the Commonwealth and share in any way the Common weal; but that the curse of our times is that many do not share it, that they are outcasts from it and have neither security nor splendour; that they share care with the high and obscur-ity with the low, but wealth or comfort with neither.'[41] It is these people whom he refers to, in the poem's sub- or parallel title, as 'the unemployed'. In doing so, he is using a word which was both new and contentious in the 1880s. Reporting on some recent political distur-bances on 15 October 1887, *The Times* noted that 'the Unemployed, as they term themselves, have begun to show in force a little sooner than they were expected'.[42] In calling themselves 'the Unemployed', the people in question were implying that society had a duty to provide them with work; and Hopkins' adoption of this contentious word in a poem celebrating the value of physical labour implies that he agrees with their point of view. In one sense the introduction of the Unemployed towards the end of the poem is prepared for by the min-atory undercurrents of the first ten lines; but in another sense their arrival leads to a severe formal and thematic dislocation in the poem.

The extent of this dislocation can be seen if 'Tom's Garland' is compared with the poem which may well have directly inspired it, the sonnet Ford Madox Brown wrote to accompany his painting 'Work':

> Work! which beads the brow and tans the flesh
> Of lusty manhood, casting out its devils!
> By whose weird art, transmuting poor men's evils
> Their bed seems down, their one dish ever fresh,
> Ah me! For lack of it what ills in leash
> Hold us. Its want their pale mechanic levels
> To workhouse depths, while Master Spendthrift revels
> For want to work, the fiends soon him immesh.
> Ah! beauteous tripping dame with bell like skirts
> Intent on thy small scarlet-coated hound
> Are ragged wayside babes not lovesome too?
> Untrained their state reflects on thy deserts
> Or they grow noisome beggars to abound,
> Or dreaded midnight robbers, breaking through.[43]

The movement from praise of work to fear of 'dreaded midnight robbers' is strongly reminiscent of the trajectory of Hopkins' poem, and there are other common features; just as Tom is 'all for' his meal and his bed, Brown suggests that for the labourer the most rudimentary bed 'seems down' and the homeliest of meals 'ever fresh'. But there are also significant differences between the two poems. For Brown, lack of wholesome labour causes all of society's ills; it reduces the 'mechanic' to 'workhouse depths', but also creates 'Master Spendthrift' whose leisure and resources makes him a prey to the 'fiends'. The sestet of his poem implies that a return to proper charitable sentiment on the part of the wealthy would prevent the transformation of 'ragged wayside babes' into 'noisome beggars' and 'midnight robbers'. Hopkins' poem, in contrast, omits all reference to the relation between work and the wealthier classes of society; this act of omission obscures the nature of the relation between the classes, and means that 'the unemployed' emerge at the end of the poem as a mystifyingly alien and unassimilable element. They are 'undenizened' – literally denied rights of citizenship – and transformed (in the severely elliptical closing lines) into sub-human creatures.[44] In addition, where Brown comfortably includes all ranks in a conventional fourteen-line sonnet, Hopkins distends and even distorts his sonnet in an attempt to deal with the problem of the 'unemployed'. A poet as sensitive to all aspects of the form of poetry as

Hopkins would not have adopted the 'caudated' sonnet without intending the reader to notice its iconic significance, and the 'codas' to the poem represent, as Richard Isomaki puts it, a 'test of inclusion or exclusion'; the unemployed and their violent progeny are both within and outside society, just as the 'codas' to the poem are both within and outside the sonnet form.[45]

Hopkins' poem, unlike Brown's, does not have a single perspective or framework; it has at its heart an unresolved conflict between two diametrically opposing ways of viewing the ordinary workmen who are its subject. On the one hand, its language of 'dogs' and 'wolves' links up with a persistent tendency towards a kind of reactionary neo-Darwinism in late nineteenth-century political discourse; the idea that the conditions of urban life, especially if they are not associated with wholesome physical labour, will eventually produce a literal 'reversion' or degeneration to a lower state of being.[46] The two faces of the ordinary labourer in the poem have a kind of Jekyll-and-Hyde quality, with the image of robust but honest Tom dissolving and being replaced by that of snarling 'Manwolf'.[47] But, as we have already seen, these ideas about racial degeneration are already present in the 'underthought' of 'Harry Ploughman', and in that setting they become part of an implied argument about the shape of an ideal society in which physical labour assumes its rightful and honourable place. Seen in this light, the suggestions of 'reversion' at the end of 'Tom's Garland' might be seen as savagely critical, not of the unemployed themselves, but of a society which allows some of its members to become 'undenizened' by refusing them their fundamental right to labour. The two parts of the poem can be seen as occupying different temporal or logical positions, with one a portrait of the ideal worker as he might be, and the other a portrait of the reality of 'the age'. The disjunction between the two parts of the poem illustrates how far the late nineteenth century is from embodying a real and living organic society; the full humanity on offer to ordinary workmen in such a society is implicitly contrasted with the limited and dehumanising reality of their own time. In this respect, then, the poem seems continuous with the Utopianism of Ruskin and Morris; Hopkins' Tom lives in a kind of Utopia, a 'world turned upside down', or at least seen upside down, in which garlands are worn on the soles of the shoes.[48] Hopkins' 'Commonwealth' and Morris' *Commonweal* are not as far apart as some critics have supposed.

The urgency of Hopkins' political sonnets comes from the fact that he is using the form to grapple with and work out his views, not to invest them with a spurious permanence and authority.[49] From what we know of his thinking at this time he seems to have been genuinely ambivalent about the various movements for social justice which emerged in the late nineteenth century. Critics and biographers have been quick to play down the significance of what he called his 'red letter' to Bridges, written in the aftermath of the Paris Commune, in which he reluctantly confesses himself a Communist; Robert Bernard Martin, for instance, sees the letter as the product of temporary estrangement between Hopkins and his friend, and reassures the reader that '[there] was little of the communist or socialist in Hopkins' make-up'.[50] But the 'underthought' of 'Tom's Garland' calls this judgement into question. Alongside the patriotic indignation of Milton's and Wordsworth's sonnets, it is also possible to detect the distant sound of Shelley's radical (and radically innovative) *Ode to the West Wind*:

> The style of the 'ode to the west wind' with its 'pestilence-stricken multitudes' and lines like 'yellow, and black, and pale, and hectic red', and 'black rain, and fire, and hail will burst; oh, hear!' resembles the style of 'Tom's Garland' in its abrupt, dynamic and intensive wildness. 'Wild' was a favourite word for Hopkins, as it was for Shelley. It would be understandable if, with Shelley's style, some of his radical fervour had slipped into the 'underthought' of Hopkins's poem. It is not fanciful to feel in the lines of 'Tom's Garland' the thought – 'hoard, unheard' – of Shelley's 'England in 1819': 'Rulers who neither see, nor feel, nor know,/ But leech like to their fainting country cling'.[51]

Zonneveld's suggestion that Hopkins' adoption of Shelley's 'style' induced an identification with his 'radical fervour' highlights the importance of the associations the political sonnet had built up throughout the century. Hopkins inherited from his precursors a form with elements of patriotic fervour, democratic sentiment and medievalism, and attempted (to use his own metaphor) to 'forge' from these a poetry which would encapsulate his own deeply held but profoundly contradictory political beliefs.

4
The Devotional Sonnet

In the Elizabethan period, the religious sonnet followed on from and to a certain extent developed out of the amatory sonnet; the conventions established in the latter were self-consciously transferred to the former in the attempt to find a contemporary idiom for religious devotion. This order of priority is reversed in the nineteenth century, with the religious sonnet appearing earlier than its amatory counterpart. The main reason for this can, again, be traced to the pre-eminence of Wordsworth. If, as Arline Golden has suggested, 'the power of the Wordsworthian-Miltonic sonnet' prevented 'the renascence of the amatory sonnet' until the appearance of *Sonnets from the Portuguese*, it also enabled the development of a specifically religious sonnet which gained in currency and popularity throughout the century.[1] This sonnet does not derive directly from Wordsworth's own specifically religious poems – although the much-derided *Ecclesiastical Sonnets* foreshadow, as we shall see, some of the main lines of the development of religious poetry – but rather from the atmosphere of reverence which suffuses his meditative poetry, and which was recognised by Wordsworth's contemporaries as the counterpart of the religious revival of the early nineteenth century in the sphere of feeling. Wordsworth's 'natural piety' modulates into the meditative and introspective sonnets of Christina Rossetti and Gerard Manley Hopkins, which function as a space in which the poets can reflect on and examine the progress of their own souls.

The poetic sensibilities of both Rossetti and Hopkins were formed to a large extent by the movement for renewal in the Church of England variously known as the 'Tractarian' or 'Oxford' movement.[2] This resurgence of Anglican fervour was sparked off by radical reforms of the late 1820s and early 1830s which seemed to weaken the link between church and state.[3] In formulating their response to these attacks, leading members of the Movement like John Keble and John Henry Newman saw themselves as participating in a more general movement of 'spiritual awakening' heralded by the work of Scott, Coleridge and Wordsworth.[4] Like the Lake poets, the founders of the Movement wanted to inspire in people a reverence for the values embodied in ancient forms and traditions. One of the first manifestations of the Movement was John Keble's phenomenally successful volume *The Christian Year* (1827), in which he provides poems to accompany the various festivals and observances of the liturgical year.[5] Keble was the principal poet and theorist of poetry amongst the Movement's adherents, recognising in it an important conduit for the transmission of feeling and the development of religious sentiment; and he acknowledged Wordsworth as his master in this respect, describing Wordsworth as a 'true philosopher and inspired poet' in the dedication to the *Lectures on Poetry* he gave during his time as Professor of Poetry at Oxford.[6] Wordsworth, in his turn, knew and admired Keble's poetry, and recognised it as a legitimate (if inferior) offshoot of his own. He is reputed to have said that *The Christian Year* 'was so good he only wished he could have written it himself to make it better';[7] and it is more than likely that he directly inspired Keble's book through the example of his *Ecclesiastical Sonnets*.[8]

Wordsworth was prompted to produce this typically loose grouping of poems describing the growth of the national church and its rituals by a walk through the grounds of Sir George Beaumont's estate at Coleorton to see the progress of a new church that was being built. The combination of 'one of the most beautiful mornings of a mild season' and the 'cherishing influences of the scene' led Wordsworth to produce some sonnets 'as a private memorial of that morning's occupation'; but these became a series of one hundred and two sonnets under the pressure of external events: 'The Catholic Question, which was agitated in Parliament about that time, kept my thoughts in the same course; and it struck me that certain points in the Ecclesiastical History of our Country might advantageously be presented to view in verse.'[9] These poems were a product of the very controversies which were stirring Keble and his fellow clergymen into action, and it is not surprising in this case to find that they anticipate to a large extent the structures of feeling characteristic of the Oxford Movement. The Movement was keen to stress the national and organic character of the Church of England, claiming it as in some ways the only true survivor of the universal Catholic faith destroyed by schism and Papal pretensions during the Middle Ages and Reformation, and Wordsworth mirrors this perception by structuring his sonnets around the venerable metaphor of the river of faith flowing on and gathering strength. The sources of this river lie in the obscure but profound religious sentiments of pre-Christian England, and this legacy can still be felt in the church being built by Sir George Beaumont, which is erected amongst the 'forest oaks of Druid memory' (III, xxxix, l. 7). Foreign influences are almost invariably presented as damaging or distorting; Rome enters English history as a conqueror and persecutor, prefiguring later 'Papal abuses' (I, iii; vi; viii; xxxvii). This emphasis on tradition and continuity leads Wordsworth to omit the Civil War and Commonwealth from his history altogether; these extremely contentious episodes 'from which Historians shrink' (II, iii, l. 14) fall into the gap between sections II and III.[10] In addition, like the Tractarians, Wordsworth seems to lament certain aspects of the Reformation:

> Would that our scrupulous Sires had dared to leave
> Less scanty measure of those graceful rites
> And usages, whose due return invites
> A stir of mind too natural to deceive;
> Giving to Memory help when she would weave
> A crown for Hope! – I dread the boasted lights
> That all too often are but fiery blights,
> Killing the bud o'er which in vain we grieve.
> Go, seek, when Christmas snows discomfort bring,
> The counter Spirit found in some gay church
> Green with fresh holly, every pew a perch
> In which the linnet or the thrush might sing,
> Merry and loud and safe from prying search,
> Strains offered only to the genial Spring. (III, xxxiii)

The emphasis here on the role of 'rites' and 'usages' in prompting feelings of religious devotion is consistent with the Tractarian attitude towards ritual (Tractarians were often caricatured as ritualists by opponents); and in fact Wordsworth's call to celebrate what he calls 'the ritual year/ Of England's Church' and its 'stupendous mysteries' in a later poem (III, xix) directly anticipates the project of *The Christian Year*.[11] Again, the scepticism about 'boasted lights' in this poem undermines one of the key terms of Protestant theology, the 'inner light' of faith and private judgement. Wordsworth's sestet reworks Shakespeare's famous image from Sonnet 73 – 'Bare ruined choirs where late the sweet birds sang' (l. 4) – to imagine a new national church in which the 'sweet birds' are lured back by the delusive hints of 'genial Spring'. There are other such moments in the *Ecclesiastical Sonnets*,[12] but Margaret Johnson is probably overstating the case when she describes the sequence as articulating a typically Tractarian 'desire for renewal of Catholicism without any accompanying Romanism'.[13] The narrative of the *Ecclesiastical Sonnets* is a fundamentally Protestant one, and becomes more so with subsequent revisions.[14] What Wordsworth is expressing in the sequence is an ambivalence which only later resolves itself into competing factions and doctrinal disputes, an adherence to the Church of England and its institutions which looks back beyond the Reformation while still recognising the historical importance of that event.

As well as finding in Wordsworth's poetry a strong precursor for their own feelings about the national church, the Tractarians also found in his critical writings a theory of poetry which they could adapt to their own purposes. Wordsworth famously defined poetry (in the Preface to *Lyrical Ballads*) as 'the spontaneous overflow of powerful feeling'; but for the Victorians generally, and the Tractarians in particular, this definition omitted the presence of an equal and opposite force of 'reserve' or concealment. The drive towards expression is impeded 'by an instinctive delicacy which recoils from exposing them [powerful feelings] openly, as feeling that they can never meet with full sympathy'. In sophisticated and cultured minds, the result of this conflict is poetry, which is defined by Keble as '*the indirect expression in words, most appropriately in metrical words, of some overpowering emotion, or ruling taste, or feeling, the direct indulgence whereof is somehow repressed.*' Expressing such emotions and feelings through the complex mediating forms of poetry indicates that they are 'so far under controul [sic], as to leave those who feel them at liberty to pay attention to measure and rhyme, and the other expedients of metrical composition'.[15] In the lectures he gave as Professor of Poetry at Oxford, Keble developed these insights into a systematic theory of poetry linking different genres to different forms of feeling. The sonnet represents one of the most complex and difficult forms, and therefore testifies to the depth of the feelings which it is attempting both to express and to repress:

> Since this particular form prescribes such scanty limits (for by inviolable rule it never exceeds fourteen lines); and since it submits itself to the further difficult law that the lines must not only be of equal length, but also rhyme at definite intervals, and these intervals stand in uneven relation to each other, we cannot but wonder how

it has come to pass that so many eager and enthusiastic temperaments have voluntarily submitted to these restraints. For, besides Petrarch to whom I have just referred, Dante Alighieri spent pains upon this form of poetry, and yielded to none in his scrupulous strictness: so too did the renowned Michael Angelo Buonarroti, a man of unfettered and colossal genius, whom no rules, not to say of any particular art, but of any and every art easily held: so too did our own Spenser, at once the tenderest and most dignified of poets: not to mention more recent instances, not unworthy assuredly to be enrolled among this company. I am persuaded, indeed, that it was by no mere chance, but by a deeply-rooted instinct, that such men as these adopted this form, because the fact that it was unusually stringent enabled it to soothe and compose their deepest emotions and longings without violating a true reserve.[16]

This emphasis on the proportional relation between depth of feeling and technical difficulty creates a discursive space for the religious sonnet in particular, since (as Keble acknowledges in his essay 'Sacred Poetry') religious feelings are both very deeply held and liable to misunderstanding and even ridicule by others.[17]

Another Tractarian theorist of 'reserve', Isaac Williams, put this theory into practice in his influential collection *The Cathedral, or the Catholic and Apostolic Church in England*, first published in 1838.[18] In the Preface to his 1815 Poems, Wordsworth describes his poetry as constituting a single entity and compares the overall effect to a cathedral. Williams' collection is avowedly based on a similar conceit, but uses the sonnet as one of its building-blocks.[19] At the entrance to the Cathedral, for instance, we find three doors called 'Obedience', 'Faith' and 'Repentance'; and the poet draws out the lesson of the 'lowly door' of Repentance for his readers in a series of three conjoined sonnets:

> So daily may'st thou less become
> In thine own eyes, and thus beguil'd
> Into the likeness of a child,
> The narrow gate shall give thee room:
> As dawns the light of thy last home,
> The wreaths of Eden, sin-defil'd,
> Drop off, but thou art reconcil'd
> To sorrow, leaving some, and some
> Before thee gone, and waiting thee,
> Where relics of lost Paradise

> Are gathering; thus made lowly wise,
> Till Life's dark porch shall set thee free,
> And there shall break upon thine eyes
> The temple of Eternity. ('Repentance', 29–42)[20]

In a collection significantly indebted to the example of Herbert's *The Temple*, it is not fanciful to see in these octosyllabic lines a visual and metrical representation of the strait gate through which the penitent must pass.[21] Williams is making the 'narrow room' of the Miltonic-Wordsworthian sonnet even narrower, and reinforces the point by using the same metre for the equally narrow door of Faith. He is also, incidentally, inventing the stanza of Tennyson's *In Memoriam*; lines 5–8 could very easily slot into Tennyson's poem, and this affinity highlights *In Memoriam*'s status as a repressed or disguised sonnet sequence.[22]

As a committed Tractarian, Williams offers a subtly different reading of ecclesiastical history from Wordsworth's, one which acknowledges the attractions of Roman Catholicism while claiming to prefer the homely simplicity of the national church:

> Dear Church, our island's sacred sojourner,
> A richer dress thy Southern sisters own,
> And some would deem too bright their flowing zone
> For sacred walls. I love thee, nor would stir
> Thy simple note, severe in character,
> By use made lovelier, for the lofty tone
> Or hymn, response, and touching antiphone,
> Lest we lose homelier truth. The chorister
> That sings the summer nights, so soft and strong,
> To music modulating his sweet throat,
> Labours with richness of his varied note,
> Yet lifts not unto Heaven a holier song,
> Than our home bird that, on some leafless thorn,
> Hymns his plain chaunt each wintry eve and morn.[23]

Williams here translates the differences between Protestant and Catholic churches into differences of climate; the 'Southern' churches with their 'richer dress' are contrasted with the forms of worship natural to the more austere climate of 'our island'. This doctrinal *legerdemain* is complemented by another reworking of the Shakespearean trope used by Wordsworth in 'Regrets'. Shakespeare's line 'Bare ruined choirs where late the sweet birds sang' underlies the sestet's contrast between the opulence of pre-Reformation musical worship and the 'plain chaunt' of the Anglican bird perched on its 'leafless thorn'. In describing the 'home bird' in its 'wintry eve and morn', however, Williams establishes a set of connotations which run counter to the argument of his poem. The loss of the music of 'summer nights' is clearly a matter of regret, regardless of the poet's attempts to claim that he prefers the austerity (to anticipate slightly) of the bleak midwinter. Such contradictions are typical of the structure of feeling of the early phase of Tractarianism, and indicate something of the inevitability of its eventual drift southward and Romeward.

Sonnets are also used prominently in the Tractarian collection *Lyra Apostolica* (1836), but this volume aims at an explicitly polemical reworking of the Romantic inheritance rather than a delicate expression of devotional sentiment. The procedure is exemplified in Richard Hurrell Froude's 'Sight against Faith':

'And Lot went out, and spake unto his sons-in-law, that married his daughters, and said, Up! get you out of this place; for the Lord will destroy this city. But he seemed as one that mocked unto his sons-in-law.'[24]

> 'Sunk not the sun behind yon dusky hill
> Glorious as he was wont? The starry sky
> Spread o'er the earth in quiet majesty,
> Discernest thou in its clear deep aught of ill?
> Or in this lower world, so fair and still,
> Its palaces and temples towering high;
> Or where old Jordan, gliding calmly by,
> Pours o'er the misty plain his mantle chill?
> Dote not of fear, old man, where all is joy;
> And heaven and earth thy augury disown;
> And time's eternal course rolls smoothly on,
> Fraught with fresh blessings as day follows day.
> The All-bounteous hath not given to take away;
> The All-wise hath not created to destroy.'[25]

This complacent utterance by one of Lot's sons-in-law, refusing to heed the warning of the imminent destruction of Sodom and Gomorrah, contains, as Margaret Johnson points out, a number of verbal echoes of one of Wordsworth's ubiquitous 'Westminster Bridge' sonnet; the 'quiet majesty' of the scene and the 'palaces and temples' are reminiscent of the London glimpsed by Wordsworth at dawn. But, as Johnson notes, these echoes assume a menacing quality in this context, and their effect is to '[direct] the threat of apocalypse toward the England of the precursor poem'.[26] A similarly pugnacious rewriting of a Romantic precursor can be seen in Newman's 'Progress of Unbelief':

> Now is the Autumn of the Tree of Life;
> Its leaves are shed upon the unthankful earth,
> Which lets them whirl, a prey to the winds' strife,
> Heartless to store them for the months of dearth. (ll. 1–4)

This is typical of many of Newman's contributions to *Lyra* in its invocation of a mood of autumnal gloom, but the leaves which 'whirl' at the wind's behest specifically recall the dominant image of Shelley's 'Ode to the West Wind'. For Newman the leaves are not harbingers of hope but the last remnants of a national faith which has all but disappeared, displaced by the worship of a 'household Baal' which feeds on the withered stalks of the Tree of Life. Such doctrinal overwritings of the Romantics in *Lyra Apostolica* highlight the Tractarians' aim of appropriating and redirecting the 'spiritual awakening' of Romanticism for their own purposes.

Tractarianism as it existed within Oxford University was, of course, an exclusively masculine affair; but as the movement broadened into a general Anglican renewal there was significant scope for the involvement of women. Some critics have, indeed, argued that Tractarianism outside Oxford was specifically adapted to and directed towards the sensibilities of women. Kathleen Jones, for instance, suggests that the Anglican convents established by Tractarians 'offered women opportunities to teach and nurse and give service to others – a practical alternative to the life of the governess, which was all that Victorian society could offer its surplus population of unmarried women'; and Jan Marsh argues that the 'religious atmosphere' generated by the preaching of leading Tractarian figures like Edward Bouverie Pusey was 'particularly targeted at young women'.[27] It might also be argued that the poetics of Tractarianism created a space uniquely adapted to the requirements of Victorian women writers. As Cynthia Scheinberg points out, there has been a tendency amongst critics to overlook or misrepresent the strength of the religious impulse behind much Victorian women's writing: 'women writers who actively supported religious institutions and affiliations' are seen as 'necessarily didactic, submissive, unenlightened, and uncreative reproducers of male religious hierarchy'.[28] Such characterisations, she suggests, underestimate the complexity of the interaction between religion and patriarchy; just as Anglican religious communities provided opportunities for activity and community in otherwise isolated female lives, so Tractarian poetics validated what was regarded at the time as the specifically female orientation towards decorum and concealment. And the sonnet, in particular, represented a privileged point of intersection between feminine and Tractarian poetics. We have already seen (in Chapter 2) the affinity between the sonnet form and the feminine poetics of secrecy and concealment. In the case of religious poetry inspired by and drawing on the Tractarian movement this affinity is sanctioned and given added authority by the doctrine of reserve. By virtue of its complex and impersonal form, the sonnet allows the writer to express her deepest devotional feelings in a way which distances them from her.

This complex interplay of revelation, concealment and devotion is illustrated by Dora Greenwell's sonnet 'Reserve':

> Now would I learn thee like some noble task
> That payeth well for labour; I would find
> Thy soul's true Dominant, and thus unwind
> Its deeper, rarer harmonies, that ask
> Interpreting; for like a gracious mask
> Is thy calm, quiet bearing; far behind
> Thy spirit sits and smiles in sunshine kind,
> And fain within that fulness mine would bask:
> Set if thou wilt this bar betwixt thy tide
> Of feeling and the world that might misknow
> Its strength; use ever with the crowd this pride,
> 'Thus far, and yet no farther shall ye go;'
> But not *with me*, dear friend, whose heart stands wide
> To drink in all thy Being's overflow.[29]

Our first impulse might be to read this as an autobiographical or confessional poem, with the 'reserve' in question being the 'gracious mask' put on by the addressee in his dealings with the world. The speaker imagines herself as a privileged interpreter, able (in a musical metaphor reminiscent of Elizabeth Barrett Browning) to discern the 'Dominant' and thus to work out the key of the addressee's complex harmonies. But the title also refers to this poem itself; it is, in its reticence, an example of the quality of 'reserve' that it both praises and seeks to overcome. There is, moreover, also a temptation, authorised by the context of Greenwell's other poetry, to see this not as a confessional or autobiographical poem but as a devotional one, employing the venerable trope of Christ the lover; like Rossetti and Hopkins later in the century, Greenwell might be asking why her God remains aloof and distant even to her, whose 'heart stands wide/ To drink in all [his] Being's overflow'. The sonnet's inherent reserve does not allow us to say for certain which of these notes is the dominant one.

The lives of the female members of the Rossetti family were profoundly influenced by the Oxford Movement and its aftermath. The Rossetti sisters and their mother attended the avowedly Puseyite Christ Church in Albany Street; Christina worked with former prostitutes at the St. Mary Magdalene Penitentiary in Highgate; and her sister Maria Francesca eventually became a nun in one of the newly established Anglican convents. Given the fact that the overwhelming majority of Christina Rossetti's poetry is religious and devotional in orientation, it is a little surprising that the links between her poetry and that of her Tractarian mentors should not have been examined in more detail. G.B. Tennyson describes her as 'the true inheritor of the Tractarian devotional mode in poetry', adding: 'Most of what the Tractarians advocated in theory and sought to put into practice came to fruition in the poetry of Christina Rossetti'; and Joel Westerholm offers a spirited defence of the aesthetic quality of Rossetti's late collection *Verses*.[30] More recently, Emma Mason has suggested that Christina might have read Keble's 'Review' of Lockhart's *Life of Scott* in the copies of *The British Critic* kept at her church's library, and so had direct access to the most straightforward version of Keble's theory of poetry.[31] Most critics, however, have preferred to concentrate on the personal, quasi-autobiographical and proto-feminist utterances of her early poetry, in comparison with which the later, explicitly religious verse can seem drearily conventional. Indeed, a number of critics have been tempted to see Rossetti's religiosity merely as the expression (or in Freudian terms the sublimation) of her stunted and repressed emotional and sexual life.[32] But there is no necessary contradiction between attention to the personal or autobiographical significance of Rossetti's poetry and attention to its devotional dimension; these two impulses are entirely compatible with one another, as a study of her sonnets makes clear. In her work the well-established tradition of seeing the sonnet as a privileged vehicle for autobiographical utterance meets the Tractarian doctrine of reserve to produce poetry which is both deeply personal and carefully depersonalised.

It is unquestionably the 'personal' note that predominates in Rossetti's early collections. Her earliest attempts at the sonnet form focus on states of mind and feeling which are incipiently religious but often lack an explicitly Christian framework. Poems like 'Remember' and 'After Death' express a longing for an intermediate state of life-in-death which allows the speaker to feel the pathos of her own departure from a life she seems to find increasingly wearisome. Christina Rossetti is in these poems the direct descendant of the Elizabeth Barrett Browning of 'Past and Future': 'I would not if I could undo my past,/ Tho' for its sake my future is a blank' ('"They Desire a Better Country"', ll. 1–2). What is lacking in Rossetti, however, is Barrett Browning's triumphant rewriting of this trope; she remains 'The Prisoner', vowed to a renunciation of the world which is both intensely painful and sublime.[33] In some of these early sonnets – the pair entitled 'A Portrait', for instance – the renunciation of the world is explicitly linked to later translation to the sphere of glory, but in others the balance of feeling is equally poised, or indeed emphasises the loss of the possibility of happiness in this life rather than the potential for joy in the next:

In progress

Ten years ago it seemed impossible
     That she should ever grow so calm as this,
     With self-remembrance in her warmest kiss
And dim dried eyes like an exhausted well.
Slow-speaking when she has some fact to tell,
     Silent with long-unbroken silences,
     Centred in self yet not unpleased to please,
Gravely monotonous like a passing bell.
Mindful of drudging daily common things,
     Patient at pastime, patient at her work,
Wearied perhaps but strenuous certainly.
Sometimes I fancy we may one day see
     Her head shoot forth seven stars from where they lurk
And her eyes lightnings and her shoulders wings.

William Michael Rossetti's note to this poem suggests that it might be about a lady Christina first knew in Newcastle-upon-Tyne, but it is impossible to read it without thinking of William's famous description of his sister as a 'fountain sealed'.[34] Indeed, William's description may well derive from this poem, which describes its self-denying subject as 'an exhausted well' with 'dim dried eyes'. In a conventionally religious sonnet, the monotony and drudgery of the life described here would be atoned for by a miraculous transfiguration: 'O lily flower, O gem of priceless worth,/ O dove with patient voice and patient eyes… Thou bowest down thy head with friends on earth/ To raise it with the saints in Paradise' ('A Portrait', 23…28). Here, however, patience is merely another form of monotony – 'Patient at pastime, patient at her work' – and the transfiguration, when it arrives, is both comical and grotesque in its violent intensity. Even the title is ambivalent; the candidate for sainthood is for most of the time not 'in progress' anywhere, imprisoned as she is by her inveterate self-denial; but she can also be seen as a work 'in progress', a study in the making of a saint.

Part of the difference in emphasis between 'A Portrait' and 'In Progress' can unquestionably be linked to the fact that one was selected for publication and the other was not. Rossetti is one of many late nineteenth-century poets – Clough, Dickinson, Hopkins – who left behind them a significant amount of unpublished material, and for whom writing appears to have occupied an intermediate territory between self-expression and private therapy.[35] Rossetti's unpublished work is similar in its preoccupations and interests to her published work, but tends to be a little less consolatory and perhaps also less guarded in its account of the poet's feelings.[36] Another way of putting this is to suggest that, in the unpublished poems, the principal 'veiling' device employed by the poet is the refusal to expose her inmost thoughts and feelings to public view at all. In such cases there is less need for the devices of literary concealment outlined by Keble; the struggle between the desire for expression and the demands of 'modest reserve' ends in victory for the latter.

Rossetti's early collections make relatively sparing use of the sonnet, but as her poems become more explicitly and consistently religious in orientation the sonnet becomes one of her stock forms.[37] The late collection *A Pageant and Other Poems* (1881) includes a prefatory sonnet explaining the presence in it of 'many sonnets', and shows Rossetti experimenting with different combinations or groupings of sonnets. One such grouping of three sonnets is headed 'The Thread of Life', and follows a typically Rossettian trajectory from isolation and regret through to recognition of and acquiescence in the divine will. Anticipating the speaker in Wallace Stevens' poem 'The Idea of Order at Key West', the poet hears in the 'irresponsive silence of the land' and the 'irresponsive sounding of the sea' the message that she too should 'stand aloof', 'bound with the flawless band/ Of inner solitude' (1, ll. 1...6); but this solitude has become a limiting and debilitating distance from the possibility of earthly pleasure:

> Thus am I mine own prison. Everything
> Around me free and sunny and at ease:
> Or if in shadow, in a shade of trees
> Which the sun kisses, where the gay birds sing
> And where all winds make various murmuring;
> Where bees are found, with honey for the bees;
> Where sounds are music, and where silences
> Are music of an unlike fashioning.
> Then gaze I at the merrymaking crew,
> And smile a moment and a moment sigh
> Thinking: Why can I not rejoice with you?
> But soon I put the foolish fancy by:
> I am not what I have nor what I do;
> But what I was I am, I am even I.

Several critics have commented on the obsessive and repetitive quality of Rossetti's verse – what Eric Griffiths calls '[moments] when her verbal needle seems stuck in a groove' – and have suggested that such moments are an integral part of the bleak sublimity achieved by her best poetry.[38] The repetition of the personal pronoun in this poem, and especially the forest of 'I's in the last two lines, succeeds in objectifying and even reifying it so that it seems no longer a mere cipher for the self but a mould into which the self must fit. Like Rimbaud, Rossetti appears to be saying '"Je" est un autre', and it is precisely the 'I' she has created for herself through her poetry that has become her 'prison'.

This tendency towards repetition and doubling also manifests itself in Rossetti's development of the sonnet of sonnets in *Monna Innominata*, and indeed the double sonnet of sonnets in *Later Life*.[39] In both cases each individual sonnet mirrors the organising principle behind the sequence as a whole. The second 'sonnet' of *Later Life*, for instance, seems in its 'octave' to suggest a sinful nostalgia for the beauty of the world. The poet remembers the rapture of hearing a nightingale singing at Lake Como one summer: 'June that night glowed like a doubled June' (21, l. 14). This self-indulgence is, however, brought to an end by sonnet 23, the 'volta' of the second 'sonnet', which reminds her of the instability and transience of earthly things:

Beyond the seas we know, stretch seas unknown
Blue and bright-coloured, for our dim and green,
Beyond the lands we see, stretch lands unseen
With many-tinted tangle overgrown;
And icebound seas there are like seas of stone,
Serenely stormless as death lies serene;
And lifeless tracts of sand, which intervene
Betwixt the lands where living flowers are blown.
This dead and living world befits our case
Who live and die: we live in wearied hope,
We die in hope not dead; we run a race
To-day, and find no present halting-place;
All things we see lie far beyond our scope,
And still we peer beyond with craving face.

Rossetti's is a quiet poetry which forces us to listen very carefully for minute changes in tone and texture. Here for instance the word 'blown' at the end of the octave releases a careful ambiguity which sums up the poet's dilemma; the flowers are 'blown' by the wind but are also 'blown' in the older sense of exhausted or past their prime; they are both beautiful and dying. In this respect they encapsulate the 'dead and living world' which the poet is both deeply attracted to and compelled to resist, and anticipate the intimations of immortality in the sestet's ambiguous formulation: 'We die in hope not dead'. Our hope is not dead when we die; but there is also a suggestion that if we die in hope, then we will not die at all. From this point onwards the sequence focuses with Rossetti's usual intensity on the moment of death and its implications. Sonnet 27 – the penultimate sonnet of the second 'sequence' – describes what it calls the 'helpless charmless spectacle' of death, and in its emphasis on the physical reality of death seems to echo the doubt raised in its own penultimate line about the speaker's eventual salvation; she is, she laments, 'no saint rejoicing on her bed.' The 'volta' of the sequence represents, then, a decisive moment in its intellectual and emotional trajectory, calling the speaker back from her delusive dreams of earthly beauty towards the impending reality of death.

In her critical biography of Christina Rossetti Jan Marsh compares *Later Life* to Donne's *Holy Sonnets*, and the overwhelming impression left by both sequences is of poets desperately struggling to maintain their Christian faith in the face of doubt, despair and suffering. There may, indeed, be a reminiscence of one of Donne's most famous sonnets – 'Batter my heart, three-person'd God' – in the first sonnet of the second grouping. After having suggested that women should 'fear to teach and bear to learn,/ Remembering the first woman's first mistake' (15, ll. 1–2), Rossetti goes on to imply that her unworthy and treacherous love will nevertheless be requited: 'Love pardons the unpardonable past:/ Love in a dominant embrace holds fast/ His frailer self, and saves without her will.' (15, ll. 12–14) This rewriting of Donne's trope – 'Nor ever chaste, except you ravish me' – implies a profound and indeed abject identification with the role created for women by the most patriarchal strain of Victorian Anglicanism, and more than justifies Scheinberg's fear that religious women poets risk being seen as 'submissive, unenlightened, and uncreative reproducer[s] of male religious hierarchy'.[40] There is, however, little evidence of Donne's influence elsewhere in the sequence, or indeed in Rossetti's poetry as a whole; and Marsh's comparison forces us to ask why the religious sonnet writers of the nineteenth century failed on the whole to look back to their Elizabethan and Metaphysical forbears for inspirations. Here again the strength of the tradition of Tractarian piety and 'reserve' seems to have been the main obstacle. Keble famously argued against originality and 'what is technically called *effect*' in sacred poetry, and criticised his seventeenth-century precursors for attempting to draw attention to themselves rather than their subject matter.[41] Religious poetry should 'quiet and sober the feelings of the penitent', not animate them with verbal pyrotechnics and far-fetched comparisons.[42] Rossetti seems to have taken this advice to heart; her poetry is (as noted earlier) quiet and self-restrained, at times almost to the point of inaudibility; and although she indulges in word-play it is almost always of a solemn kind. Her most characteristic trope is to take a word and develop it with a variant of itself or with its own negation; when she writes '[love] pardons the unpardonable past' (*Later Life*, 15, l. 12) the repetition of the first word in the second reinforces the paradox by making the word self-cancelling, rather like a quantity in algebra that appears on both sides of the equation. Such tropes – 'I am sick of where I am and where I am not' (*Later Life*, 17, l. 9) – reinforce the sense of imprisonment within a small and shrinking universe of meaning which characterises most of Rossetti's religious poetry.[43]

Keble's notion of an inversely proportional relation between attention to technique and sincerity of impulse in religious poetry also informs the work of the poet who is in many respects Christina Rossetti's successor, Gerard Manley Hopkins. A key question in the reading of Hopkins' devotional sonnets has always been the relation between formal and doctrinal orthodoxy in them. The so-called 'terrible' sonnets, written towards the end of Hopkins' life, seem to articulate a spiritual crisis and at the same time abandon the extravagant formal experimentation which characterises most of his output in this form; as Jennifer Wagner puts it in her perceptive reading of the sonnets, 'the peculiar "dialect" of poetic voice that we associate with Hopkins falls away in these poems', to be replaced by echoes of Milton and Wordsworth.[44] Critics have, as a result, been tempted to read these sonnets as uniquely personal utterances; their relative 'artlessness' makes us feel that we have in them the key to Hopkins' heart.[45] This reading of the 'terrible' sonnets is unquestionably connected to the biographical tendency we have seen at work in the nineteenth-century response to the sonnet, but it is also sanctioned by the Kebelian tradition within which Hopkins was working. If the 'terrible' sonnets are indeed the outward manifestation of a spiritual crisis then they must offer themselves to God in all humility, without allowing 'what is technically called *effect*' to distract the reader from their main purpose.

When G.B. Tennyson wrote his book on Tractarian poetry in 1981 the idea of Hopkins as a Tractarian poet was still something of a novelty, but since that time numerous biographical and critical studies have reinforced his connections with the Oxford Movement.[46] By the time he arrived at Balliol College Oxford Tractarianism had mutated into 'Ritualism', a self-conscious revival of the beliefs and practices of pre-Reformation Catholicism; like Newman before him, Hopkins was unable to accept the logic of Anglo-Catholicism, and ended up converting to Roman Catholicism. His aesthetic and intellectual affiliations were, however, largely formed by his High Anglican environment. One indication of this is the fact that he remained an admirer of Christina Rossetti's poetry throughout his life.[47] He seems to have been particularly taken by the asceticism and renunciation of the world which are dominant motifs of her work. Rossetti's poem 'The Convent Threshold' is the imagined farewell of a young woman about to take the veil: 'Your eyes look earthward,' she informs her 'love', 'mine look up' (l. 17). One of Hopkins' earliest literary efforts was an 'answer' to this poem, called 'A Voice from the World'; and its stark opposition between this world and the life to come seems to have become one of the structuring tensions of his mature poetry.[48] His 'slaughter of the innocents' – the burning of much of his early poetry in the wake of his decision to become a Catholic priest – and the intermittent and almost secretive nature of much of his poetic production thereafter indicates just how strongly he felt the conflict between aesthetic pleasure and beauty on the one hand and the need to focus on the next world on the other.

In the sonnet form, however, Hopkins seems to have found a way of articulating and (in part) reconciling this tension. Despite his willingness to experiment, Hopkins adheres all the way through his poetic career to a rigid Petrarchan orthodoxy as far as the structure of the sonnet is concerned. Even in his 'caudated' and 'curtal' sonnets the octave/sestet division is rigidly respected; he is, as he says in a letter to Dixon, 'dogmatic' on this point: '[When] one goes so far as to run the rhymes of the octet into the sestet a downright prolapsus or hernia takes place and the sonnet is crippled for life'.[49] This concern with form seems, as Jennifer Wagner points out, to have come from a belief that beauty is essentially a 'relation of comparison' or 'likeness tempered by difference'.[50] The sonnet, with its intricate patterns of likeness and unlikeness and its mathematically quantifiable proportions, becomes for Hopkins something like a Platonic ideal of beauty.[51] The asymmetrical relation between its two parts renders it ideal for articulating both the conflict between this world and the claims of the next, and the resolution of that conflict in the transcendent beauty and glory of God. Hopkins' prototypical sonnet design is, therefore, one in which the octave sets out the beauty and glory of this world, and the sestet reorients the reader towards recognition and praise of God, whose beauty and power are imperfectly imaged in the natural world:

> Nothing is so beautiful as spring –
>> When weeds, in wheels, shoot long and lovely and lush;
>> Thrush's eggs look little low heavens, and thrush
> Through the echoing timber does so rinse and wring
> The ear, it strikes like lightnings to hear him sing;
>> The glassy peartree leaves and blooms, they brush
>> The descending blue; that blue is all in a rush
> With richness; the racing lambs too have fair their fling.
>
> What is all this juice and all this joy?
>> A strain of the earth's sweet being in the beginning
> In Eden garden. – Have, get before it cloy,
>
> Before it cloud, Christ, lord, and sour with sinning,
>> Innocent mind and Mayday in girl and boy,
> Most, O maid's child, thy choice and worthy the winning.

From the unusual clarity and straightforwardness of the opening line we move into an octave in which Hopkins attempts to give us some sense of the intricate beauty of Spring. One of the key differences between Hopkins' poetic world and Christina Rossetti's is that the schematic and formulaic winter and spring landscapes of her poetry are replaced in his by an attempt to remake language into new shapes more adequate to his perception of the glory and the energy of the natural world.[52] Words hover between verbs and nouns ('leaves and blooms'), novel metaphors are offered for the effect of the natural world on the human senses ('rinse and wring'), and, most obviously, there is an insistent use of alliteration and assonance. As J. Hillis Miller points out in his chapter on Hopkins in *The Disappearance of God*, these verbal resemblances and echoes are seen by Hopkins as images in miniature of the patterns underlying the apparent variety of the natural and phenomenal world; language too has a hidden order which mirrors or echoes the order of the world.[53] In contrast to the octave's attempt to render the intricate freshness and beauty of spring, the sestet tries to 'look up'; such beauty as spring possesses is merely a trace of the original beauty of the unfallen world in 'Eden garden' (yet another repetition, this time of a syllable); and we end with an exhortation to Christ to rescue '[innocent] mind and Mayday in girl and boy' from the possibility of being '[soured] with sinning' by engagement with the natural world.[54]

Such abrupt changes of perspective between octave and sestet are equally apparent in the 'curtal' sonnet, the form Hopkins describes in his 'Author's Preface' as 'constructed in proportions resembling those of the sonnet proper, namely 6 + 4 instead of 8 + 6, with however a half line tailpiece (so that the equation is rather $12/2 + 9/2 = 21/2 = 10 \; 1/2)'$.[55] It is important to realise that the proportions of the 'curtal' sonnet are therefore identical to those of the regular sonnet; its ratio between octave and sestet of 12:9 is the same as the usual sonnet ratio of 8:6 (both being different ways of expressing the ratio 4:3, which gives for Hopkins the fundamental proportion of the sonnet).[56] These curtal sonnets exploit the potential for sublimity in the 'upward' movement of the sestet, most strikingly in 'Pied Beauty':

> Glory be to God for dappled things –
>   For skies of couple-colour as a brinded cow;
>   For rose-moles all in stipple upon trout that swim;
> Fresh-firecoal chestnut-falls; finches' wings;
>   Landscape plotted and pieced – fold, fallow, and plough;
>   And áll trádes, their gear and tackle and trim.
>
> All things counter, original, spare, strange;
>   Whatever is fickle, freckled (who knows how?)
>   With swift, slow; sweet, sour; adazzle, dim;
> He fathers-forth whose beauty is past change:
>   Praise him.

In a letter to Bridges, Hopkins states that in some of his sonnets he has attempted to combine what he calls 'counterpoint' with 'sprung rhythm', and an important part of the sublimity achieved by the 'sestet' in this curtal sonnet comes from this combination of two different metrical systems.[57] Any attempt to read line four as traditional iambic pentameter, for example, breaks down at the semi-colon; 'falls' and the first syllable of 'finches' are both stressed, and as a result the first of these words must be allowed to expand to take up the time usually occupied by two syllables in a single foot. This conjunction of two seemingly incompatible metrical systems – 'the most delicate and difficult business of all', according to Hopkins[58] – mirrors the poem's emphasis on the doubleness of things; they are both themselves, in all their originality and strangeness, and also aspects of the one unchanging God who 'fathers' them 'forth'. Moreover, the use of sprung rhythm allows Hopkins to make the last half-line, with its two stressed syllables, expand itself to cover the time taken by four or even six syllables earlier in the poem; it is, as J. Hillis Miller puts it, 'like two great concluding chords in a fugue', both echoing the assertion made in the opening lines and adding to it all the resonance derived from the intervening description of the bewildering diversity of the natural world.[59] The very shortness or incompleteness of both the line and the sonnet makes them, in a gesture familiar to Hopkins from the aesthetics of Ruskin, a more fitting tribute to the creator who exceeds them by an infinite margin.

In Hopkins' curtal and caudated sonnets, then, we see what Jennifer Wagner calls his 'restless stretching and contracting of the sonnet form is an effort to study the inscape... of the form itself'.[60] But he is not always entirely comfortable within the 'narrow room' of the sonnet, as 'The Caged Skylark' makes clear:

As a dare-gale skylark scanted in a dull cage
Man's mounting spirit in his bone-house, mean house, dwells –
That bird beyond the remembering his free fells;
This in drudgery, day-labouring-out life's age.

Though aloft on turf or perch or poor low stage,
Both sing sometímes the sweetest, sweetest spells,
Yet both droop deadly sómetimes in their cells
Or wring their barriers in bursts of fear or rage.

Not that the sweet-fowl, song-fowl, needs no rest –
Why, hear him, hear him babble and drop down to his nest,
But his own nest, wild nest, no prison.

> Man's spirit will be flesh-bound when found at best,
> But uncumbered: meadow-down is not distressed
> For a rainbow footing it nor he for his bónes rísen.

A number of critics have noted the reminiscence of Milton's sonnet 'Upon his Blindness' here – 'Doth God exact day-labour, light-denied/ I fondly ask?' (ll. 7–8) – but fewer have recognised the allusions to Wordsworth's 'Prefatory Sonnet'.[61] The caged skylark is 'beyond the remembering his free fells'; both it and the human spirit it images 'droop deadly sometimes in their cells/ Or wring their barriers in bursts of fear and rage'. These hermits are clearly not contented with their 'cells', a point the poem reinforces by noting that it is only a freely-chosen dwelling, a 'wild nest', which is 'no prison'. Hopkins is, then, capable at certain moments of seeing the sonnet form not as an instance of harmonious beauty and proportion, but (like Wordsworth and Elizabeth Barrett before him) as an iconic representation of imprisonment; and this antagonistic relation to the sonnet is at its most intense in the 'terrible' sonnets. Their reversion to a sober interpretation of Petrarchan form is both an admission of defeat and a gesture of humility which acknowledges the wayward and unruly spirit behind the desire to alter the proportions of the hermit's cell. This conscious self-restraint is accompanied by a thematic emphasis on 'selving', on the process by which things express or become themselves, which Hopkins saw at work in the world and continually attempted to overcome.[62] Sonnets like 'Pied Beauty' attempt to show that the 'original, spare, strange' world finds its ultimate unity in God. In the terrible sonnets, in contrast, the self is trapped by and within itself; there is no transcendent or unifying vision:

> I wake and feel the fell of dark, not day.
> What hours, O what black hours we have spent
> This night! what sights you, heart, saw; ways you went!
> And more must, in yet longer light's delay.
>
> With witness I speak this. But where I say
> Hours I mean years, mean life. And my lament
> Is cries countless, cries like dead letters sent
> To dearest him that lives alas! away.
>
> I am gall, I am heartburn. God's most deep decree
> Bitter would have me taste: my taste was me;
> Bones built in me, flesh filled, blood brimmed the curse.

Selfyeast of spirit a dull dough sours. I see
The lost are like this, and their scourge to be
As I am mine, their sweating selves; but worse.

This is a '[wringing]' of the 'barriers in bursts of fear or rage' which revisits or inverts many of Hopkins' typical motifs. Coming to it immediately after 'The Caged Skylark', it is impossible not to be struck by the word 'fell' in the first line; there are many possible meanings (the embodiment of darkness as a physical presence; the typically creative transformation of an adjective ('fearsome') into a noun), but Wordsworth's 'bees that soar for bloom/ High as the highest peak of Furness fells' can also be detected in the background, mocking the poet's wretched self-imprisonment.[63] In addition, where the earlier poem saw the human frame as an encumbrance which would eventually be transformed and triumphed over at the resurrection, this sonnet makes the bones, flesh and blood the very symbols of the poet's imprisonment in himself. In what seems almost a blasphemous parody of the Eucharist, the poet is given his own 'flesh' and 'blood' to eat rather than those of his Saviour: 'my taste was me'. There is, moreover, none of the shift of perspective between octave and sestet which characterised the earlier sonnets. The poet remains trapped within himself, forced to 'sour' his 'dull dough' with 'selfyeast';[64] and the miraculous 'selving' which in earlier poems proved the identity of God and man in Christ here becomes mere excretion or 'sweating' of the self.[65]

'Perhaps the most remarkable aspect of these poems', remarks Robert Bernard Martin in reference to the 'terrible' sonnets, 'is the sense of contained anarchy, of inchoate, almost unspeakable emotion given verbal form':

And no less remarkable is that Hopkins should have picked the sonnet out for the purpose. Whether or not he thought out the matter, the fact is that he chose one of the most disciplined verse forms because it best held his explosive emotions in check. These poems shock doubly because of the contrast the decorum of the sonnet form and the dark energy pulsing against its restraints.[66]

But, as Hopkins states in a letter to Bridges on the subject of the apparent similarities between his own metrical experiments and those of his American contemporary Walt Whitman, '[in] a matter like this a thing does not exist, is not *done* unless it is wittingly and willingly done; to recognise the form you are employing and to mean it is everything.'[67]

When placed in the tradition of Christian poetry emanating from Wordsworth and Keble, it becomes clear that Hopkins knew exactly what he was doing in the 'terrible' sonnets; utilising a form which had been used throughout the century to impose the maximum level of restraint or 'reserve' on the expression of personal emotion. The relatively plain and unadorned language of these sonnets also conforms to Kebelian precept; like the ideal 'sacred poetry' described by Keble, the 'terrible' sonnets seem to be written with a 'total carelessness about originality and what is technically called *effect*' with the aim of 'unburthening' the poet of his deepest and most sincere feelings about God.[68]

5
'Illegal Attachments': The Amatory Sonnet Sequence

Part of the reason for the rather belated revival of the amatory sonnet sequence was unquestionably the dominance of the Miltonic-Wordsworthian sonnet, but there were aspects of the amatory tradition itself which rendered it problematic for nineteenth-century poets and critics.[1] Its origins in the work of Petrarch and his numerous imitators gave it associations with insincerity and impropriety which proved difficult to eradicate, and the biographical emphasis in sonnet criticism which helped to mitigate the first offence only increased the seriousness of the second.[2] Ever since the Abbé Jacques François de Sade revealed in the eighteenth century that Petrarch's 'Laura' was not, as had often been supposed, a mere Platonic idealisation of beauty but a married woman, it became more difficult to see Petrarch's love poetry as an arid intellectual game, but also more difficult to justify its existence on moral grounds.[3] In his posthumously published introduction to *The Book of the Sonnet*, Leigh Hunt notes that numerous sonnet sequences from the earlier periods of the form's existence 'turn upon illegal attachments... [nobody] would dream, from [Petrarch's] three hundred sonnets, that there was a gentleman of the name of De Sade, who had a right to ask him "what he meant"'.[4] Byron's observation in *Don Juan* is equally pointed:

> There's doubtless something in domestic doings,
>> Which forms, in fact, true love's antithesis;
> Romances paint at full length people's wooings,
>> But only give a bust of marriages;
> For no one cares for matrimonial cooings,
>> There's nothing wrong in a connubial kiss:
> Think you, if Laura had been Petrarch's wife,
> He would have written sonnets all his life? (III, ll. 57–64)

The first stage in the rehabilitation of the amatory sonnet sequence was, then, to rescue it from this association with 'illegal attachments' and to show that it was compatible with the celebration of 'domestic doings'; and gestures in this direction can be detected in the critical writing on Petrarch and early Italian poetry which preceded and contributed towards the form's eventual revival.[5] Thomas Campbell's 'Life' of Petrarch, for instance, includes an apology for the nature of the passion which animated his subject's poetry: 'The love of Petrarch was misplaced, but its utterance was at once so fervid and delicate, and its enthusiasm so enduring, that the purest minds feel justified in abstracting from their consideration the unhappiness of the attachment, and attending only to its devout fidelity.'[6] Walter Savage Landor, similarly, admits that attempts 'to solicit the wife of another' may appear 'inconsistent' with Petrarch's reputation as a 'purifier both of language and of morals', but suggests that this 'custom of the Tuscan race' should not blind us to the poet's 'chastity': 'Love is the purifier of the heart; its depths are less turbid than its shallows'.[7] This attempt to separate Petrarch's form from its adulterous connotations leads logically to its use for the celebration of married love in Elizabeth Barrett Browning's *Sonnets from the Portuguese*, and it is tempting to see in this movement a 'domestication' or *embourgeoisement* of the form.[8] Such a reading, however, underestimates the complexity of the Victorian reinvention of the amatory sonnet sequence. At its best, the new Petrarchanism 'exploits the traditional confusion between true emotion and sonnet convention', and indeed the amatory sonnet's traditional associations with impropriety, in ways which question dominant Victorian notions of love, marriage and sexuality.[9]

This complexity is, as we have seen, already present in the sequence which revives the form for the nineteenth century; Elizabeth Barrett Browning's celebration of married love is also an inversion of traditional gender roles. Its transgressive potential can also be seen in a work published in the same year as *Sonnets from the Portuguese*: Tennyson's *In Memoriam*. Tennyson's poem is not, of course, a sonnet sequence in the conventional sense (nor indeed is it a love poem in the conventional sense), but it is a poem in which the background presence of the amatory sonnet makes itself felt. A review from *The Times* of 28 November 1851, believed to be by Manley Hopkins, the father of the poet, shows that critics were aware from the outset of the affinities between Tennyson's elegy and Shakespeare's sonnets.[10] The reviewer congratulates Tennyson on avoiding the pastoral scenes of Milton and Spenser in his elegy and focusing instead on 'domestic interiors', but criticises him for introducing a tone of 'amatory tenderness' into his lament for his dead friend:

> Surely this is a strange manner of address to a man, even though he be dead:
>
> > So, dearest, now thy brows are cold,
> > > I see thee what thou art, and know
> > > Thy likeness to the wise below,
> > Thy kindred with the great of old.
> >
> > But there is more than I can see,
> > > And what I see I leave unsaid,
> > > Nor speak it, knowing death has made
> > His darkness beautiful with thee.
>
> Very sweet and plaintive these verses are; but who would not give them a feminine application? Shakspeare [sic] may be considered the founder of this style in English. In classical and Oriental poetry it is unpleasantly familiar. His mysterious sonnets present the startling peculiarity of transferring every epithet of womanly endearment to a masculine friend, – his master-mistress, as he calls him by a compound epithet, as harsh as it is disagreeable... We really think that floating remembrances of Shakspeare's sonnets have beguiled Mr. Tennyson.[11]

These 'floating remembrances' of Shakespeare clearly worry the reviewer because they activate the dormant suggestions of transgressive sexuality in both sequences. In writing a poem to his dead friend, Tennyson is following directly in the tradition of Petrarch (whose Laura died during his sonnet-writing marathon), but in making his addressee a man he is blurring gender boundaries; it is noteworthy that the reviewer objects in particular to the compound noun 'master-mistress'.[12] These anxieties are, however, alleviated by the suggestion that Tennyson has merely been 'beguiled' into adopting an inappropriate literary convention; he is not, the reviewer implies, expressing his deepest feelings, but identifying himself too fully with his great precursor. The background presence of Shakespeare's sonnets allows Tennyson both to indulge and to distance himself from the expression of feelings which contradict many of the most deeply-held beliefs and values of his society, and perhaps gives rise (through a strategy of overcompensation) to the poem's aggressive masculinisation of its language of fearless intellectual inquiry.[13]

There is a similarly sophisticated use of the amatory sonnet tradition in George Meredith's brutally honest analysis of the breakdown of a marriage, *Modern Love* (1861).[14] Meredith, like Elizabeth Barrett Browning, translates the love sonnet to the domestic sphere, but does so in order to demonstrate the incongruity rather than the appropriateness of the juxtaposition. The 'medieval cult of love' which produced Petrarch's sonnets has, Meredith suggests, become a mere '"sentimental passion" which preserves the cult's gestures and rituals without the premises underlying them.'[15] The main 'premise' of this cult was, of course, the unattainability of the loved object, and Meredith underlines the absurdity of attempting to make grand passions out of 'matrimonial cooings' by placing the question of adultery at the centre of his sequence. Its disruptive power is highlighted by the fact that it is literally unnameable:

> You like not that French novel? Tell me why.
> You think it quite unnatural. Let us see.
> The actors are, it seems, the usual three:
> Husband, and wife, and lover. She–but fie!
> In England we'll not hear of it. (XXV, ll. 1–5)

But, as the speaker says at the end of this sonnet, it is the Anglo-Saxon rejection of this reality which is 'unnatural': 'Unnatural? My dear, these things are life:/And life, some think, is worthy of the Muse' (ll. 15–16). The characters in the poem are forced to contort themselves into ever more unnatural shapes by their inability to escape from a language they no longer believe in, and the result is a loss of authenticity which leads to self-division, conflict, and eventually death.

Like many of the more interesting sonnet sequences of the century, *Modern Love* is in fact a hybrid into which elements of the novel and the dramatic monologue enter.[16] This novelistic quality can be seen primarily in the sequence's shifts between first and third person narration; like the novelists, Meredith allows himself the luxury of an 'inside view' of the principal character in order to allow us to share his perspective, while at the same time retaining for himself the novelist's privilege of omniscience. The poem consists of fifty sonnets which are not 'legitimate' (appropriately perhaps given their subject matter); instead of the usual octave-sestet division, we instead get a sixteen-line stanza consisting of four independent Petrarchan quatrains.[17] It is worth noting that both Meredith and his critics were happy to accept this form as a 'sonnet' from the outset, suggesting perhaps an increasing willingness on the part of both writers and commentators to entertain non-formal definitions of the sonnet.[18] Although it predates the coining of the term 'sonnet sequence' by a decade, it is appropriate to call Meredith's poem a sequence because it has a much higher level of integration than previous series or groupings; there is a narrative (although it takes some piecing together on the part of the reader), and a common vocabulary and set of images. Some of these images are, as we might expect, derived from the courtly love tradition, and they are often used with a savage inversion of their traditional meaning. Thus 'Madam', the protagonist's wife, is (in true Petrarchan fashion) a 'star', but one whose 'light is overcast', both in the sense of being dimmed by her real or imagined adultery and in being 'cast' onto her lover instead of her husband: 'Only mark/ The rich light striking out from her on him!' (III, l. 14; ll. 5–6). The very first line of the sequence alerts us to 'Madam's' eyes, another Petrarchan *topos*, but these are now 'guilty gates' which shut out rather than include the protagonist (II, ll. 2–3). In both these cases the poem is highlighting the effect of seeing things from the point of view of the member of the 'usual three' usually excluded from the Petrarchan sonnet sequence, the cuckolded husband. What seems from the point of view of the lover like brilliance and passion looks to the husband like deception and exclusion. Yet paradoxically the husband's ability to insert his wife into the template of courtly love provided by these sonnets enables him to see her with 'the eyes of other men' (VII, ll. 9–10), and so renews his desire for what has once again become maddeningly unattainable:

> Familiar was her shoulder in the glass,
> Through that dark rain: yet it may come to pass
> That a changed eye finds such familiar sights
> More keenly tempting than new loveliness. (V, ll. 6–9)

This 'changed eye' enables the husband to play the role of the lover, to see his wife as other men might see her, and so introduces an element of adultery into the marital relationship itself; the brief reconciliation towards the end of the poem (XLI–XLIII) anticipates those moments in Hardy where sexual relations between an estranged husband and wife blur the supposedly absolute boundary between lawful sexual relations and adulterous passion.

In his relationship with the lover he takes in revenge for his wife's actions the protagonist switches to a more traditional role, that of suitor for the affections of 'My Lady'; but his attempts to employ the language of courtly love in a non-ironic sense are throughout undercut by his inability to allow himself to indulge in the illusions which the role seems to demand. He is willing to play 'the game of sentiment'

(XXVIII, l. 3) with her, but remains aware throughout that '[a] kiss is but a kiss now! and no wave/ Of a great flood that whirls me to the sea' (XXIX, ll. 13–14). This is partly because of his own age and experience, but partly also because he knows too much about the springs of human passion:

> What are we first? First, animals; and next
> Intelligences at a leap; on whom
> Pale lies the distant shadow of the tomb,
> And all that draweth on the tomb for text.
> Into which state comes Love, the crowning sun:
> Beneath whose light the shadow loses form.
> We are the lords of life, and life is warm.
> Intelligence and instinct now are one.
> But nature says: 'My children most they seem
> When they least know me: therefore I decree
> That they shall suffer.' Swift doth young Love flee,
> And we stand wakened, shivering from our dream.
> Then if we study Nature we are wise.
> Thus do the few who live but with the day:
> The scientific animals are they. –
> Lady, this is my sonnet to your eyes. (XXX)

Love is 'the crowning sun' of life which makes us momentarily forget 'the distant shadow of the tomb'; but once Love has made us forget that shadow it leaves us, and forces us to live with the decisions we have taken while blinded by its influence. This play on sun and shadow prepares the reader for the bathos of the final line; the poet is refusing to be conventionally 'blinded' by his Lady's eyes, and can offer only this '[strange] love talk' (XXXIII, l. 16) in place of the expected tribute.[19] This continual undercutting of the language of romantic love is summarised in sonnet XLV, which exploits the possibilities of the sixteen-line stanza to produce a perfectly symmetrical poem:

> It is the season of the sweet wild rose,
> My Lady's emblem in the heart of me!
> So golden-crowned shines she gloriously,
> And with that softest dream of blood she glows;
> Mild as an evening heaven round Hesper bright!
> I pluck the flower, and smell it, and revive

> The time when in her eyes I stood alive.
> I seem to look upon it out of Night.
> Here's Madam, stepping hastily. Her whims
> Bid her demand the flower, which I let drop.
> As I proceed, I feel her sharply stop,
> And crush it under heel with trembling limbs.
> She joins me in a cat-like way, and talks
> Of company, and even condescends
> To utter laughing scandal of old friends.
> These are the summer days, and these our walks.

The first half of this sonnet, with its elevated neo-Elizabethan diction, comes as close as anything in *Modern Love* to a non-ironic use of the language of the amatory sonnet; but it is 'sharply' deflated by the contemporary idiom introduced with the arrival of 'Madam'. The 'sweet wild rose' is transformed from an emblem of 'My Lady' into a real flower, and then brutally (and comically) crushed by Madam, whose 'trembling limbs' reveal her imperfectly suppressed passion. There is a double satirical movement here: the separation between romance and marriage is made abundantly clear by the opposing halves of the poem; and the language of romance is itself shown to be untenable in the prosaic modern world.

Yet the language of romance is also very difficult to escape. The husband recognises in his 'Lady' 'that rare gift/ to beauty, Common Sense' (XXXI, ll. 13–14) and so feels free to offer her his disillusioned observations, but he also recognises that the 'pure daylight of honest speech' would be (and indeed is) a 'fatal draught' for Madam (XLVIII, ll. 7–8). The suggestion here is that some women force men to share, or at least pretend to share, their romantic illusions, and then blame men if they point out the discrepancies between illusion and reality:

> Oh, had I with my darling helped to mince
> The facts of life, you still had seen me go
> With hindward feather and with forward toe,
> Her much-adored delightful Fairy Prince! (X, ll. 13–16)

Men are, then, forced by women to play the 'Fairy Prince', to enter a world of conventional sentiments and pieties which masks and distorts reality, and will continue to be forced to do so until women change: 'More brain, O Lord, more brain! or we shall mar/ Utterly this fair garden we might win' (XLVIII, ll. 3–4). This incipiently misogynistic outlook is reinforced by some of the poem's repeated images; the 'little gaping snakes' of the first sonnet, for instance, reappear throughout in ways designed to identify the wife as a reincarnation of Eve. The poem's discursive alignment again anticipates Hardy, who characteristically sees women as both the main victims of conventional morality and its most aggressive defenders.[20]

Meredith's sequence stands alone in many respects; it made little impact on first publication, and its incorporation of the language of contemporary life and satirical tone set it apart from most of the amatory sonnet sequences that appeared during the second half of the nineteenth century.[21] During this period, and particularly during the last third of the century, when there was a veritable effusion of amatory sonnet sequences, the sonnet begins to acquire a self-consciously archaic quality; it loosens its connection with its Wordsworthian-Miltonic heritage, and indeed becomes through its association with the Renaissance in Italy and England one of the areas in which the emergent cultural values of the *fin-de-siècle* do battle with the Puritanism of this heritage.[22] This clash of values is highlighted by the controversy which surrounded the publication of Dante Gabriel Rossetti's 'Sonnets and Songs Towards a Work to be Called "The House of Life"' in 1870. Largely because of his cultural heritage – his father Gabriele Rossetti was a political refugee and Dante scholar who became Professor of Italian at King's College London – Dante Gabriel understood the Italian tradition with an intensity and inwardness not available to most of his fellow English poets. When he attempted to transfer this intensity to his sequence on the growth and death of love, he produced poetry which scandalised many of his contemporaries with its overt emphasis on sensuality and physical love. The poet and journalist Robert Buchanan launched an (anonymous) attack on him, accusing him of being the founder and leader of a 'Fleshly School of Poetry', and took particular exception to a sonnet entitled 'Nuptial Sleep':

> At length their long kiss severed, with sweet smart:
> >   And as the last slow sudden drops are shed
> >   From sparkling eaves when all the storm has fled,
> So singly flagged the pulses of each heart.
> Their bosoms sundered, with the opening start
> >   Of married flowers to either side outspread
> >   From the knit stem; yet still their mouths, burnt red,
> Fawned on each other where they lay apart.

> Sleep sank them lower than the tide of dreams,
>   And their dreams watched them sink, and slid away.
> Slowly their souls swam up again, through gleams
>   Of watered light and dull drowned waifs of day;
> Till from some wonder of new woods and streams
>   He woke, and wondered more: for there she lay.

Although Rossetti takes pains to underline the fact that this poem is about married love – as can be seen (for instance) in the bizarre and overdetermined conceit of the 'married flowers' (l. 6) – the sonnet is uncompromisingly straightforward in its description of the physical reality of this married love.[23] There can be no ambiguity about the meaning of the various physical details represented in the octave. The couple's separation after the 'long kiss', their 'flagging' pulses after prolonged physical exertion, the comparison between this flagging and the shedding of the 'last slow sudden drops' from the eaves of a house after a storm, and the 'sundering' of the their bosoms all suggest the immediate aftermath of sex.

Buchanan accuses Rossetti of representing 'merely animal sensations' in this poem, and of '[extolling] fleshliness as the distinct and supreme end of poetic and pictorial art' throughout his work.[24] In defending himself against these charges Rossetti reminds his antagonist that 'Nuptial Sleep' is simply one 'sonnet-stanza' in a larger and as yet uncompleted work called *The House of Life*, and that the sequence contains a number of different views of love, including poems such as 'Love-Sweetness' (XXI) in which 'the passionate and just delights of the body are declared... to be as naught if not ennobled by the concurrence of the soul at all times'.[25] He insists, that is to say, on the spirituality of the married love represented in his poems as well as on its physical dimension; and this is also apparent in his bold, even reckless use of a religious vocabulary to describe this love. 'Love's Testament', for instance, included in its first incarnation an extraordinary comparison between the lovers' embrace and the Eucharist, a comparison which recalls in its extravagance the worst excesses of Crashaw: 'O thou who are Love's hour ecstatically/ Unto my lips dost evermore present/ The body and blood of Love in sacrament' (III, ll. 1–3). In some respects both 'Nuptial Sleep' and 'Love's Testament' take the Victorian 'domestication' of the sonnet to its logical conclusion. For Rossetti's contemporaries like Charles Kingsley and Coventry Patmore, there was a sacramental element to 'married love', and Rossetti might simply be seen here as emphasising his belief in the holiness of this particular relationship. But where Patmore and Kingsley were, in their published writings at least, content with hints and metaphors to describe the sexual side of marriage, Rossetti introduces into the celebration of married love a physical reality which renders its combination of sexual frankness and religious sentiment strange and slightly disturbing.[26] Buchanan's response picks up on a conflict of values within Rossetti's own work, a conflict which was to be developed in the work of his immediate successors, between the 'medieval' values of his Victorian precursors and the more worldly and sensual 'Renaissance' values explicitly formulated by Pater and Symonds.

Rossetti was sufficiently shaken by Buchanan's criticisms to omit 'Nuptial Sleep' from the completed *House of Life*, which was first published in 1881.[27] In its final form, the sequence consists of one hundred and two sonnets, not all of which, as Rossetti reminds Buchanan in his defence of the earlier version, have to do with love; nearly half of the poems '[treat] of quite other life-influences'.[28] It is divided into two unequal sections: the sixty sonnets of 'Youth and Change' deal with love and loss, while the forty-one sonnets of 'Change and Fate' reflect on the relations between life and art, and between the various different versions of the self that appear in a retrospective survey of the poet's life.[29] Each of the sonnets is, as Rossetti puts it in his prefatory sonnet, a 'moment's monument', fixing and immortalising 'one dead deathless hour' for future contemplation; and the poem is an attempt to see whether or not meaning can be gleaned from or imposed upon such 'monuments' by the reflecting consciousness. The elegiac and autobiographical dimensions of the poem have led some critics to compare it to *In Memoriam*;[30] like Tennyson, Rossetti uses the records of his past experiences to see if it is possible for men to 'rise on stepping-stones/ Of their dead selves to higher things' (*In Memoriam*, I, ll. 3–4). There is, however, a more important formal precedent for *The House of Life* in Dante's *Vita Nuova* (New Life), which Rossetti translated into English as part of *The Early Italian Poets* (1861).[31] Rossetti notes in his introduction that 'Vita Nuova' might be more accurately rendered 'Early Life', and like the first part of Rossetti's own sonnet sequence it consists of reflections on 'Youth and Change'.[32] Dante gives us, in prose narrative interspersed with sonnets, 'the Autobiography or Autopsychology of [his] youth till about his twenty-seventh year', and in particular the story of his youthful idealisation of and even fixation on Beatrice Portinari.[33] There are substantial similarities between this narrative and the 'story' (insofar as it can be recovered) of *The House of Life*; in both cases idealisation of Love is followed by change, the death of the beloved, the advent of a new love, and finally some kind of mystical communion with the beloved. Dante's poem also serves as a formal and stylistic model for Rossetti's.[34] *The House of Life* is as self-consciously archaic in its form as Rossetti's painting *The Girlhood of Mary Virgin*, and the most striking aspect of this archaism is Rossetti's use of the device of personification. This device, and in particular the representation of 'Love' as a corporeal presence in the poem, has variously irritated, amused and perplexed Rossetti's critics, but the extent of its indebtedness to *Vita Nuova* has not, perhaps, always been sufficiently appreciated.[35] In *Vita Nuova* Dante makes 'Love' a young man who has 'lordship' over the poet, and who sometimes exercises this lordship in unpredictable and frightening ways:

> A day agone, as I rode sullenly
> > Upon a certain path that liked me not,
> > I met Love midway while the air was hot,
> Clothed lightly as a wayfarer might be.
> And for the cheer he showed, he seemed to me
> > As one who hath lost lordship he had got;
> > Advancing tow'rds me full of sorrowful thought,
> Bowing his forehead so that none should see.
> Then as I went, he called me by my name,
> > Saying: 'I journey since the morn was dim
> > > Thence where I made thy heart to be – which now
> I needs must bear unto another dame.'
> > Wherewith so much passed into me of him
> > > That he was gone, and I discerned not how.[36]

Love is bearing the poet's heart (which Love had made him leave with Beatrice) away from her and to another; and in so doing implicitly suggesting, as Dante's prose paraphrase makes clear, that the poet's love for Beatrice was 'feigned' and so can be easily transferred. This combination of allegory and eerie metamorphosis can be seen in a number of the poems in *The House of Life*, most notably in the first of the mini-sequence entitled 'Willowwood' (XLIX–LII) dealing with death and loss:

> I sat with Love upon a woodside well,
> > Leaning across the water, I and he;
> > Nor ever did he speak nor looked at me,

> But touched his lute wherein was audible
> The certain secret thing he had to tell:
>   Only our mirrored eyes met silently
>   In the low wave; and that sound came to be
> The passionate voice I knew; and my tears fell.
>
> And at their fall, his eyes beneath grew hers;
> And with his foot and with his wing-feathers
>   He swept the spring that watered my heart's drouth.
> Then the dark ripples spread to waving hair,
> And as I stooped, her own lips rising there
>   Bubbled with brimming kisses at my mouth. (XLIX)

Rossetti's Love is just as capricious and enigmatic as Dante's; he is shown here gazing into the 'woodside well' with the poet, and then metamorphosing into the face of the beloved. In personifying Love (and other 'accidents of substance'), then, Rossetti is directly imitating Dante's practice in *Vita Nuova*, and the primary function of this imitation is to indicate the cultural affiliations of his work.[37] Like the ostentatious symbolism and flattened perspective of his paintings, Rossetti's personifications and allegorical encounters are the outward and visible signs of his desire to associate himself and his work with the moral, intellectual and spiritual qualities of European Catholic civilisation.

One manifestation of this archaism is a renewed objectification of the beloved, something against which Barrett Browning and to a certain extent Meredith had struggled in their respective sequences. In the tenth poem of the sequence, 'The Portrait', a picture of the beloved is celebrated partly as an emblem of the poet's possession of and control over her: 'Her face is made her shrine. Let all men note/ That in all years (O Love, thy gift is this!)/ They that would look on her must come to me' (X, ll. 12–14). A great deal of *The House of Life*, and indeed of Rossetti's poetry in general, is indebted to Robert Browning, but the poet of 'My Last Duchess' must have been uncomfortable with his disciple's 'monumentalisation' of the object of his desire.[38] Such objectification leads to 'fetishisation' of the feminine, which becomes goddess, muse, and even demon, but never fully equal human being:[39]

> Of Adam's first wife, Lilith, it is told
>   (The witch he loved before the gift of Eve,)
>   That, ere the snake's, her sweet tongue could deceive,
> And her enchanted hair was the first gold.

And still she sits, young while the earth is old,
   And, subtly of herself contemplative,
   Draws men to watch the bright web she can weave,
Till heart and body and life are in its hold.

The rose and poppy are her flowers; for where
   Is he not found, O Lilith, whom shed scent
And soft-shed kisses and soft sleep shall snare?
   Lo! as that youth's eyes burned at thine, so went
   Thy spell through him, and left his straight neck bent
And round his heart one strangling golden hair.

                  (LXXVIII, 'Body's Beauty')

This poem 'answers' sonnet XXXVI, 'Life-in-Love', in which the poet contemplates 'all love hath to show/ For heart-beats and for fire-beats long ago': the beloved's 'golden hair undimmed in death' (ll. 10–11; 14). This love-relic is transformed in the later sonnet into something 'enchanted', a 'strangling golden hair' around the heart of the unwitting youth. Meredith in his bleaker moments compares 'Madam' to Eve, but Rossetti goes further, invoking the rabbinical fable of Adam's first wife Lilith to provide himself with a more menacing archetype. She is (punningly) a 'witch', Penelope, and the serpent itself, as the riot of sibilance in lines 10–11 underlines; unlike Eve, who is the instrument of guilt and (in the longer view) also of redemption, Lilith acts on her own initiative to destroy the youth.[40]

Perhaps the most significant expression of this tendency comes in sonnet XCIV, 'Michelangelo's Kiss', in which the iconic figure of Vittoria Colonna – the figure claimed, as we have seen, by both Felicia Hemans and Elizabeth Barrett Browning as a poetic ancestor – is transformed back into the silent 'Muse and dominant Lady' of the 'Great Michelangelo' (ll. 7; 1) in a gesture which emphasises Rossetti's remasculinisation of the Petrarchan sonnet sequence. It is tempting to read Christina Rossetti's *Monna Innominata*, published in the same year as *The House of Life*, as a typically oblique response to this aspect of her brother's work. Like her brother, Christina was a student of the early Italian sonnet, contributing an article on Petrarch to the *Imperial Dictionary of Universal Biography* in which she assesses the evidence for the real existence of 'Laura'.[41] Her 'sonnet of sonnets' does not, however, aim to provide a 'voice' for Laura, or indeed for Beatrice, but for the 'bevy of unnamed ladies, "donne innominate" sung by a school of less conspicuous poets':

Had such a lady spoken for herself, the portrait left us might have appeared more tender, if less dignified, than any drawn even by a devoted friend. Or had the Great Poetess of our own day and nation only been unhappy instead of happy, her circumstances would have invited her to bequeath to us, in lieu of the 'Portuguese Sonnets,' an inimitable 'donna innominata' drawn not from fancy but from feeling, and worthy to occupy a niche beside Beatrice and Laura.[42]

This refusal to 'voice' the *donne* of Dante and Petrarch is a typically Christina-ish gesture of humility; an unhappy Elizabeth Barrett Browning could have been a new Laura, but an unhappy Christina Rossetti relegates herself to the ranks of the unknown ladies of Petrarch's largely unknown precursors. There is, however, a slightly arch tone to this introduction; the 'bevy of unnamed ladies' summons up an incongruous image of a group of fashionably dressed society ladies at odds with the idealising and spiritualising tone of the poems in which they are addressed; and it is not at first glance easy to see why the portrait given by the Lady herself should be 'less dignified' than the one given by her admirer. This arch tone seeps into the sonnet sequence itself, providing some resistance to its otherwise relentless march towards defeat and self-abnegation.

Providing a voice for the unknown and silent women of the courtly love sonnet represents an implicit challenge to the gaps and omissions of that tradition. By not allowing the 'Lady' to speak and presenting her as cruel and aloof, the Petrarchan sonnet encourages the view that women's love is essentially frivolous, shallow and vain, and not the equal of men's. This is certainly how Christina's 'Lady' imagines the future will view her:

> Many in aftertimes will say of you
> 'He loved her' – while of me what will they say?
> Not that I loved you more than just in play,
> For fashion's sake as idle women do. (11, ll. 1–4)

In *Monna Innominata* there is a constant vigilance about the relative weight or value (to use two of the recurring metaphors of the sequence) of the respective loves of speaker and beloved, and a repeated insistence on their equality. The speaker dreams of a time when she and her beloved will be '[as] happy equals in the flowering land/ Of love, that knows not a dividing sea' (7, ll. 3–4), but as the sequence progresses it gradually becomes apparent that such equality is not yet possible. The

beloved claims a religious vocation which the speaker cannot successfully resist or share, and so leaves her forced into passivity and resignation. She struggles with this attitude for much of the sequence, but is
eventually pushed back by it into the '[silence] of love that cannot sing
again' (14, l. 14).

In the first 'quatrain' of the sequence a number of topics familiar
from the history of the amatory sonnet sequence are revisited – first
meetings, imaginary encounters in dreams – but it is not until the
fourth sonnet that the first troubling suggestions of inequality are
introduced:

> I loved you first: but afterwards your love
>> Outsoaring mine, sang such a loftier song
> As drowned the friendly cooings of my dove.
>> Which owes the other most? (4, ll. 1–4)

There might be an echo of Byron's contempt for 'matrimonial cooings'
in the speaker's characterisation of her own songs here as well as a
reminiscence of one of the ways in which Dante's Beatrice is
described;[43] and the question in line 4 invites a pointed if not yet an
overtly ironic intonation. It becomes apparent in the next sonnet that
the beloved's 'loftier song' is prompted by and directed towards a love
of God. This interplay between the languages of love and devotion is
problematised in the next 'quatrain' of sonnets, in which the poet
struggles with the competing impulses to support her lover on the one
hand and to bemoan her own fate on the other.[44] In sonnet 5, for
instance, she commends her lover to 'Him whose noble service setteth
free', but adds, with a hint of bitterness: 'So much for you; but what for
me, dear friend?' (5, l. 9). She resolves to continue loving him, but this
resolution teeters on the brink of irony by the last line, in which she
reminds herself that 'woman is the helpmeet made for man' (5, l. 14).
And in line 8, the 'volta' of the sequence, she imagines herself as
Esther, the Jewish heroine who succeeded in overturning the Persian
king Ahasuerus' edict against her people:

> 'I, if I perish, perish' – Esther spake:
>> And bride of life or death she made her fair
>> In all the lustre of her perfumed hair
> And smiles that kindle longing but to slake.
> She put on pomp of loveliness, to take
>> Her husband thro' his eyes at unaware;

> She spread abroad her beauty for a snare,
> Harmless as doves and subtle as a snake.
> She trapped him with one mesh of silken hair,
>   She vanquished him by wisdom of her wit,
>   And built her people's house that it should stand:
>
> If I might take my life so in my hand,
>   And for my love to Love put up my prayer,
>   And for love's sake by Love be granted it![45]

Like Dante Gabriel's Lilith, Esther has a deadly attractiveness about her; she is willing to use her beauty to 'take/ Her husband thro' his eyes at unaware', and to '[trap] him with one mesh of silken hair'. But, unlike Lilith, Esther is not only a demon but also a liberator of her people. Through her subtle employment of her sexual power and her ruthlessness – in the Bible she requests that her enemy Haman's ten sons should be hanged on the gallows he has prepared for her guardian Mordecai – she has 'built her people's house that it should stand'. In comparing herself to Esther, then, the speaker is imagining a sphere of action in which the 'tension between sexual desire and spiritual desire' might be successfully resolved 'from a woman's point of view'.[46] But, as Cynthia Scheinberg points out in her astute analysis of the role of this sonnet in the sequence, such a resolution is not available to the speaker:

> In contrast to the speaker's self description in Sonnet 7:9: 'My heart's a coward though my words are brave,' Esther's earthly desires and her religious goals are linked; Esther's words and actions are brave and divinely sanctioned, whereas the speaker sees the disjunction between the language of desire she produces in her poetry and her own actions, or rather lack of ability to act on her desire.[47]

She cannot become an 'Esther'; there is no positive value ascribed to sensuality or female agency in the Christian ascetic tradition espoused by her lover, and as a result she finds herself forced, in the concluding 'sestet' of poems, to resign herself to a fruitless, unrequited love. There are moments of dissatisfaction with this role – the phrase 'honoured excellence' (9, l. 3) seems suspiciously fulsome, as does the praise of 'that nobler grace,/ That readier wit than mine, that sweeter face' (12, ll. 4–5) possessed by an imaginary successor in her beloved's affections – but the dominant tone is given by the speaker's grim determination to accept the renunciation of the prospect of earthly pleasure. Like Dante, she sees herself sailing 'con miglior corso e con migliore stella' ('With better course and with a better star') towards the final destination of God's eternal love.[48] Her situation is summed up in the closing sonnet: 'Youth gone and beauty,' she asks, 'what remains of bliss?' (l. 3):

> The longing of a heart pent up forlorn,
> A silent heart whose silence loves and longs;
> The silence of a heart which sang its songs
> While youth and beauty made a summer morn,
> Silence of love that cannot sing again. (14, ll. 10–14)

The speaker's heart is 'pent up', trapped in its own unacted desire, and 'forlorn' because it knows that its desire can never be realised; its songs, like its youth and beauty, belong in the past. This dismal conclusion is underlined by the parallels between the opening and closing sonnets. In the first sonnet separation is a keen pleasure, the 'pang of parting' (l. 10) – it is typical of Christina Rossetti to notice that 'pang' is literally separated by 'parting' – which gives rise to the possibility of future desire. But there is a curious double consciousness at work in the last two lines of the sonnet: 'Ah me, but where are now the songs I sang/ When life was sweet because you called them sweet?' (1, ll. 13–14) These lines seem to combine the voice of the speaker when she believes her beloved will come back to her with the later, disillusioned voice which knows he is not coming back. This momentary intrusion of the perspective attained at the end of the sequence suggests another reason for the speaker's eventual silence. She values her songs because her beloved values them; life is sweet for her 'because he calls them sweet'. When he is no longer interested in her song, she lapses into silence. As so often in Christina Rossetti's work, there is a kind of Pyrrhic victory in this complete self-abnegation, a sublimity in a self-denial so absolute that it ends up effacing the speaker's very existence.

Some recent critics have found it difficult to reconcile *Monna Innominata*'s bold reclamation of the unspoken history of female desire and subjectivity with its apparently quiescent ending.[49] One way of explaining this apparent contradiction is suggested by Christina's description of her treatment of this subject as 'semi-historical'.[50] Although it is largely free of the cumbersome allegorical machinery and self-conscious archaism of *The House of Life, Monna Innominata* is on one level a poem set in the past which attempts to explain why women of equal 'poetic aptitude' to men failed to produce their half of the courtly love story. It does not necessarily imply that 'silence' would be the fate of a contemporary 'innominata'; indeed, Rossetti's comparison in her preface between her sequence and Elizabeth Barrett Browning's suggests the opposite conclusion – that the kind of equality dreamt of by the speaker of *Monna Innominata* is at least a possibility in the nineteenth century. This historical dimension is, however, muted by the poem's contemporary idiom and the presence in it of so many of Christina's habitual themes, images and preoccupations; the mottoes from Dante and Petrarch are the only tangible connection to the cultural context in which it is supposed to take place. Most readers have, in consequence, followed Christina's brother William Michael in reading *Monna Innominata* as a work of disguised autobiography. In a note to the poem in his edition of his sister's poems published in 1904 he states straightforwardly that her 'sonnet of sonnets' is 'a personal utterance – an intensely personal one', and adds that the 'introductory prose-note, about "many a lady sharing her lover's poetic aptitude," etc., is a blind... interposed to draw off attention from the writer in her proper person.'[51]

Such readings indicate both the strength and persistence of the biographical emphasis in sonnet criticism, and also the extent to which poets were becoming aware of the need to erect adequate defences against the increasingly sophisticated weapons of the biographically-minded critics. It was no longer enough simply to claim, as Elizabeth Barrett Browning had done, that her poems were translated from Portuguese, a claim which could be (and was) disproved in an instant. The historical shell constructed by Christina is more durable, and gives rise to a persistent and, notwithstanding her brother's comments, an ineradicable ambiguity in the sequence itself. On the one hand the amatory sonnet sequence can, as William Michael Rossetti's comments show, be read as a 'veil' for the expression of personal feeling. This metaphor of 'veiling' is widespread in the period, and illustrates the migration of concepts and techniques from the devotional to the amatory sonnet during the second half of the nineteenth century.[52] But on the other hand it is also, as John Addington Symonds points out in the preface to his collection of sonnets *Animi Figura*, a form which obliges the poet to give a personal and lyrical form to the utterance of abstract ideas and beliefs:

> That this Portrait of a Mind [i.e. *Animi Figura*] is not a piece of accurate self-delineation will be understood by students of sonnet-literature. They know that this species of poetry has lent itself in all times to the expression of impersonal thought and feeling under forms

borrowed from personal experience. The sonnet is essentially a meditative lyric. What the sonnet writer has conceived as speculation,
he is bound by the lyrical conditions of his verse to utter as emotion. What conversely has occurred to him as a particular emotion,
assumes the character of generality when he invests it with the fixed
form of this stanza. On the one hand, he escapes from the aridity of
gnomic verse by adopting the language of subjective passion. On
the other hand, he shuns the direct outpouring of individual joys
and griefs by veiling these in a complicated, artificial, stationary
structure which can only be accepted as semi-lyrical.[53]

There is in the sonnet, then, a deliberate blurring of the boundaries
between the private and the public, between sincerity and artifice; and
in his amatory sonnet sequence *Stella Maris*, published in 1884,
Symonds exploits the complexities of this interaction to the full. He
creates a poem which hides behind a series of defences against successful biographical reading – some of them only recently breached – to
become a meditation on the impossibility of achieving perfect love in
any human relationship.

Symonds had much more to hide than Meredith or the Rossettis.
Ever since the revelations in Phyllis Grosskurth's 1964 biography, and
the publication of most of his *Memoirs* in 1984, he has come to be seen
as the classic case-study in Victorian sexual pathology.[54] This biographical material shows someone in a deep state of internal conflict; on the
surface a respectable married man of letters with four daughters, he
struggled throughout his life with homosexual drives which it was
impossible and even illegal for him to acknowledge openly.[55] One of
the interesting things about Symonds' career, however, is that he never
gave up trying to explain and justify his sexual preferences to an over-
whelmingly hostile public, albeit in disguised and indirect forms. He
was one of the major participants in what recent scholars and critics of
this period have described as a 'counterdiscourse' of homosexuality,
using his copious writings on cultural and literary subjects as a way of
defining and explaining his sexual orientation:

> To write blatantly about homosexuality in his works on history and
> literature would have been both intellectually renegade and politic-
> ally risky. As a consequence, when he felt compelled to speak, he
> usually used an oblique approach in which he cunningly allied
> ingenuousness and craft... Reading carefully, his audience might
> none the less discern his sexual interests.[56]

This 'counterdiscourse' was articulated for Symonds and many others through a revived Hellenism, and its outlines have been traced in (for instance) the language of 'Platonism' current in late nineteenth-century Oxford.[57] The role of the sonnet in its development has, however, not yet been fully recognised. The Renaissance sonnet offered, in the work of Michelangelo and Shakespeare, two hugely significant examples of the fleeting emergence of a homosexual counterdiscourse at an earlier stage of cultural history; and it is their example which underlies Symonds' own practice in his amatory sonnets.

Symonds' interest in Michelangelo's sonnets was prompted, as he explains in the introduction to his 1878 translation, by the appearance in 1863 of a new Italian edition edited by Guasti which went back to the original manuscripts and discovered that these had been extensively bowdlerised by the poet's first editor, a great-nephew also called Michelangelo Buonarroti: 'The more he studied his great ancestor's verses, the less he liked or dared to edit them unaltered. Some of them expressed thoughts and sentiments offensive to the Church. In some the Florentine patriot spoke over-boldly. Others exposed their author to misconstruction on the score of personal morality.'[58] It was clear that some of the love poems were addressed not, as Elizabeth Barrett Browning, Dante Gabriel Rossetti and many others had believed, to the elderly Vittoria Colonna, but to a male friend called Tommaso de' Cavalieri. In one of the sonnets, on the traditional topic of 'Love's Lordship', Michelangelo even puns on Cavalieri's name in Italian:

> Se vint' e pres' i' debb' esser beato,
> maraviglia non è se, nud' e solo,
> resto prigion d'un Cavalier armato. (XXXI)

Symonds' translation attempts to retain the pun by capitalising the word 'Knight', though there is also a certain coyness in translating 'nudo' (naked) as 'bare':

> If only chains and bands can make me blest,
> no marvel if alone and bare I go
> an armèd Knight's captive and slave confessed.[59]

Michelangelo's sonnets were, for Symonds, moulded in this and other respects by the spirit of 'Platonism' abroad in the Renaissance. Symonds' profound interest in the Renaissance – a term which he did a great deal to popularise in England – was prompted by the fact that it represented a revival not just of the forms of classical learning, but also of many of the frankly pagan and sensual values and beliefs of anti-quity. In the work of Plato Michelangelo and his contemporaries found a new understanding of the relation between earthly beauty and its heavenly archetype:

> Nothing is more clear than that Michelangelo worshipped Beauty in the Platonic spirit, passing beyond its personal and specific manifes-tations to the universal and impersonal. This thought is repeated over and over again in his poetry; and if we bear in mind that he habitually regarded the loveliness of man or woman as a sign and symbol of eternal and immutable beauty, we shall feel it of less importance to discover who it was that prompted him to this or that poetic utterance.[60]

But Platonism was not simply an idealising doctrine; it was also a defence of love between men. Symonds make the significance of this term clearer in his essay on 'The Dantesque and Platonic Ideals of Love', in which he argues that Platonic love, 'the affection of a man for a man' described in the *Phaedrus* and *Symposium*, is the equivalent of the 'chivalrous love' which prompted Dante's sonnets to Beatrice in the *Vita Nuova*. Both forms of love were prone to debasement and misconstruction; chivalrous love was 'wholly extra-nuptial and anti-matrimonial' in character, and Greek love was mixed up with a 'for-midable social evil'. But 'in its origin and essence' Greek love was 'masculine, military, chivalrous... neither an effeminate depravity nor a sensual vice'; and like the love celebrated by Dante, it was in its highest form 'a state of the soul, not an appetite'.[61]

In Michelangelo's sonnets, then, Symonds found evidence for his belief in the equivalence of 'chivalric' and Platonic love; and there was an analogous instance within the English literary tradition for him to draw on. We have already seen in the critical response to Tennyson's *In Memoriam* something of the transgressive potential of Shakespeare's sonnets, and their use of the language and conventions of the amatory sonnet in poems overtly addressed to a man seemed to some a parallel instance of the diffusion of 'Platonic' doctrines during the Renaissance. This is certainly how the sonnets are presented in Oscar Wilde's strange and typically playful narrative *The Portrait of Mr. W.H.*, in which the narrator takes up and develops 'Cyril Graham's' theory that the sonnets are addressed to a boy actor in Shakespeare's company called 'Willie Hughes'. He comes to realise that in the sonnets we have 'the soul, as well as the language, of neo-Platonism', and argues that 'it is only when we realise the influence of neo-Platonism on the Renaissance that we can understand the true meaning of the amatory phrases and words with which friends were wont, at this time, to address each other'.[62] Wilde makes the connection between Platonism, Michelangelo and Shakespeare explicit:

> Michael Angelo, the 'haughtiest spirit in Italy' as he has been called, addresses the young Tommaso Cavalieri in such fervent and passionate terms that some have thought that the sonnets in question must have been intended for that noble lady, the widow of the Marchese of Pescara [Vittoria Colonna], whose white hand, when she was dying, the great sculptor's lips had stooped to kiss. But that it was to Cavalieri that they were written... is evident not merely from the fact that Michael Angelo plays with his name, as Shakespeare plays with the name of Willie Hughes, but from the direct evidence of Varchi, who was well acquainted with the young man... Strange as these sonnets may seem to us now, when rightly interpreted they merely serve to show with what intense and religious fervour Michael Angelo addressed himself to the worship of intellectual beauty, and how, to borrow a fine phrase from Mr. Symonds, he pierced through the veil of flesh and sought the divine idea it imprisoned.[63]

There is of course no 'Willie Hughes' in reality; Wilde makes the search for him, which ultimately costs the life of Cyril Graham, a metaphor for the strength of the desire that he and his contemporaries have to locate their own distinctive complex of sexual orientation and aesthetic sensibility within the mainstream of the European cultural tradition.

It is the examples provided by Michelangelo and Shakespeare that inspire the 'Platonism' of *Stella Maris*, the amatory sonnet sequence set in Venice which Symonds published in 1884. Part of the purpose of this sequence is, as Symonds acknowledges in his *Memoirs*, to provide a disguised record of his relationship with Angelo Fusato, a Venetian gondolier, during the spring of 1881;[64] and the poem takes advantage of the 'veil' of the sonnet sequence to defend itself from prurient biographical reading while at the same time inviting initiates to decode its hidden meanings. The first line of defence is provided by the preface to *Vagabunduli Libellus*, which retrospectively embeds *Stella Maris* within Symonds' earlier collection *Animi Figura*. In a sense unknown to Symonds' contemporaries, and indeed to any of his readers until the publication of the *Memoirs* in 1984, this manoeuvre is faithful to the experiences underlying the poetry; Symonds lists in his private autobiography the sonnets written about his relationship with Fusato, and these include 'L'Amour de l'Impossible' and several others from *Animi Figura* as well as many of those in *Stella Maris* itself.[65] However, the main function of the preface is to stress the 'fictitious character' of the events portrayed in both volumes. Symonds claims that he has written *Stella Maris* in order to complete the portrait of the 'abnormal personality' depicted in *Animi Figura*: 'The portrait of a beauty-loving and impulsive but at the same time self-tormenting and conscientious mind... was incomplete and inexplicable without the episode of passionate experience set forth in "Stella Maris"'[66] Moreover, even within *Stella Maris* itself, the sonnets written to and about Fusato are concealed within what Symonds in his *Memoirs* calls an 'artificial context framed to render publication possible'; the story of a 'love 'twixt man and maid, lawless, unwed' (LXIII, l. 1) and its predictably disastrous outcome.[67] Many of the sonnets written about Fusato have, as Symonds laments in one of his uncomfortably Freudian metaphors, been 'mutilated in order to adapt them to the female sex' in this process.[68]

The result of these acts of concealment and mutilation is a melodramatic and occasionally incoherent narrative. Symonds reminds his readers that the sonnet 'is not designed for continuous narration, but for the crystallization of thought around isolated points of emotion, passion, meditation, or remembrance', but is obviously sufficiently conscious of the absence of narrative coherence to provide a brief summary of the action in the preface to the volume. It deals, he tells us, with a 'somewhat arrogant' and overly analytical hero who is first 'overmastered' by passion, but then allows 'his acquired habits of self-analysis' to produce 'doubt and conflict at the very moment of fruition' as he 'becomes aware of a discord not only between his own tone of feeling and that of the woman who attracted him, but also between the emotion she inspired and his inalienable ideal of love'. Finally, '[in] a moment of disillusionment he roughly rejects what he had ardently desired, because he finds himself on the verge of disloyalty to his superior nature.'[69] It is possible to recognise the outlines of the sequence in this description, but a number of unresolved inconsistencies remain. Symonds' usual habit is not to alter the gender of the beloved but to leave it unspecified, and this has the effect of making those sonnets overtly addressed to a woman look as if they were about a different character (as indeed in some respects they are). There is, moreover, a troubling and unresolved ambiguity in the nature of the speaker's relationship with this woman. There are strong suggestions in sonnets xl and xlv that she is a prostitute – 'For gold she sells herself. Thine is the shame!' (XL, l. 14) – yet this seems incompatible with the portrait of her both before and after their moment of consummation, which implies a 'respectable' relationship.[70] Again, the 'beloved' of the earlier sonnets is insistently identified with Venice (for example in XVII), yet after the 'moment of fruition' she is summarily despatched from the city (presumably back to England), and ends up suffering the typical, melodramatic fate of the 'fallen woman': 'They write me, Stella, write me thou art mad!/ Strange truth to say, this comforts me somewhat' (LII, ll. 1–2). The sententious observations on love with which the poem ends incongruously invoke the vocabulary of marriage, and offer a 'moral' with little obvious relevance to the action:

> Love, be it high or low,
> Is no light-wingèd slight indifferent thing,
> But a close bond wedding two selves in one;
> However disparate those selves may grow
> Toward diverse issues. Beauty thus doth bring
> Man back through love to law no life may shun.
>
> (LXVII, ll. 9–14)

The echoes of Meredith's 'union of this ever-diverse pair' here are typical of the poem's tendency to slip into the idiom of *Modern Love* whenever it deals with the frustrations and disappointments of explicitly heterosexual relationships.[71]

This 'artificial context', however, does not completely obscure the original impulse behind the poem. The terms in which the 'beloved' is described in the gender-neutral sonnets – 'the rhythm of thy strength at rest' (XXI, l. 9) – clearly imply that the object of the speaker's affections is male. Moreover, embedding the sonnets to Fusato within a story of 'lawless' heterosexual love has the effect of dividing the poet's relationship with the beloved into two moments which correspond to the 'ideal' and the 'real' moments of Platonic love; a (masculine or ungendered) moment of desire and intense longing, which generates enraptured poetry, and a (feminine) moment of carnal lust which brings only shame, disgust and disappointment.[72] An example of the first moment is provided by sonnet VII:

I saw thee first, and knew not I should love thee,
    Pacing the meadows where narcissus flowers
Star the green grass, and clustering stars above thee
    Hung the white blossoms of acacia bowers.
Those rathe acacia branches wove a slender
    Lattice of light and trembling leaves to shield thee;
Soft was the shade, and soft the shadowy splendour
    Of sunbeams shed through flowers that half concealed thee.
Lap-full of stars, white buds and golden, fragrant
    With perfume of the spring in all their bloom,
Singing a morning song to match the vagrant
    Larks high in air above that leafy gloom,
Star of my soul, thou stood'st, and far before thee
Slept the blue sea, heaven's broad blue caverns o'er thee.

It is interesting to note that this beautiful and haunting poem is not
identified as one of the 'Fusato' sonnets by Symonds; it idealises and
spiritualises love by extracting it from any particular situation. The
context of 'Platonic' love is hinted at by the fact that the beloved is
first seen amidst 'narcissus flowers', aligning him with the beautiful but
doomed boy of Greek myth. Indeed the octave as a whole, with its delicate portrait of the unselfconscious beloved at one with and protected
by nature, is reminiscent of a scene in Greek mythology. Conversely,
the 'chivalric' tradition is invoked by the star motif which is, of course,
present in the title of the sequence. The narcissus flowers '[star] the
green grass', anticipating the identification of the speaker as the '[star]
of my soul' in the penultimate line. It is also perhaps significant that
this is a relatively rare example of a Shakespearean sonnet in what is a
largely if loosely Petrarchan sequence. The use of the Shakespearean
form may be a gentle reminder of the formal precedent provided by
the work of the great English Renaissance writer for a sequence which
intermingles heterosexual and homosexual desire.

    This 'ideal' character is, however, lost in those poems which deal
with the consummation of the relationship. These poems demonstrate
in a very literal way the equivalence between homosexual sex and
'extra-nuptial' relationships asserted in 'The Dantesque and Platonic
Ideals of Love', and indeed superimpose these two kinds of love one
upon the other in a remarkably graphic way:

She was a woman; therefore was she one,
    Worshipping whom a man of woman born

> Shrinks like a guilty thing surprised by morn
> From thoughts of self and sin's dominion.
> I clasped her in my arms; yet might not shun
>   The awful oath of that allegiance sworn
>   To Beauty, when the soul was less forlorn
>   Circling with gods round heaven's unfaltering sun.
> I drank her lips; as thirsty flowers drink rain,
>   Kisses I drank sweeter than honey-dews;
>   Yet though their arrowy perfume smote my brain,
> Love lurked not there, whose breath lifts earth to heaven;
>   Love, for whose sake man's frailties are forgiven,
>   Love cried: Less than Love's best thou shalt refuse! (XXXIX)

For the post-Freudian reader, the opening quatrain betrays itself almost too easily; the speaker, remembering that he is 'a man of woman born', 'shrinks' from the prospect of sexual relations with a woman 'like a guilty thing surprised', the echo of Wordsworth reinforcing the puritanical revulsion from the prospect of physical love.[73] But the 'original' version of this poem, transcribed in the *Memoirs*, reveals the extent to which Symonds has literally projected one form of desire onto the other here:

> I am not dreaming. He was surely here
>   And sat beside me on this hard low bed;
>   For we had wine before us, and I said –
> 'Take gold: 'twill furnish forth some better cheer.'
> He was all clothed in white; a gondolier;
>   White trousers, white straw hat upon his head,
>   A cream-white shirt loose-buttoned, a silk thread
> Slung with a charm about his throat so clear.
> Yes, he was here. Our four hands, laughing, made
>   Brief havoc of his belt, shirt, trousers, shoes:
> Till, mother-naked, white as lilies, laid
>   There on the counterpane, he bade me use
> Even as I willed his body. But Love forbade –
>   Love cried, 'Less than Love's best thou shalt refuse!'[74]

This poem reveals the secret of the otherwise baffling 'gold' motif in *Stella Maris*; Fusato is clearly willing to sell his sexual favours. The encounter in the unpublished version ends not with sex, however, but with an agonised recognition that 'Love' in its highest form requires the speaker to 'refuse' what is being offered on the grounds that it is not 'Love's best'. In both sonnets, then, the moment of real or potential consummation is a moment of disappointment and even degradation. What human beings are looking for are not instances of love and beauty, but the Platonic essences from which these instances are derived; and the gap between the ideal and reality leads inexorably to disillusionment. As the speaker puts it in sonnet XXIII, human beings are always seeking to 'delude desire/ With possible fruition' (ll.1–2), always (like Narcissus) mistaking the image reflected in water for the thing itself.

In *Stella Maris*, then, we find a very sophisticated and self-conscious form of 'veiling' which both excludes the uninitiated and provides subtle clues for those who might respond appropriately to its hidden story. This veiling even extends to the title of the volume to which Symonds retrospectively assigns the sequence. In linking *Stella Maris* to *Animi Figura* his main purpose is, as we have seen, to insist on its status as fiction; but he also informs the reader that the title of the earlier collection comes from the *Agricola* of Tacitus, and its context there leaves no doubt about its personal application:

> This, too, is what I would enjoin on daughter and wife, to honour the memory of that father, that husband, by pondering in their hearts all his words and acts, by cherishing the features and lineaments of his character rather than those of his person. It is not that I would forbid the likenesses which are wrought in marble or in bronze; but as the faces of men, so all similitudes of the face are weak and perishable things, while the fashion of the soul is everlasting, such as may be expressed not in some foreign substance, or by the help of art, but in our own lives.[75]

It is typical of Symonds, and indeed of the whole 'Hellenising' movement of which he was a part, to use classical culture and allusion, for so long regarded as expressions of the highest form of civilisation, as a coded language for the articulation of forbidden desire. In alluding to the difficulties of his own domestic circumstances in this way he underlines just how inadequate the language of 'embourgeoisement' or 'domestication' is to describe the Victorian amatory sonnet sequence. Far from reinforcing dominant ideologies of gender and sexuality, each of the sequences examined in this chapter challenges or disrupts those ideologies in some significant way. The rediscovery of the Petrarchan sonnet was part of a broader rediscovery of alternative values and beliefs embedded within the literary tradition of Europe, and it provided a forum in which the subversive potential of these values could be explored in relative safety.

6
'Thought's pure diamond': The Sonnet at the End of the Century

The years around 1880 saw a 'Sonnettomania' to rival that of the closing decades of the previous century.[1] 'Into whatsoever ballroom you went,' writes Max Beerbohm in '1880', his satirical portrait of the high noon of the aesthetic movement, 'you would surely find, among the women in tiaras and the fops and the distinguished foreigners, half a score of comely ragamuffins in velveteen, murmuring sonnets, posturing, waving their hands.'[2] Beerbohm no doubt had in mind young men like Wilfred Scawen Blunt, whose *Sonnets and Songs* appeared (under the aesthetic pseudonym Proteus) in 1875. The volume's fashionably yellow front cover is decorated with a sun-motif, and the motto: 'By thy light I live'. Proteus is (to use the terms of Gilbert and Sullivan's *Patience*) more of a 'fleshly' than an 'idyllic' poet; his volume consists of reminders that '[the] day of love is short, and every bliss/ Untasted now is a bliss thrown away'.[3] He also, as his dedication to the sun implies, follows Swinburne in looking to a revived Paganism as an alternative source of values to Christianity. 'Truce to thee, soul' laments the effect of Christian asceticism on humanity, and looks forward to a time when the physical and sensual side of existence will be accepted and celebrated: 'Poor Body, I must take some thought of thee' (l. 14).

Something of the appeal of the form to poets like Proteus is indicated in one of the many 'sonnets on the sonnet' written towards the end of the century, in this case by John Addington Symonds:

> There is no mood, no heart-throb fugitive,
>> No spark from man's imperishable mind
>> No moment of man's will, that may not find
>> Form in the Sonnet; and thenceforward live

A potent elf, by art's imperative
      Magic to crystal spheres of song confined; –
      As in the moonstone's orb pent spirits wind
      'Mid dungeon depths day-beams they take and give.
Spare thou no pains; carve thought's pure diamond
      With fourteen facets scattering fire and light: –
      Uncut, what jewel burns but darkly bright?
And Prospero vainly waves his runic wand,
      If spurning art's inexorable law,
      In Ariel's prison-sphere he leave one flaw.[4]

According to Symonds, the sonnet has the magical ability to confine in 'crystal spheres of song' any 'mood or heart-throb fugitive', any thought or desire that springs from 'man's imperishable mind'; it is, to use Dante Gabriel Rossetti's more famous formulation, a 'moment's monument'. Symonds' sonnet also, however, reflects on the relation between art and nature in this process in ways which illustrate some of the tensions and contradictions at the heart of the aesthetic project. The trope of jewellery suggests a co-operative relation between nature and art. Before 'thought's pure diamond' can 'burn' as it ought to, it must first be cut into 'fourteen facets scattering fire and light'; the material is furnished by nature, but the polish and brilliance come from human art. However, the other metaphors in the sonnet suggest (in a figure which reaches back to Wordsworth) that the sonnet is a kind of imprisonment of experience; life is reduced to a 'potent elf' and 'confined' to the 'crystal spheres of song'. If the sonnet has formal perfection, it is the perfection of 'Ariel's prison-sphere'. Such metaphors point to one of the recurring themes of the aesthetic sonnet and the critical language generated by it; the relation between the 'monumentalised' individual moments of experience and the life as a whole. It is not coincidental that this is the period in which the sonnet sequence is finally recognised, named and described as a distinct and distinctively modern form. Poets of this period are always attempting to combine their individual sonnets into larger groupings to see if their fragmentary records of experience will cohere into a convincing fiction of identity.

In his essay on 'The Poetry of Michelangelo', Walter Pater indicates some of the reasons for the association of the sonnet with particularly intense moments of perception or feeling during this period. Michelangelo's sonnets are, like Shakespeare's, the key that unlocks the mystery of his personality, but they are even more valuable than Shakespeare's because they do not represent his habitual mode of expression. They are not written 'to support a literary reputation' but 'occasional and informal'; they often appear in the margins of his drawings, 'arresting some salient feeling or unpremeditated idea as it passed'.[5] Like Raphael in Robert Browning's 'One Word More', another painter turned sonnet-writer, Michelangelo is '[using] nature that's an art to others,/ Not, this one time, art that's turned his nature' in order to voice his uniquely vivid and personal experience of love: 'Once, and only once, and for one only,/ So to be the man and leave the artist,/ Gain the man's joy, miss the artist's sorrow.'[6] The fascination of such moments for Pater and Browning is in the combination of the profoundly artistic temperament and the intense moment of experience. Without the artistic temperament – the 'sensibility' and receptiveness so prized by the aesthetes – the moment would slip by unregarded; once apprehended, the sonnet, to use a metaphor derived from the photographic process, becomes a kind of 'developing solution' which renders it visible.[7]

The sonnets of Michelangelo are, then, the records of a life lived at the highest level of sensitivity to experience, and so, in Pater's terms, a life of the utmost value. For the Pater of the resounding and enormously influential 'Conclusion' to the first edition of *The Renaissance*, life is nothing more than a series of impressions, and each one of these impressions is 'the impression of the individual in his isolation, each mind keeping as a solitary prisoner its own dream of a world'. These impressions are not, moreover, cumulative; our life 'fines itself down' to 'a single sharp impression, with a sense in it, a relic more or less fleeting, of such moments gone by'. This 'continual vanishing away' makes it all the more important that we attune ourselves to the passing moment:

> Every moment some form grows perfect in hand or face; some tone on the hills or the sea is choicer than the rest; some mood of passion or insight or intellectual excitement is irresistibly real and attractive to us, – for that moment only. Not the fruit of experience, but experience itself, is the end. A counted number of pulses only is given to us of a variegated, dramatic life. How may we see in them all that is to seen in them by the finest senses? How shall we pass most swiftly from point to point, and be present always at the focus where the greatest number of vital forces unite in their purest energy?
>
> To burn always with this hard, gemlike flame, to maintain this ecstasy, is success in life... While all melts under our feet, we may

well grasp at any exquisite passion, or any contribution to knowledge that seems by a lifted horizon to set the spirit free for a
moment, or any stirring of the senses, strange dyes, strange colours,
and curious odours, or work of the artist's hands, or the face of one's
friend. Not to discriminate every moment some passionate attitude
in those about us, and in the very brilliancy of their gifts some
tragic dividing of forces on their ways, is, on this short day of frost
and sun, to sleep before evening.[8]

Pater's hypnotic prose reverberates in the work of his contemporaries
and immediate successors. When Symonds, in the first of his sonnets
on the sonnet, describes the form as '[a] gem which, hardening in the
mystical/ Mine of man's heart, to quenchless flame hath leapt' (ll. 3–4)
he is remembering the 'hard, gemlike flame' of Pater's ecstatic votary;[9]
and images of weaving and unweaving, twilight and shadow become
recurring motifs in the sonnets of the last quarter of the nineteenth
century.

The effect of this exaltation of the moment of intense experience is
the kind of literary impressionism seen in Theodore Watts-Dunton's
'Foreshadowings':

> The mirrored stars lit all the bulrush spears,
> And all the flags and broad-leaved lily-isles;
> The ripples shook the stars to golden smiles,
> Then smoothed them back to happy golden spheres.
> We rowed – we sang; her voice seemed, in mine ears,
> An angel's, yet with woman's dearest wiles;
> But shadows fell from gathering cloudy piles
> And ripples shook the stars to fiery tears.
> God shaped the shadows like a phantom boat
> Where sate her soul and mine in Doom's attire;
> Along the lily-isles I saw it float
> Where ripples shook the stars to symbols dire;
> We wept – we kissed, while starry fingers wrote,
> And ripples shook the stars to a snake of fire.

Here the Neo-Platonic motif of the star reflected in the water – familiar
from *Stella Maris* – is used to produce a meditation on the intangibility
of desire and the transience of human life. Like the star, which assumes
many shapes in the water, from 'golden smiles' during the optimistic
moment of the octave to 'a snake of fire' in the sestet, everything in

this poem teeters on the edge of symbolism. The boat in which the lovers ride is imaged in the water 'in Doom's attire', perhaps as the boat that takes souls across Lethe, the river of forgetfulness, in classical mythology; and the 'snake of fire' at the end of the poem sounds an apocalyptic note about the indulgence of earthly desire. This is clearly a moment of intense experience, but equally clearly a moment which refuses to yield its secrets; it is valuable in and for itself.

Watts-Dunton, the friend and companion of Swinburne, wrote extensively on the sonnet, and attempted to demonstrate its natural affinity with certain heightened states of mind and feeling. His most famous formulation of this idea comes in another 'sonnet upon the sonnet', 'The Sonnet's Voice':

> You silvery billows breaking on the beach
> Fall back in foam beneath the star-shine clear,
> The while my rhymes are murmuring in your ear
> A restless lore like that the billows teach;
> For on these sonnet-waves my soul would reach
> From its own depths, and rest within you, dear,
> As, through the billowy voices yearning here,
> Great nature strives to find a human speech.
> A sonnet is a wave of melody:
> From heaving waters of the impassion'd soul
> A billow of tidal music one and whole
> Flows in the 'octave;' then returning free,
> Its ebbing surges in the 'sestet' roll
> Back to the deeps of Life's tumultuous sea.

In this much-anthologised poem, Watts-Dunton manipulates metre as well as form to reinforce his message that the structure of the sonnet resembles the ebb and flow of the sea (which in its turn resembles the movement of the 'impassion'd soul'). The second line begins with a spondee which reverses, albeit temporarily, the metrical flow of the poem and so mirrors the 'falling back' it describes; and the double enjambment of lines 10–12 builds up a pressure which is released by the semi-colon in line 12, to 'ebb' gently to the end of the poem.[10] This 'wave' theory is adopted enthusiastically by T. Hall Caine, the compiler of one of the most significant anthologies of the period, the 1882 volume *Sonnets of Three Centuries*.[11] Caine sees Watts-Dunton as having provided 'a new model' for the sonnet 'grounded in a fixed law of nature' which has the effect of freeing it both from scholastic restrictions and from the imputation that it is merely imitative of the Italian model: 'Here it is seen that the "sonnet-wave" – twofold in quality as well as movement – embraces flow and ebb of thought or sentiment, and flow and ebb of music. For the perfecting of a poem on this pattern the primary necessity, therefore, is, that the thought chosen be such as falls naturally into unequal parts, each essential to each, and the one answering the other.'[12] There is, then, an inherent fitness about the form of the sonnet for representing certain moods of the mind, those characterised by a moment of intense feeling or experience followed by reaction to or reflection on that experience. As John Addington Symonds puts it in the preface to *Animi Figura* (1882), '[the] equipoise between the two parts of the stanza lends itself admirably to dialectic, whether this process of debate be conceived as a dialogue between two persons, or as a conversation carried on within the meditative mind.'[13]

One consequence of this 'wave theory' is that, as a non-formal definition, it frees the sonnet from some of the restrictions imposed by convention. For Symonds, recent critical opinion manifests 'unanimity of opinion' in accepting '[great] varieties in the structure of the sonnet... as equally legitimate'.[14] Watts-Dunton is equally clear about the implications of his 'wave theory'; although he advocates a reasonable strictness in the octave (to correspond to the building of the wave), he argues that the Petrarchan sestet should be 'absolutely free, save that the emotions should govern the arrangement of the verses'.[15] This represents, in some respects, a return to the position at the beginning of the century, when Coleridge described the sonnet as 'a small poem, in which some lonely feeling is developed', and Nathan Drake praised his contemporaries for freeing themselves from the shackles of unnecessary adherence to an arbitrary, imported form.[16] And, as at the beginning of the century, the end of the century sees a great deal of formal experiment within the sonnet. In the case of Symonds and Watts-Dunton, such experiment is primarily to do with the rearrangement of the rhyme scheme, but in other poets it also occasionally takes the form of a 'stretching' of the sonnet itself. Wilfred Scawen Blunt routinely calls fifteen- and sixteen-line poems sonnets, and expands the 'Last Sonnet' of his *Sonnets and Songs* to twenty lines. Gerard Manley Hopkins goes even further, reaching twenty-four lines in the late sonnet 'That Nature is a Heraclitean Fire and of the Comfort of the Resurrection'. With his intense interest in the formal properties of the sonnet and his willingness to experiment with its structure, Hopkins is in many respects typical of the period in which he was writing; and it is one of the ironies of literary history that he might have been recognised as a poet by his contemporaries had it not been for the unfortunate intervention of Dante Gabriel Rossetti. T. Hall Caine includes three poems by Hopkins' friend Richard Watson Dixon in his anthology, praising Dixon as 'probably by far the most striking instance of a living poet deserving the highest recognition yet completely unrecognised'; but two other poems which Dixon had sent in on behalf of another unknown poet – Hopkins – were rejected on the advice of Rossetti.[17] Had Hopkins' work been included alongside that of Rossetti, Watts-Dunton, and others, his affinities with his contemporaries might have been more obvious, even in his most extreme and experimental moments.[18]

In the Preface to *Animi Figura* John Addington Symonds asks: 'What are the just conditions of the sonnet-sequence?'[19] This was a question that fascinated a number of late nineteenth-century poets and critics. In his essay on the sonnet Richard Chenevix Trench credits Wordsworth with having invented the idea of 'a poem made up of a succession of Sonnets, each complete in itself, but each at the same time constituting, so to speak, a stanza of that larger poem whereof it forms a part; just as in a bracelet made up of a string of cameos, or mosaics, each may be a perfect little picture in itself, while at the same time contributing to the beauty and perfection of a larger whole'.[20] The sonnet sequence seemed to offer a way out of the 'crystal sphere' of heightened but solitary experience; reinserted into a sequence, the individual sonnet once again became alive and active with anticipations and reflections. But it also drew attention to the incipient incompatibility between the highly-wrought artifice of the sonnet as a form and the open-endedness and untidiness of experience. Symonds registers something of the tension between the 'monumentalising' tendencies of the form and the commitment to organic process in the answers he provides to his own question. It is unclear whether the best sonnet sequences are the ones in which the individual sonnets can be detached from the whole, or the ones in which the sonnets effectively fuse into a single poem:

It is clear that the first and larger portion of Shakespeare's sonnets form a single poem. Though we may detach each stanza for separate consideration, many of these suffer more from isolation than any single one of Petrarch's *In Morte di Madonna Laura* would do. Wordsworth's *River Duddon* and Mrs. Browning's *Portuguese Sonnets* are sequences, liable to injury in like manner, but not in the same degree, by dismemberment. And the most perfect sonnets which have been published during the last quarter of a century, Mr. D.G. Rossetti's *Willow Wood*, are linked together by a chain so delicate that severance is almost mutilation. Still, in all these cases, the essential quality of the sonnet, as hitherto recognised, has been preserved. The continuous argument has been so ordered that each step is presented in a separate and self-sufficient poem. The sonnet has not passed into a strophé.[21]

Shakespeare's sonnets, or at least 'the first and larger portion' of them – the ones addressed to the mysterious 'Mr. W.H.' – 'form a single poem'. Given the cultural prestige of Shakespeare, we might expect his sonnet-sequence to represent the highest form of the genre, and the descriptions of Petrarch, Wordsworth and 'Mrs. Browning' which follow would appear to confirm this expectation. Their sequences are less organic, and therefore less damaged by 'dismemberment', than Shakespeare's. Only Rossetti in *Willow Wood*, the central sequence of *The House of Life*, has succeeded in producing poems 'linked together by a chain so delicate that severance is almost mutilation'. Yet Symonds concludes, apparently contradicting this emphasis on the interconnectedness of the sequence, that in all of these cases each sonnet remains 'a separate and self-sufficient poem', not a mere 'strophé' of a larger poem.

This uneasy oscillation between the claims of the individual poem and those of the larger sequence is illustrated by the restless groupings and regroupings of Rossetti's *House of Life*. In trying to find the appropriate shape for the 'monuments' to thirty years or so of his life Rossetti repeatedly but inconclusively addresses the question of the relation between art and life. As he redrafted and expanded the poem, Rossetti added a metaphorical substructure – an 'underthought', in Hopkins' terms – comparing the different moments of his life to seasons of the year;[22] but, as 'Love's Last Gift', the last poem of Part I makes clear, the work of art which emerges from this organic process stands apart from it:

> Love to his singer held a glistening leaf,
>   And said: 'The rose-tree and the apple-tree
>   Have fruits to vaunt or flowers to lure the bee;
> And golden shafts are in the feathered sheaf
> Of the great harvest-marshal, the year's chief,
>   Victorious Summer; aye and 'neath warm sea
>   Strange secret grasses lurk inviolably

> Between the filtering channels of sunk reef.
> All are my blooms; and all sweet blooms of love
>   To thee I gave while Spring and Summer sang;
>   But Autumn stops to listen, with some pang
> From those worse things the wind is moaning of.
> Only this laurel dreads no winter days:
> Take my last gift; thy heart hath sung my praise.'

At this pivotal moment in the sequence we are moving from Spring and Summer – the seasons of love's birth and fruition – into Autumn and Winter, the seasons of foreboding and decline. But the evergreen 'laurel' that love offers the poet 'dreads no winter days'; the reward for the singer is an escape from the inevitability of 'hourly change' by means of what Rossetti, in the first sonnet of the next section, calls 'Art's transfiguring essence' (LX, l. 11). Yet the status of the poet's own productions is in doubt. Are they 'blooms of love' like the fruits, flowers and '[strange] secret grasses' of nature? Or are they human arte-facts, like the laurel wreaths used to crown the heads of poets in class-ical antiquity? The sestet of sonnet LX, 'Transfigured Life', offers a similarly incoherent image:

> So in the song, the singer's Joy and Pain,
>   Its very parents, evermore expand
> To bid the passion's fullgrown birth remain,
>   By Art's transfiguring essence subtly spann'd;
>   And from that song-cloud shaped as a man's hand
> There comes a sound as of abundant rain. (ll. 9–14)

The song is the 'child' of profound human experiences which eventu-ally supersedes the traces of its origin in the development of its own distinct identity; but it is also a 'song-cloud shaped as a man's hand' which has the ability to produce 'a sound as of abundant rain'. This baffling movement from child to cloud to 'man's hand' to mimic rain bears witness to the strength of Rossetti's ultimately unsuccessful search for an image which will bridge the divide between life and art.

It is, moreover, unclear whether or not the final 'monument' which emerges from these moments has more than provisional status. On the one hand the poem's 101 sonnets divided into two unequal parts sug-gests a very self-conscious and formal patterning analogous to the sonnet itself.[23] On the other hand, however, the poem consistently highlights the uncertainty of its own 'retrospective aesthetic reordering of experience';[24] to use the Dantean metaphor favoured by Rossetti, it suggests that there are various possible 'paths' through life which cannot be easily or definitively identified:

From Dawn to Noon

As the child knows not if his mother's face
　　　Be fair; nor of his elders yet can deem
　　　What each most is; but as of hill or stream
At dawn, all glimmering life surrounds his place:
Who yet, tow'rd noon of his half-weary race,
　　　Pausing awhile beneath the high sun-beam
　　　And gazing steadily back, – as through a dream,
In things long past new features now can trace: –

Even so the thought that is at length fullgrown
　　　Turns back to note the sun-smit paths, all grey
And marvellous once, where first it walked alone;
　　　And haply doubts, amid the unblenching day,
　　　Which most or least impelled its onward way, –
Those unknown things or these things overknown. (LXXX)

In the octave of this poem there are suggestions, through the meta-phors of childhood and emerging daylight, of progress towards order and certainty, with things 'long past' gradually revealing new aspects of themselves. This optimistic account of change is, however, under-mined by the sestet's 'doubts' about which of the 'sun-smit paths' was decisive in shaping the self. Rossetti's inspired coinage 'overknown' suggests that some things have become too familiar, too readily accepted as part of the poet's account of his own identity; while other things are simply 'unknown', motives which remain opaque to the observer even in his current position. The speaker cannot, then, be sure that he has understood the shape of his own life; indeed, as poems like 'He and I' indicate, he cannot even be sure that the successive selves documented in the various poems add up to a single coherent personality. In this respect each individual sonnet becomes something like an elegy, achieving 'a kind of monumentality that cannot preserve the living past, or even give coherence to the dead hours and lost selves, but at least preserve and enshrine past incarnations of the self.'[25]

It is perhaps this 'inherently monumental' quality which makes the sonnet's connection with elegy so strong during the latter part of the century.[26] There is again a resemblance here to the position at the very end of the previous century; many late nineteenth-century sonnet writers take a morbid and almost voluptuous pleasure in the contemplation of death which would have been familiar to Charlotte Smith. The sonnet as elegy elides the kinds of difficulties and contradictions Rossetti faces in *The House of Life*; the 'hourly change' which perplexes and ultimately defeats Rossetti's attempts to transform his own life into art has ceased, and the pattern of a life can be summarised and commemorated. Rossetti's own death in 1882 prompted a sequence of four octasyllabic sonnets by Francis Thompson which take up the poet's self-identification with Dante; and the death of Robert Browning in 1889 led Swinburne to produce seven sonnets of mingled lament and celebration of the poet's life.[27] Although an extremely influential figure in other respects, Swinburne was only an occasional sonnet-writer. It might have been for this reason that his close friend Watts-Dunton identified himself so strongly with the sonnet, thereby avoiding (like Tennyson's brother Charles) direct comparison with his more illustrious contemporary. Given this general indifference to the sonnet, and indeed Robert Browning's known aversion to the form, it is therefore interesting that Swinburne chooses the sonnet as the vehicle for his impressions. The poems are dated 13–15 December 1889, the three days following Browning's death; and the decision to affix dates to them is designed to signify their status as crystallised moments of grief. Over the three days they form a miniature *In Memoriam*; the three 'December 14' sonnets constitute a moment of grief and denial, while the 'December 15' sonnets see this grief transformed into a public commemoration of the poet's life and achievements. There is, moreover, a conscious incorporation into these 'spontaneous' outpourings of some typical motifs of elegy. The volume in which they appear is called *Astrophel*, the title of Spenser's lament for the death of Sidney, and the dispraise of death in sonnet 2 is a reworking of a typically Renaissance theme. Similarly, the poem on Venice, the city in which Browning died, recalls the 'Vienna' sections of Tennyson's elegy on the death of Hallam; in both cases the city is 'blamed' for the death of the beloved:

> Blithe and soft and bland,
> Too fair for storm to scathe or fire to cleave,
> Shone on our dreams and memories evermore
> The domes, the towers, the mountains and the shore
> That gird or guard thee, Venice: cold and black
> Seems now the face we loved as he of yore.
> We have given thee love---no stint, no stay, no lack:
> What gift, what gift is this thou hast given us back? (ll. 7–14)

The vestigial presence of these literary archetypes reminds us that, like *In Memoriam*, Swinburne's sequence implicitly claims to evolve its structure out of lived experience; what looks at first like a spontaneous outpouring of grief eventually reveals itself as 'like a statue solid-set/ And moulded in colossal calm' (*In Memoriam*, 'Epilogue', ll. 15–16). And in this respect it is typical of the late-Victorian sonnet sequence, which both exploits and conceals the ineradicable tension between the language of spontaneity and sincerity so central to nineteenth-century poetics and the flagrant artifice of the sonnet's conventions.

In his note on Elizabeth Barrett Browning's poetry, Hall Caine asks by what right she is 'worthy to ride in the very van of English sonnet-writers, with Shakespeare, Milton, Wordsworth and Keats, as an Amazon in noble alliance with these male warriors', and concludes that 'her right of rank with the foremost is founded upon claims somewhat dissimilar from those advanced by her great fellows':

> She has written nothing which quite touches the summits of possibility in sonnet-excellence... But the so-called sonnets from the Portuguese are among the most perfect *series* of love-poems in our language, and it is in the nature of things that a sonnet of the supreme order can rarely be one of an inter-related series, but is oftenest a thing wholly self-inclusive, being the outcome of a special inspiration which is born with it and consumed by it... [The *Sonnets from the Portuguese*] are, in the highest sense, essentially *woman's* love-poetry – essentially feminine in their hyper-refinement, in their intense tremulous spirituality, and above all, in that absolute saturation by the one idea, which bears out Byron's familiar dictum that '- love is in man's life a thing apart,/ 'Tis woman's whole existence'.[28]

So keen is he to establish gender boundaries in this area that he contradicts prevailing opinion (and indeed himself) in this paragraph. If, as he asserts, 'a sonnet of the supreme order can rarely be one of an inter-related series' where does this leave Shakespeare's sonnets, universally regarded at the end of the century as the highest example of the form? And if a 'sonnet of the highest order' is 'the outcome of a special inspiration which is born with it and consumed by it', then surely Elizabeth Barrett Browning's sequence, which betrays an 'absolute saturation by... one idea', should be capable of attaining this status. This attempt to designate the amatory sonnet sequence as a peculiarly feminine form highlights both the persistence and the complexity of gender distinctions during this period. On the one hand, women poets were no longer subject to the kind of routine segregation and denigration suffered by the 'poetesses' earlier in the century; all of the major sonnet anthologies include work by a large number of women poets, and poets like Alice Meynell, Mathilde Blind and Augusta Webster enjoyed considerable literary reputations.[29] On the other hand, however, subtle distinctions and redefinitions of the kind indicated by Hall Caine were continually devised in order to demarcate a specifically 'male' kind of achievement in this form. William Sharp, for instance, cannot keep a note of condescension out of his voice when he praises the work of A. Mary F. Robinson: 'In 1884 was published *The New Arcadia*, a book that deservedly attracted very considerable attention; though some of Miss Robinson's most discriminating friends doubted the advisability of her attempting the reform of the condition of the agricultural classes by means of poetic special pleading'.[30] Similarly, his extravagant praise of Dante Gabriel Rossetti – 'the one English poet whose sonnet-work can genuinely be weighed in the balance with that of Shakespeare and with that of Wordsworth' – seems designed in part to exclude the claims of his most significant precursor in the amatory sonnet sequence.[31]

This desire to maintain gender boundaries in an era when many of them were being transgressed and realigned can be seen at work in William Michael Rossetti's introduction to Augusta Webster's post-humously published sonnet sequence *Mother and Daughter*. Rossetti uses as his epigraph to the volume Theodore Watts-Dunton's remarks on 'George Eliot, Mrs. Webster, and Miss Cobbe, who, in virtue of lofty purpose, purity of soul, and deep sympathy with suffering humanity, are just now far ahead of the men – bending their genius, like the rainbow, as a covenant of love over "all flesh that is upon the earth"'.[32] Rossetti's brief introductory remarks continue in this chivalrous vein:

> Nothing certainly could be more genuine than these Sonnets. A Mother is expressing her love for a Daughter – her reminiscences, anxieties, and hopeful anticipations. The theme is as beautiful and natural a one as any poetess could select, uniting, in the warm clasp of the domestic affections, something of those olden favourites, *The Pleasures of Memory* and *The Pleasures of Hope*. It seems a little surprising that Mrs. Webster had not been forestalled – and to the best of my knowledge she never *was* forestalled – in such a treatment. But some of the poetesses have not been Mothers.[33]

The pointed closing remark is consistent with the *fin-de-siècle* feeling that female independence and intellectual emancipation were inconsistent with marriage and motherhood.[34] In developing the theme of motherhood and the 'domestic affections', in contrast, Webster was cultivating the proper sphere of the 'poetess' who lived in a realm of 'lofty purpose' and 'purity of soul' far from the degraded world of men. Had Rossetti read Webster's sequence a little more closely, however, he might have seen that she expresses some reservations about this masculine view of women's love:

Love's Mourner

'Tis men who say that through all hurt and pain
The woman's love, wife's, mother's, still will hold,
And breathes the sweeter and will more unfold
For winds that tear it, and the sorrowful rain.
So in a thousand voices has the strain
Of this dear patient madness been retold,
That men call woman's love. Ah! they are bold,
Naming for love that grief which *does* remain.

Love faints that looks on baseness face to face:
Love pardons all; but by the pardonings dies,
With a fresh wound of each pierced through the breast.
And there stand pityingly in Love's void place
Kindness of household wont familiar-wise,
And faith to Love – faith to our dead at rest.

What has been celebrated by men as 'woman's love, wife's, mother's' appears to the woman herself as a 'dear patient madness' which does in some sense survive 'all hurt and pain' but only in the form of 'faith to Love – faith to our dead at rest'. When women seem to continue to love, what they are actually doing is mourning the death of love, a love which has been killed by the repeated 'wounds' it has suffered. This fleeting allusion to Christ on the cross highlights the underlying ambivalence of Webster's image; in comparing herself to Christ, the suffering woman takes on the classically feminine role of victim and martyr. She becomes one of George Eliot's Comtean priestesses, sacrificing herself for the greater good of humanity – in this instance, for the greater good of her daughter; and it is significant in this respect that the most obvious precursor for a sonnet sequence on the domestic affections (again, not noted by Rossetti) is George Eliot's *Brother and Sister*.[35]

There is a similarly ambivalent use of the sonnet to represent a typically feminine experience in the work of A. Mary F. Robinson, the poet
to whom we saw William Sharp condescending earlier.[36] In her sonnet
'Neurasthenia' Robinson attempts to provide an account from within
of the defining female malady of the age. This nervous disorder, induc-
ing 'feelings of fatigue and lassitude, with vague physical symptoms
such as headache, muscle pain, and subjective sensory disturbances',
was often viewed as one of the unfortunate consequences of women's
increasingly strident rejection of their traditional roles as wife and
mother: 'Doctors linked what they saw as an epidemic of nervous dis-
orders including anorexia, neurasthenia, and hysteria with the changes
in women's aspirations'.[37] In making this the subject of her sonnet,
then, Robinson is invoking some of the most profound anxieties of a
very anxious period:

> I watch the happier people of the house
>   Come in and out, and talk, and go their ways;
> I sit and gaze at them; I cannot rouse
>   My heavy mind to share their busy days.
>
> I watch them glide, like skaters on a stream,
>   Across the brilliant surface of the world.
> But I am underneath: they do not dream
>   How deep below the eddying flood is whirl'd.
>
> They cannot come to me, nor I to them;
>   But, if a mightier arm could reach and save,
> Should I forget the tide I had to stem?
>   Should I, like these, ignore the abysmal wave?
>
> Yes! in the radiant air how could I know
> How black it is, how fast it is, below?

Neurasthenia is here presented as a kind of *reductio ad absurdum* of
the aesthetic attitude to experience. Robinson leaves the gender of the
speaker unspecified, but the nature of her malady and the domestic
setting of the first quatrain imply a female persona. The world has
become a 'brilliant surface' with which she feels no connection; in a
dizzying switch of perspective, the second quatrain presents the
speaker as watching this 'surface' from beneath the sheet of ice upon
which the skaters 'glide'. The poem reworks the 'wave' metaphor so
characteristic of the period to produce an incipiently psychoanalytical
language of surface and depth, concealment and revelation; beneath

the calm exterior of everyday life lurks an 'eddying flood', an 'abysmal wave' of terrifying ferocity and power. The experience of the speaker, confined within the house by a debilitating and possibly psycho-somatic medical condition, invites comparison with the situation of the narrator of Charlotte Perkins Gilman's *The Yellow Wallpaper*; but the polemical force of the poem is mitigated by the vestigial fantasy of rescue in the sestet. Were a 'mightier arm' to 'reach and save' her, the speaker implies that she would be 'cured' of her disorder, and, like the rest of humanity, be able to ignore or forget the chaotic energy that lurks just below the surface.

Robinson's sonnet, with its emphasis on disease and disorder, sug-gests that the always blurred and indistinct line between aestheticism and decadence has probably been crossed. One of the characteristic features of the decadence is its perverse pleasure in what Mathilde Blind calls '[the] hectic beauty of decay'.[38] Poets seek out moments of decline, loss and fragmentation to enshrine in their sonnets, and find them even in the most innocuous-seeming places:

To-day

> 'Widower of yesterday! why stand aloof?
>> Know me thy child, and know me too thy bride;
>> Thou must beget thy issue from my side.
> The loom thou wroughtest, joy thee in the woof!
> The plate thou gravedst, now behold the proof;
>> All days but print afresh the yester-trace,
>> Save each impression grows more poor and base:
> Take me, who shalt take worse to thy life's roof.'
>
> Then spat I out the ashes of my youth; –
> 'Thou liest a lie embittered with the truth!
>> But one part in to-morrow's blood thou hast:
> From many morrows and one higher me
> The days shall be bred out to purity,
>> And build on the drained marshes of the past.'[39]

Francis Thompson here manages to make the 'moment' of the aes-thetic sonnet something menacing and even disturbing. The speaker in the octave – presumably the 'To-day' of the title – represents the addressee as the 'widower of yesterday' who is forced to marry and beget children with his own daughter. This example of 'strict domestic economy', to quote E.M. Forster on the Ptolemies of Egypt, introduces the language of racial degeneration which provides the connecting

thread for the rest of the sonnet.[40] Punning on the language of printing, the first speaker describes today as the 'proof' of yesterday, with
each successive 'impression' of the original growing 'more poor and
base'. The sestet, however, vigorously denies this suggestion that the
present and future are somehow determined by the past; 'to-morrow's
blood' is partly composed of the impressions of the past, but it can be
'bred out' by 'one higher me' to a new 'purity'. This pestilence can
be eradicated by the construction of a kind of garden-city of the mind;
the new self will be built 'on the drained marshes of the past'.

Thompson's poem illustrates the 'decadent' sonnet's greater openness than its aesthetic forerunner to the dominant social and cultural
debates of its epoch. His work also indicates the extent to which
Wordsworth and Milton had been displaced by Shakespeare and Keats
as models for sonnet writers by the end of the century. In many of his
poems he cultivates an almost unreadable pseudo-Elizabethan diction
inlaid with Keatsian motifs: 'When I perceive the fullest-sailèd sprite/
Lag at most need upon the lethèd seas,/ The provident captainship oft
voided quite,/ And lamèd lie deep-draughted argosies'.[41] Thompson's
combination of formal archaism and an almost undisciplined openness
to the intellectual cross-currents of his era is reminiscent of Hopkins,
whose work Thompson may indeed have known;[42] and this again
helps to illustrate some of the connections between Hopkins and the
other poets of his time. The sonnets of both Thompson and Hopkins
are 'decadent' both in the sense that they reflect the typical concerns
of the epoch, and in the sense that they show the sonnet 'going to
seed' in the attempt to contain moments of death and disintegration
within a tight formal structure. Parallels with 'To-day' can be seen in
Hopkins' almost contemporary 'Spelt from Sibyl's Leaves', perhaps the
most extraordinarily experimental sonnet of the whole century:

> Earnest, earthless, equal, attuneable, vaulty, voluminous, . .
> stupendous
> Evening strains to be tíme's vást, womb-of-all, home-of-all,
> hearse-of-all night.
> Her fond yellow hornlight wound to the west, her wild hollow
> hoarlight hung to the height
> Waste; her earliest stars, earl-stars, stárs principal, overbend us,
> Fíre-féaturing heaven. For earth her being has unbound, her
> dapple is at an end, as-
> tray or aswarm, all throughther, in throngs; self ín self steepèd
> and páshed—qúite

Disremembering, dísmémbering áll now. Heart, you round me
                                                    right
With: Óur évening is over us; óur night whélms, whélms, ánd
                                              will end us.
Only the beak-leaved boughs dragonish damask the tool-smooth
                                    bleak light; black,
Ever so black on it. Óur tale, O óur oracle! Lét life, wáned, ah lét
                                              life wind
Off hér once skéined stained véined varíety upon, áll on twó
                                    spools; párt, pen, páck
Now her áll in twó flocks, twó folds—black, white; right, wrong;
                              reckon but, reck but, mind
But thése two; wáre of a wórld where bút these twó tell, each off
                                    the óther; of a rack
Where, selfwrung, selfstrung, sheathe- and shelterless, thóughts
                        agaínst thoughts ín groans grínd.

There are a number of familiar motifs here, not least in the title –
the Sibyl makes regular appearances in *fin-de-siècle* poetry – and in the
twilight setting. Twilight both transfigures the visual environment in
ways which make it available for symbolic reading and provides an
image of the encroachment of the knowledge of death into human life.
Its arrival is a reminder that '[our] evening is over us; our night whelms,
whelms, and will end us'. These motifs are, however, transfigured
in Hopkins' work; whereas his contemporaries see in the brevity of
human life an injunction to 'seize the day' and fill it with valuable
impressions and sensations, he represents this same brevity as a
reminder of the overriding importance of the life to come. The classical
image of the 'weaving' of fate, the 'loom' of Thompson's poem, is literally undone; the pagan oracle is Christianised as 'our tale... our oracle',
a story not of the blending of human destinies but of the abrupt and
irreversible separation which will take place on the day of judgement as
the 'two spools' reel in their respective threads.

One effect of the extreme archaism of both Thompson and Hopkins
is make the sonnet the equivalent of the *recherché* poetic forms – the
stornelli and rispetti, villanelles and haikus – sought out and used by
the writers of the '80s and '90s. This is, in one sense, a way of keeping
the sonnet current; a familiar form strongly associated with the previous generation of poets is reinvented as an exotic. But is also undermines the sonnet's claim to any natural or necessary place in the poetic
order, a claim which was, as we have seen, central to its popularity for

the writers of the aesthetic movement. There is, moreover, as Hopkins in particular illustrates, an incipient contradiction in the attempt to enshrine 'the hectic beauty of decay' within the rigid confines of the sonnet. This contradiction can, at its most productive, lead to the work of a Hopkins; but during the last decade of the nineteenth century there seems to be a movement away from the sonnet and towards other, more spontaneous and immediate forms. Even Watts-Dunton admits that the sonnet is not the most appropriate form for '[the] function of giving spontaneous voice to the emotions and passions of the poet's soul'; and Bernard Bergonzi in his anthology of poetry of the period suggests that it is supplanted by the quatrain, which 'as a terse enclosed unit, provided the best means of conveying the significant, isolated "moment" that was a dominant element in the poetics of the time'.[43] The new poets of the nineties – Housman, Yeats – do not really use the sonnet at all; Yeats, indeed, deliberately avoids the form in his beautiful adaptation of Ronsard's sonnet 'Quand vous serez bien vieille':

> When you are old and grey and full of sleep,
> And nodding by the fire, take down this book,
> And slowly read, and dream of the soft look
> Your eyes had once, and of their shadows deep;
>
> How many loved your moments of glad grace,
> And loved your beauty with love false or true,
> But one man loved the pilgrim soul in you,
> And loved the sorrows of your changing face;
>
> And bending down beside the glowing bars,
> Murmur, a little sadly, how Love fled
> And paced upon the mountains overhead
> And hid his face among a crowd of stars.

The basic stanza of this poem is the Petrarchan quatrain, and the vestigial but unrealised presence of the Petrarchan sonnet can be felt throughout. By refusing the conventional octave-sestet division Yeats denies his readers the satisfaction of closure and finality, offering them instead something which gestures outwards beyond the amatory sonnet and towards higher and more intangible areas of experience. Ronsard's poem ends with a conventional *carpe diem* – 'Cueillez dès aujourd'huy les roses de la vie' – but Yeats finishes on a more enigmatic (and egocentric) note; his poet is not (like Ronsard's) in his grave, but pacing the mountains in rapt communion with the stars.[44]

There were, moreover, social and political changes towards the end of the 1890s which led to a widespread rejection of the aesthetic and decadent attitudes of the previous two decades, and with it a rejection of their habitual forms of artistic expression. One such change was unquestionably prompted by the arrest and trial of Oscar Wilde, an incident which according to one historian of the period brought the 'decadent' movement to a sudden and emphatic halt.[45] Perhaps more important, however, was the outbreak of the Boer War at the end of the decade, which led to a feverish national preoccupation with Britain's imperial destiny. As A. Mary F. Robinson puts it in the preface to her *Collected Poems* (1902), 'I send forth this little book with scant expectance of immediate success. Entirely lyrical, intellectual, or romantic, these little poems must sound as the merest tootling of Corydon's reed-pipe in ears accustomed to the martial music of our times.'[46] One instrument of this 'martial music' was the sonnet, which rediscovered its Miltonic-Wordsworthian heritage of masculine patriotic invocation. In his sonnets on Rhodes, for instance, Watts-Dunton celebrates the imperialist adventurer as the Clive of Africa:

> For see! – for hear! – how race is trampling race
> Where'er the white man's tempered breezes blow! –
> Hear England saying, 'He won a breathing space
> For English lungs where skies of azure glow' –
> Hear Freedom saying, 'He gave me a brooding place
> Where, 'neath the flag I love, my limbs shall grow.'[47]

Others, however, remember that the genuine Miltonic-Wordsworthian strain includes moral reflection and self-criticism as well as patriotic rabble-rousing. The case of Thomas Hardy is an instructive one in this respect. As is well known, Hardy became a prolific poet during the last thirty years of his career, having more or less given up poetry for novel-writing during the years between 1870 and 1895. His early work from the 1860s includes a number of sonnets (such as the Meredith-inspired amatory mini-sequence *She to Him*), but his later work uses the form extremely sparingly. He is, however, tempted into the form in October 1899 for two poems on the embarkation of British troops at Southampton on their way to the Boer War:

> Here, where Vespasian's legions struck the sands,
> And Cerdic with his Saxons entered in,
> And Henry's army leapt afloat to win

> Convincing triumphs over neighbour lands,
>
> Vaster battalions press for further strands,
> To argue in this selfsame bloody mode
> Which this late age of thought, and pact, and code,
> Still fails to mend. – Now deckward tramp the bands,
>
> Yellow as autumn leaves, alive as spring;
> And as each host draws out upon the sea
> Beyond which lies the tragical To-be,
> None dubious of the cause, none murmuring,
>
> Wives, sisters, parents, wave white hands and smile,
> As if they knew not that they weep the while.

It is characteristic of Hardy to see things in a 'vaster' timeframe than his contemporaries, and his first thought on seeing the departure of British troops is to remember the invasions that have created Britain and Britishness. His emphasis on the irony and pathos of war is typified by the first line of the sestet. In this autumnal setting the bands are '[yellow] as autumn leaves' but also 'alive as spring'; and the telescoping of the two seasons becomes a tragic prolepsis. There is, moreover, no 'murmuring', no shade or nuance of emotion, just the stark contrast between the innocent 'white hands' of the crowds at the dockside and the 'tragical To-be' lying in wait for so many of their loved ones.

In focusing on the sea as an emblem of British power and vulnerability Hardy is echoing one of the dominant motifs of Wordsworth's early sonnets; and there are some perhaps surprising similarities in the position of the sonnet at the beginning and the end of the century. These similarities should not be overstated; one enormous difference is the absence of a figure to do for the sonnet in the twentieth century what Wordsworth had done for it in the nineteenth. In addition, Hardy and Watts-Dunton did not have to 'rediscover' the patriotic sonnet; imperialism was, as we have already seen, part of the characteristically *fin-de-siècle* complex of attitudes and beliefs.[48] At the beginning of the twentieth century, however, as at the beginning of the nineteenth, it is possible to say that the sonnet becomes one of the most sensitive registers of a larger cultural reaction. Its reversion to a simpler, plainer, more 'masculine' strain signifies in both cases the attempt to overwrite the legacy of a 'decadent' movement by appropriating one of its principal forms of expression.

Notes

Introduction

1 Introduction to the facsimile reprint of *The Germ* (1901; rpt. Oxford: Ashmolean Museum, 1992), p. 20. The poem in question is 'Her First Season'.
2 Christina Rossetti, *The Complete Poems*, eds R.W. Crump and Betty S. Flowers (London: Penguin, 2001), p. 854.
3 This equation was made explicit by some writers towards the end of the nineteenth century; see ch. 6 below, pp. 146–7.
4 In 'Scorn not the sonnet': 'with this key/ Shakespeare unlocked his heart' (ll. 2–3); see ch. 2 below.
5 See ch. 4 below for a discussion of Keble's theory of 'reserve' in relation to the sonnet.
6 See ch. 1 below, pp. 18–23.
7 Jan Marsh ed., *Dante Gabriel Rossetti: Collected Writings* (London: J.M. Dent, 1999), p. 494.
8 See for instance Browning's sonnet 'Why I am a liberal' (1885), published in response to a request and not included by Browning in the collected edition of his poems.
9 In *Culture and Anarchy* (1869), ch. 2.
10 See William T. Going, 'The Term "Sonnet Sequence"', *Modern Language Notes* 62 (1947), 400–2, and ch. 6 below. I have tended to use 'series' rather than 'sequence' for sonnet groupings written before the last quarter of the century.
11 The 'obvious affinity' between the sonnet sequence and the lyric sequence is noted by John Woolford in his illuminating discussion of the lyric sequence in *Browning the Revisionary* (Houndmills, Basingstoke: Macmillan, 1988), p. 89.
12 See ch. 6 below, pp. 140–1.
13 Raymond Williams, *Marxism and Literature* (Oxford: Oxford University Press, 1986), part II, ch. 8.
14 In 'The Sonnet's Voice' (1881); see ch. 6 below, pp. 138–9.
15 'Cavalcanti' (1934) in T.S. Eliot ed., *Literary Essays of Ezra Pound* (1954; rpt. London and Boston: Faber and Faber, 1985), p. 170.

Chapter 1   The Wordsworthian Sonnet Revival: *Poems in Two Volumes* (1807)

1 Lee M. Johnson, *Wordsworth and the Sonnet*, Anglistica XIX (Copenhagen: Rosenkilde and Bagger, 1973), p. 10.
2 See Stuart Curran, *Poetic Form and British Romanticism* (Oxford: Oxford University Press, 1986), ch. 3; Daniel Robinson, 'Reviving the Sonnet: Women Romantic Poets and the Sonnet Claim,' *European Romantic Review* 6 (1995), 98–127.

3 Cited in Alun Jones ed., *Wordsworth's Poems of 1807* (Basingstoke: Macmillan, 1987), p. 159; Wordsworth's account is corroborated by one of Dorothy Wordsworth's journal entries (hence the editorial emendation to the date): see Marjorie M. Barber ed., *A Dorothy Wordsworth Selection* (London: Macmillan, 1965), p. 56.

4 First published in the *European Magazine* XL (March 1787) under the pseudonym 'Axiologus'. Helen Maria Williams was herself a poet, and identified herself strongly with the cause of the French Revolution.

5 Mary Robinson's preface is reprinted in Paula R. Feldman and Daniel Robinson eds, *A Century of Sonnets: The Romantic-Era Revival 1750–1850* (Oxford and New York: OUP, 1999), pp. 233–40; Anne Radcliffe, *A Sicilian Romance* (1790: OUP, 1993), pp. 23–24.

6 From the *Gentleman's Magazine*, 56 (1786), 333–4; cited Duncan Wu, *Romantic Women Poets: An Anthology* (Oxford: Blackwell, 1997), p. 69.

7 Nathan Drake, *Literary Hours or Sketches Critical and Narrative* (London: Cadell and Davies, 1798), pp. 61, 66–7.

8 A translation of Petrarch's sonnet beginning 'Se la mia vita dall'aspro tormento' ; first published in the *Morning Chronicle* in 1798.

9 Feldman and Robinson, *Century*, p. 15; the first edition of Smith's *Elegiac Sonnets* appeared in 1784.

10 See Bishop Hunt Jr., 'Wordsworth and Charlotte Smith', *The Wordsworth Circle* 1 (1970), 85–103.

11 Feldman and Robinson, *Century*, p. 15.

12 Ibid., p. 16.

13 Doubtfully headed 'To [?] Charles Lamb', but the words in question were intended for the poet's brother John; see Alan G. Hill ed., *Letters of William Wordsworth: A New Selection* (Oxford and New York: Oxford University Press, 1984), pp. 59–60.

14 Jennifer Ann Wagner suggests that Wordsworth 'recuperated [the] form... from a "feminization" of the genre', and traces out this 'masculine' Wordsworthian line in her study of the nineteenth-century sonnet; *A Moment's Monument: Revisionary Poetics and the Nineteenth-century English Sonnet* (London: Associated University Presses, 1996), p. 13.

15 See ch. 1 of *Biographia Literaria* for Coleridge's account of his discovery of Bowles' sonnets; the quotation is from the second version of Coleridge's sonnet to Bowles, l. 8. Coleridge's tortuous relation to the sonnet tradition is discussed in detail in Daniel Robinson, '"Work without hope": Anxiety and embarrassment in Coleridge's Sonnets', *Studies in Romanticism* 39 (2000), 81–110.

16 John Kerrigan notes the significance of this phrase in 'Wordsworth and the Sonnet: Building, Dwelling, Thinking', *Essays in Criticism* 35 (1985), 57.

17 From a letter of October 1805 to Sir George Beaumont; cited in Jones, *Poems of 1807*, p. 161.

18 *Paradise Lost*, bk vii, ll. 26–7.

19 Coleridge, 'Reflections on Having Left a Place of Retirement', l. 48.

20 Jennifer Ann Wagner also notes this dimension of the Wordsworthian sonnet: 'Wordsworth introduces to the nineteenth-century sonnet a self-reflexivity that the form had not seen since Shakespeare; [his] keen awareness of the dialectics of constraint and freedom, of miniaturization and expansion,

of resistance and potentiality, reinforces the structure of his poems with a thematization of those very dynamics': *A Moment's Monument*, p. 15.

21 Jonathan Hess, in contrast, reads the poem as an assertion of liberty which '[affirms] what it sees as the foundations of political freedom... by negating what recent scholarship has come to see as *the* symbolically central political institution of the age [i.e. prison]'; 'Wordsworth's Aesthetic State: The Poetics of Liberty', *Studies in Romanticism* 33 (1994), 24.

22 'I cannot praise a fugitive and cloistered virtue, unexercised and unbreathed, that never sallies out and sees her adversary, but slinks out of the race, where that immortal garland is to be run for, not without dust and heat'; Milton, 'Areopagitica' in K.M. Burton ed., *Milton's Prose Writings* (London and New York: Dent, Dutton, 1974), p. 158.

23 E.P. Thompson, *The Making of the English Working Class* (1963; rpt. Harmondsworth, Middx.: Penguin, 1982), p. 299.

24 Compare the image of domestic contentment around the spinning wheel in 'Michael', ll. 80–111.

25 Cp. Spenser, *Amoretti*, 71, ll. 9–12: 'But as your worke is woven all about,/ With woodbynd flowers and fragrant Eglantine:/ So sweet your prison you in time shall prove,/ With many dear delights bedecked fine'.

26 See for example Milton's 'When I consider how my light is spent': '"Doth God exact day-labour, light denied?"/ I fondly ask. But Patience, to prevent/ That murmur, soon replies...' (ll. 7–9).

27 This letter, to the Whig statesman Charles James Fox, was written in January 1801 to accompany a presentation copy of *Lyrical Ballads*; see Michael Mason ed., *Lyrical Ballads* (London and New York: Longman, 1992), pp. 42–43.

28 Herbert Sussman, *Victorian Masculinities: Manhood and Masculine Poetics in Early Victorian Literature and Art* (Cambridge: Cambridge University Press, 1995).

29 A similarity also noted by Arunodoy Bhattacharya in *The Sonnet and the Major English Romantic Poets* (Calcutta, 1976), p. 32.

30 'The Sonnets of William Wordsworth', *Quarterly Review* 69 (1841–2), 3; 4–5.

31 Leigh Hunt and S. Adams Lee eds, *The Book of the Sonnet* (Boston: Roberts Bros., 1867), I, pp. 226–7

32 Alan Liu, *Wordsworth: The Sense of History* (Stanford, California: Stanford UP, 1989), p. 431.

33 Liu suggests that this poem was originally part of a series of poems commemorating the 'Calais Tour' of 1802, a moment of great personal significance for Wordsworth in coming to terms with the legacy of his involvement in the fortunes of revolutionary France. For Liu, the 'memorial tour' is the form evolved by Wordsworth in response to his repression of History; see *The Sense of History*, pp. 474–85.

34 Stuart Curran suggests that the removal of the sonnets 'To Sleep' and the translations from Michelangelo would leave 'a surprisingly coherent pattern' constituting 'a sequence in the Petrarchan mode'; *Poetic Form*, pp. 41–2.

35 In his definition of the 'Fancy' in the Preface to *Poems* (1815); *Poems*, p. 919.

36 Liu, *Sense of History*, pp. 428, 435.

37 Preface to *Poems* (1815); John O. Haydon, *Wordsworth: The Poems* (Harmondsworth, Middx.: Penguin, 1982), II, p. 919.

38 Wagner, *Moment's Monument*, pp. 41–45.

39　See the letter to Lady Beaumont of 21 May 1807 defending sonnet 8, 'With ships the sea was sprinkled far and nigh': 'My mind wantons with grateful joy in the exercise of its own powers, and, loving its own creation, "This ship to all the rest I did prefer"' (Hill, *Letters*, p. 102).

40　Philip Cox points out this poem's satirical relation to the 'revisit' sonnet tradition; *Gender, Genre and the Romantic Poets* (Manchester and New York: Manchester UP, 1996), p. 47.

41　This contradiction also fascinated Browning; see the discussion of 'One Word More' and its importance for the 'aesthetic' sonnet in ch. 6.

42　Liu suggests that this poem represents the end of the (repressed or displaced) Calais Tour, and in its rejection of the fantastic visions conjured up by the clouds implies the poet's final surrender to respectability: 'Watching the sky's cumulus architecture... the poet feels all along that he will forget the phantom New Jerusalem because it has no earthly substance'; *The Sense of History*, p. 482.

43　For Wordsworth's involvement in the revolutionary politics of London in the 1790s see Nicholas Roe, *Wordsworth and Coleridge: The Radical Years* (Oxford: Clarendon Press, 1988).

44　Letter to Lady Beaumont, 21 May 1807; Hill, *Letters*, p. 100.

45　This sonnet obviously irritated Keats; see 'The House of Mourning Written by Mr. Scott': 'But viler Wordsworth's sonnet/ Upon Dover. Dover! Who *could* write upon it.' (ll. 13–14)

46　Nicholas Roe, *The Radical Years*, p. 29.

47　The word 'patriotism' had Jacobin connotations at this time; see *The Prelude* (1805), ix, 'Residence in France', ll. 122–5: 'I gradually withdrew/ Into a noisier world, and thus did soon/ Become a patriot; and my heart was all/ Given to the people, and my love was theirs.'

48　Francis Jeffrey, Review of *Poems in Two Volumes*, *Edinburgh Review* 11 (1807), 230.

49　*Antony and Cleopatra*, I, i, 1–2: 'Nay, but this dotage of our general's/ O'erflows the measure'.

50　The 'River Duddon' sonnets are discussed in ch. 3.

51　This form fascinated Hopkins in particular; see ch. 3.

Chapter 2　'Transcripts of the private heart': The Sonnet and Autobiography

1　Reprinted in *Leigh Hunt's Literary Criticism*, eds L.H. Houtchens and C.W. Houtchens (New York: Columbia UP, 1956), p. 359.

2　Alexander Dyce, *Specimens of English Sonnets* (London: William Pickering, 1833), p. vi.

3　The 'River Duddon' sonnets are discussed in ch. 3 below.

4　Originally published as *Ecclesiastical Sketches* in 1822; the title was later changed to *Ecclesiastical Sonnets* when thirty poems were added; see ch. 4 below.

5　*Book of the Sonnet*, I, p. 86.

6　Cp Hazlitt's barbed comment on Wordsworth in his essay 'On Milton's Sonnets' in *Table-Talk* (1821; rpt. Oxford University Press, 1910), p. 237:

'They mouth it well, and are said to be sacred to Liberty. Brutus' exclamation, "Oh virtue, I thought thee a substance, but I find thee a shadow," was not considered as a compliment, but as a bitter sarcasm. The beauty of Milton's Sonnets is their sincerity, the spirit of poetical patriotism which they breathe. Either Milton's or the living bard's are defective in this respect. There is no Sonnet of Milton's on the Restoration of Charles II. There is no Sonnet of Mr. Wordsworth's corresponding to that of "the poet blind and bold" "On the late Massacre in Piedmont".'

7   Robinson, '"Work without hope"', 82.
8   Coleridge, 'On Poesy or Art', in R.A. Foakes ed., *Lectures 1808–19 on Literature* (Princeton UP, 1987), II, p. 224.
9   *Book of the Sonnet*, I, p. 87.
10 Walter Jackson Bate, 'Keats's Style: Evolution towards qualities of permanent value' in M.H. Abrams ed., *English Romantic Poets: Modern Essays in Criticism*, 2nd ed. (OUP, 1975), pp. 413–4.
11 Jonathan Bate, *Shakespeare and the English Romantic Imagination* (OUP, 1986; rpt 1989), p. 183.
12 See eg. Miriam Allott ed., *Keats: The Complete Poems* (Harlow: Longman, 1970); Bate, *Romantic Imagination*, p. 182; Keats' sonnet alludes to Shakespeare's sonnets 64 and 107 as well as 12.
13 See below, pp. 44–6.
14 Richard Monckton Milnes ed., *The Life and Letters of John Keats* (1848; rpt. London: J.M. Dent and Sons, 1927), p. 162.
15 See T. Hall Caine ed., *Sonnets of Three Centuries: A Selection, including Many Examples Hitherto Unpublished* (London: Elliot Stock, 1882), p. 310.
16 William Sharp ed., *Sonnets of This Century* (London: Walter Scott, 1886), p. liv.
17 See ch. 6 below.
18 Both were published by Taylor and Hessey and knew and admired one another's work, though they never met; see Jonathan Bate, *John Clare: A Biography* (London: Picador, 2004), pp. 188–90.
19 From a letter of 5 January 1824 to his publisher John Taylor; cited in R.K.R. Thornton ed., *The Rural Muse, Poems by John Clare* (1835; rpt. The Mid Northumberland Arts Group and Carcanet New Press, 1982), p. 11.
20 Bate, *John Clare*, p. 379; Eric Robinson, David Powell and P.M.S. Dawson eds, *John Clare: Northborough Sonnets* (Ashington: Mid Northumberland Arts Group/Carcanet Press, 1995), p. xi. Thomas Bewick (1753–1828) was an artist famous for his woodcuts of rural life and labour.
21 'O for a life of sensations rather than of thoughts'; Keats to Bailey, 22 November 1817; Milnes, *Keats*, p. 44.
22 Cited in Bate, *John Clare*, p. 189.
23 Robinson et al., *Northborough Sonnets*, p. ix.
24 'Life', from *The Village Minstrel, and Other Poems*, 2 vols (London: Taylor and Hessey, and Stamford: E. Drury, 1821).
25 Bate, *John Clare*, p. 187.
26 John Barrell, *The Idea of Landscape and the Sense of Place: An Approach to the Poetry of John Clare* (Cambridge: CUP, 1972), pp. 166–7.
27 Ibid., p. 167.

28   Clare moved (due to financial circumstances) from Helpston to nearby Northborough in 1832.
29   The group of five sonnets entitled 'The Badger' in the *Selected Poems* is taken from a longer group in the Northborough Sonnets which describes some of the poet's activities and experiences as a child; Eric Robinson and Geoffrey Summerfield eds, *Selected Poems and Prose of John Clare* (Oxford: OUP, 1982), pp. 84–6.
30   Robinson et al. *Northborough Sonnets*, pp. 3, 4. This collection of previously unpublished poetry includes all the sonnets Clare wrote between 1832 and 1837 which were not included in either *The Rural Muse* (1835) or the *Midsummer Cushion* (a projected volume not published during Clare's lifetime).
31   'I hate the very noise of troublous man'; *Northborough Sonnets*, p. 55.
32   Barrell, *Idea of Landscape*, p. 179.
33   Sharp, *Sonnets of this Century*, p. 284.
34   Wordsworth, *Poetical Works*, 6 vols (London: Edward Moxon, 1836–7), III, p. 314.
35   Ernest de Selincourt ed., *The Letters of William and Dorothy Wordsworth: The Later Years* (Oxford: Clarendon Press, 1939), I, pp. 70–1.
36   'Alas! what boots the long laborious quest', and 'Captivity – Mary Queen of Scots'.
37   Cited in Daniel Robinson, 'Elegiac Sonnets: Charlotte Smith's Formal Paradoxy', *Papers on Language and Literature* 39 (2003); accessed through *blhttp://web1.infotrac.galegroup.com/itw/infomark/501/783/44482372w1/purl=rc1_EAIM*bg (18/02/04)
38   Duncan Wu, *Romantic Women Poets: An Anthology* (Oxford: Blackwell, 1997), p. 67; Wu cites a review from the *Gentleman's Magazine* 56.1 (1786), in which the reviewer expresses concern about the well-being of a poet who returns so obsessively to the themes of suffering, sorrow and impending death.
39   Hazlitt, 'On Milton's Sonnets', p. 235.
40   Macaulay, 'Milton' in *Critical and Historical Essays* (London: Longman, 1859), I, p. 14.
41   Ibid., I, p. 14.
42   Ugo Foscolo, 'An Essay on the Poetry of Petrarch' (1821); rpt. in Beatrice Corrigan, *Italian Poets and English Critics 1755–1859* (University of Chicago Press, 1969), pp. 81, 97.
43   Drake, *Literary Hours*, p. 64.
44   Hazlitt, 'On Milton's Sonnets', p. 236.
45   A.W. von Schlegel, *Lectures on Dramatic Art and Literature*, tr. John Black (London: Henry G. Bohn, 1846), p. 352. Schlegel's lectures quickly became well known; Leigh Hunt, for instance, referred to them in the Preface to *Foliage* (1818); see Houtchens, *Leigh Hunt's Literary Criticism*, pp. 140–141.
46   *Poems*, ii, p. 932.
47   Charles Armitage Brown, *Shakespeare's Autobiographical Poems* (London: James Bohn, 1838), p. 5.
48   Brown, op. cit., p. 45.
49   Ibid., p. 47.

50 Thomas Carlyle, 'The Poet as Hero' in *On Heroes, Hero-Worship and the Heroic in History* (London: Chapman and Hall, 1888), p. 266.

51 Houtchens, *Hunt's Literary Criticism*, p. 359.

52 John Keble, review of 'Memoirs of the Life of Sir Walter Scott', *The British Critic* xxiv (1838), 435; the importance of Keble's theory of poetry for the history of the devotional sonnet in the nineteenth century is discussed in ch. 4.

53 The term 'poetess' was widely used at the time, and has been revived during the last decade or so as a way of referring to L.E.L. and Felicia Hemans in particular; see eg. Anne Mellor, 'The Female Poet and the Poetess: Two Traditions of British Women's Poetry, 1780–1830', *Studies in Romanticism* 36 (1997), 261–76.

54 Isobel Armstrong, *Victorian Poetry: Poetry, Poetics and Politics* (London and New York: Routledge, 1993), pp. 337–9; Armstrong notes the affinity between Tractarian poetics and the 'expressive' tradition at work in women's writing.

55 From Greenwell's 1860 essay on Single Women; cited in Armstrong, *Victorian Poetry*, pp. 342–3.

56 Henceforward 'Spring', 'Autumn' and 'Sickness'.

57 See Richard Cronin, 'Felicia Hemans, Letitia Landon e il "dominio della donna"' in *Le poetesse romantiche inglesi*, eds Lilla Maria Crisafulli and Cecilia Pietropoli (Roma: Carocci, 2002), p. 250: 'è possibile che Felicia Hemans divenne la più popolare scrittrice della Gran Bretagna producendo delle poesie che mettono a nudo la vanità distruttiva dei valori più cari ai suoi lettori?' [Could Mrs Hemans possibly have become the most popular woman writer in Britain producing poems which exposed the destructive worthlessness of the values held most dear by her readers?]

58 These sonnets on Pellico and Felicia Hemans' numerous translations from the Italian poets (some of which will be dealt with below) highlight her interest in the struggle for Italian national liberation, one of the many respects in which she anticipates the work of Elizabeth Barrett.

59 From a letter of 23 November 1842 to Mary Russell Mitford; cited in Susan J. Wolfson, *Felicia Hemans: Selected Poems, Letters, Reception Materials* (Princeton and Oxford: Princeton UP, 2000), p. 590. See also her poem 'Felicia Hemans: To L.E.L., referring to her monody on the poetess', which mocks the tone and diction of L.E.L.'s poem.

60 See 'On a Portrait of Wordsworth by B.R. Haydon', published in the Athenaeum (29 October 1842) and reprinted as the third of the sonnets of 1844. There are a few sonnets in the 1838 volume, but none in the earlier collections.

61 This point is also made by Amy Billone; see '"In Silence Like to Death": Elizabeth Barrett's Sonnet Turn', *Victorian Poetry* 39 (2001), pp. 533–50.

62 *The Complete Poetical Works of Elizabeth Barrett Browning* (London: Smith, Elder and Co., 1907), p. 648; cp the letter of 30 Apr 45 to Cornelius Matthews, in which EBB calls Wordsworth 'the prince of poets', and relates an anecdote concerning his meeting with Queen Victoria with the words 'And so do queens speak to Kings!'

63 Barrett, *Poetical Works*, p. 649.

64 Marjorie Stone, *Elizabeth Barrett Browning* (Basingstoke: Macmillan, 1995), ch. 2.

65 Letter of 20 October 1842; her hatred for it intensified with time; by 1853 she was describing the whole collection as 'that horrible ghost of the Seraphim which makes me sicker than other ghosts when I see it on a table'; Scott Lewis ed., *The Letters of Elizabeth Barrett Browning to Her Sister Arabella*, 2 vols (Waco, Texas: Wedgestone Press, 2002), ii, p. 21.

66 *Poetical Works*, pp. xi–xii.

67 Letters of 15 Jan. and 7 June 1845; R. Barrett Browning ed., *The Letters of Robert and Elizabeth Barrett Browning* (London: John Murray, 1930), I, pp. 7, 91.

68 See above, pp. 17–18.

69 Barrett, *Poetical Works*, p. 649.

70 *Poetical Works*, p. xiv.

71 Isaiah 28: 11.

72 Barrett, *Poetical Works*, p. xiii.

73 Edmund Burke, *A Philosophical Enquiry into the Origin of Our Ideas of the Sublime and Beautiful* (London: R. and J. Dodsley, 1759), p. 110; on Barrett's development of the Romantic motifs of the Double and the Sublime as a way of articulating her sense of her relation to the male poetic tradition, see John Woolford, 'Elizabeth Barrett and the Wordsworthian Sublime', *Essays in Criticism* 45, 1 (1995), 36–56.

74 Amy Billone notes some verbal resemblances between this poem and Wordsworth's 'Composed upon Westminster Bridge'; 'Sonnet Turn', 541–3.

75 Vittoria Colonna's husband Ferrante D'Avalos died in 1525; she wrote a series of sonnets in his memory; see Vittoria Colonna, *Rime*, ed. Alan Bullock (Giuseppe Laterza e figli: Roma, 1982). Colonna is used as one example of the poetry of 'conjugal love' in Elizabeth Barrett's friend Anna Jameson's *The Romance of Biography; or, Memoirs of Women Loved and Celebrated by Poets*. 3rd ed. (London: Saunders and Otley, 1837), vol. 2.

76 The *Sonnets from the Portuguese* appeared immediately after Barrett's poem 'Catarina to Camoens' in the 1850 edition of her poems, as she pointed out in a letter to her sister Arabella; see Lewis, *EBB to Arabella*, I, pp. 368–9. Felicia Hemans translated twenty of Camoens' sonnets into English. The question of Barrett's indebtedness to Camoens is discussed at length in Barbara Neri, 'A Lineage of Love: The Literary Bloodlines of Elizabeth Barrett Browning's *Sonnets from the Portuguese*', *Studies in Browning and His Circle* 23 (2000), 50–69.

77 Letter of 2–3 July 1845; Daniel Karlin ed., *Robert Browning and Elizabeth Barrett: The Courtship Correspondence* (OUP, 1989), p. 78.

78 Helen Cooper, *Elizabeth Barrett Browning, Woman and Artist* (Chapel Hill and London: The University of North Carolina Press, 1988), p. 102; see also Angela Leighton, *Elizabeth Barrett Browning* (Brighton; Harvester, 1986).

79 There is an interesting account of some of the intertextual relations between the two sequences in Sharon Smulders, '"Medicated Music": Elizabeth Barrett Browning's *Sonnets from the Portuguese*', *Victorian Literature and Culture* 23 (1996), 193–213; Smulders argues that Barrett Browning actualises the trope of feminine infirmity in order to chart her own emergence from a 'genre plagued by infirmity'.

80 'The Female Poet and the Embarrassed Reader: Elizabeth Barrett Browning's *Sonnets from the Portuguese*', *English Literary History* 48 (1981), 354.
81 Cooper, *Woman and Artist*, p. 100; on the myth of rescue see Daniel Karlin, *The Courtship of Robert and Elizabeth Barrett Browning* (Oxford: OUP, 1985).
82 There are a number of other sonnets in the 1850 *Poems*, but almost none thereafter.
83 Natalie M. Houston, 'Affecting Authenticity: *Sonnets from the Portuguese* and *Modern Love*', *Studies in the Literary Imagination* 35 (2002), 99–122.
84 Now I am going to speak to you about those sonnets. I have had a letter from dear Mr. Kenyon, and he and Mr. Forster detected them as well as you – and a letter from American speaks of 'the Portuguese sonnets *so called*.' – and a letter from Mrs. Payne disapproves of the 'blind' and tells me that the open truth would have been 'worthier of me'... by which I am a little, just a little, vexed. The truth is that though they were written several years ago, I never showed them to Robert till last spring... I felt shy about them altogether... even to him. I had heard him express himself strongly against 'personal' poetry and I shrank back – As to publishing them, it did not enter my head. But when Robert saw them, he was much touched and pleased – and, thinking highly of the poetry, he did not like,... could not consent, he said, that they should be lost to my volumes: so we agreed to slip them in under some sort of veil, and after much consideration chose the 'Portuguese'. Observe – the poem which precedes them, is 'Catarina to Camoens'. In a loving fancy, he had always associated me with Catarina, and the poem had affected him to tears, he said, again and again. So, Catarina being a Portuguese, we put 'Sonnets from the Portuguese' – which did not mean (as we understood the double-meaning) *'from the Portuguese language'*... though the public (who are very little versed in Portuguese literature) might take it as they pleased. (Lewis, *EBB to Arabella*, I, pp. 368–9).
85 Margaret Reynolds has suggested that 'the tone and the imagery which colours the *Sonnets [from the Portuguese]* is derived from a fairytale stock; there are palaces inhabited by her princely lover, gifts of ruby crowns and golden thrones, magic kisses which wake the enchanted Sleeping Beauty...'; 'Love's Measurement in Elizabeth Barrett Browning's *Sonnets from the Portuguese*,' *Studies in Browning and His Circle* 21 (1997), 54–5.

Chapter 3   The Political Sonnet

1 Liu, *Sense of History*, p. 428.
2 H.F. Lowry ed., *The Letters of Matthew Arnold to Arthur Hugh Clough* (OUP, 1968), p. 64 (Arnold's emphasis).
3 Liu, *Sense of History*, p. 499.
4 *Poems* ii p. 982; Daniel Robinson argues that the River Duddon sonnets represent a self-conscious revisiting or reappropriation by Wordsworth of the 'river sonnet' tradition cultivated by Warton, Bowles, Smith and Coleridge, a tradition he had earlier attempted to distance himself from; '"Still Glides the Stream": Form and Function in Wordsworth's *River Duddon* Sonnets', *European Romantic Review*, 13 (Dec 2002), 449–64.
5 'Feelings of a Republican on the Fall of Bonaparte'; 'Political Greatness', ll. 11, 13–14.

6   Feldman and Robinson include this in Shelley's sonnets, with the observation that its 'five-part structure suggests a short sonnet sequence': see *A Century of Sonnets*, pp. 258–9. There is, however, dissent from this view in T. Hall Caine's notes to *Sonnets of Three Centuries*, in which he argues that D.M. Main's decision to print the five stanzas of the poem as a series of sonnets 'is an act which has no better effect than to cripple the matchless fashioning of the finest lyric Shelley achieved, in order to endow the author with a number of imperfect sonnets' (p. 296).

7   *The Poetical Works of Gerald Massey* (London: Routledge, Warne and Routledge, 1861), p. viii; the notice in question was first published in *Eliza Cook's Journal*, 1851. Massey was however interested in Shakespeare's sonnets, and wrote a book expounding his own theory about them: see *The Secret Drama of Shakespeare's Sonnets Unfolded, with the Characters Identified*, 2nd ed. (London (private publication for 100 subscribers), 1872).

8   Miles Taylor, *Ernest Jones, Chartism, and the Romance of Politics 1819–1869* (OUP, 2003), p. 80.

9   Text from *blhttp://lion.chadwyck.co.uk*bg; accessed 21/04/05.

10   Anne Janowitz, *Lyric and Labour in the Romantic Tradition* (CUP, 1998), p. 154.

11   'Sonnet suggested by the death of Mr. Ernest Jones', *The Freelance* (30 Jan. 1869), p. 36; cited Taylor, *Jones*, p. 4

12   *Sonnets on the War*, by Alexander Smith and by the author of 'Balder' [Sydney Dobell] (London, 1855).

13   See for instance Arthur Hugh Clough's 'Recent English Poetry', first published in the *North American Review* 77 (1853), 1–30, in which he contrasts Smith's work favourably with Matthew Arnold's *Empedocles on Etna and Other Poems*.

14   Kingsley, 'Thoughts on Shelley and Byron', from *Literary and General Lectures and Essays* (London: Macmillan, 1890); cited in Natalie M. Houston, 'Reading the Victorian Souvenir: Sonnets and Photographs of the Crimean War', *Yale Journal of Criticism* 14 (2001), 374. For a history of the 'Spasmodic' controversy see Mark A. Weinstein, *William Edmondstone Aytoun and the Spasmodic Controversy* (New Haven: Yale UP, 1968).

15   Text taken from *blhttp://lion.chadwyck.co.uk*bg; accessed 11/4/05.

16   Houston, 'Reading the Victorian Souvenir', 354; for later uses of this photographic analogy see below, ch. 6, p. 136.

17   Tennyson's indebtedness to the 'Spasmodic' poets in *Maud* has long been recognised; see Ricks, *Tennyson*, p. 1038.

18   Rpt. in *Poetical Works*. Isobel Armstrong has also highlighted the similarities between *War Waits* and *Maud*; see *Victorian Poetry*, pp. 271–4. She discounts, however, the possibility that Tennyson is alluding directly to Massey's poetry: '[Tennyson] could not have seen [Massey's] poems published in the same year as his own' (p. 272). But Massey sent Tennyson a copy of one of his previous collections, and received a reply from Emily Tennyson; and *War Waits* was reviewed as early as February 1855, several months before the appearance of *Maud* in July of that year. Smith and Dobell's *Sonnets on the War* appeared in January 1855.

19   From a letter of 6 December 1855 to Archer Gurney.

20 Miriam Allott remarks that the group of poems 'does Arnold little poetic credit, but illustrates how difficult he found it to write poetry after 1860' (Allott, *Poems*, p. 520).

21 See ch. 6 below for an extended discussion of the sonnet and the aesthetic movement.

22 The poem appears in the sonnet anthologies of both T. Hall Caine (1882) and William Sharp (1886); on these anthologies see below, ch. 6, pp. 138–40.

23 Watts-Dunton's poetry and writings about the sonnet are discussed in ch. 6, pp. 137–40.

24 The phrase comes from Hopkins' famous 'red' letter, discussed below pp. 83–4.

25 Letter of 12 January 1888; see Catherine Phillips ed., *The Oxford Authors: Gerard Manley Hopkins* (OUP, 1986), p. 271.

26 Hopkins distinguishes between the paraphrasable content of a poem and what he calls its 'underthought'; the latter is 'conveyed chiefly in the choice of metaphors etc used and often only half realised by the poet himself' (cited in Sjaak Zonneveld, *The Random Grim Forge: A Study of Social Ideas in the Work of Gerard Manley Hopkins* (Maastricht: Van Gorcum, Assen, 1992), p. 115).

27 Dennis Hardy, *Alternative Communities in Nineteenth-Century England* (London and New York: Longman, 1979), p. 79.

28 Zonneveld, *Random Grim Forge*, p. 114.

29 John Ruskin, *Unto this Last* (London: George Allen, 1898), pp. 100–2 (ch. 3, no. 54)

30 Cited in John Lucas, 'Hopkins and Symons: Two Views of the City' in John Stokes ed., *Fin de Siècle/Fin du Globe: Fears and Fantasies of the Late Nineteenth Century* (New York: St Martin's Press, 1992), p. 57. The battle of Majuba Hill took place in 1881; British troops secured a hill overlooking their Boer adversaries, but through a combination of overconfidence and poor planning allowed the Boers to retake it and capture many of their number; see Thomas Pakenham, *The Scramble for Africa* (London: Abacus, 1991), pp. 101–6.

31 Hopkins' account of 'sprung rhythm' has given rise to a good deal of confusion, mostly because it develops (without restating) Patmore's notion of poetry as constituted by 'isochronous intervals' between stresses; on this see J.P. Phelan, 'Radical Metre: The English Hexameter in Clough's *The Bothie of Toper-na-Fuosich*,' *Review of English Studies* n.s. 50 (1999), 166–187. Hopkins essentially means (a) that poetic metre in English is constituted by the number of stresses in a line rather than the number of syllables; and (b) that where two consecutive stresses occur, the first either expands or is followed by a pause to make it up to the same length as a full 'foot'.

32 Hopkins was in fact rather sarcastic about the poem, describing it as 'not worth reading'; Phillips, *Hopkins*, p. 255.

33 Letter of 29 October 1881 to R.W. Dixon; Phillips, *Hopkins*, pp. 246–8.

34 These metrical marks are reproduced in most editions of Hopkins' poetry; see eg. Phillips, *Hopkins*, pp. 381–2.

35 Ibid., p. 382.

36 Michael R.G. Spiller. *The Sonnet Sequence: A Study of its Strategies* (New York: Twayne Publishers, 1997), p. 9; see Zonneveld, *Random Grim Forge*, pp. 115–7 for an account of the poem's composition.

37 The political background to the poem is dealt with in Lucas, 'Hopkins and Symons'.
38 Phillips, *Hopkins*, p. 385; as Richard Isomaki points out, '[there] is something grotesque in Tom the giant man-boot, a synecdoche *manqué*'; 'Hopkins, Community, Functions: "Tom's Garland"' *Nineteenth-Century Literature* 47:4 (1993), 484.
39 Zonneveld, *Random Grim Forge*, pp. 122–3.
40 The link with Morris' journal is noted in Lucas, 'Hopkins and Symons', p. 54.
41 Phillips, *Hopkins*, p. 384.
42 Isomaki, 'Hopkins', p. 473.
43 Cited in Teresa Newman and Ray Watkinson, *Ford Madox Brown and the Pre-Raphaelite Circle* (London: Chatto and Windus, 1991), p. 117. There is also an odd resemblance between this poem and the closing lines of Wordsworth's sonnet on Charles II, one of the *Ecclesiastical Sonnets* (1822): 'Away, Circean revels!/ But for what gain? if England soon must sink/ Into a gulf which all distinction levels -/That bigotry may swallow the good name,/ And, with that draught, the life-blood; misery, shame,/ By Poets loathed; from which Historians shrink!'
44 The last three lines seem to mean: 'the only thing they share [with the rest of society] is "care" or anxiety; this one is made hangdog dull by despair; that one is turned into a manwolf by rage; and (picking up on the canine metaphor) the "packs" of these despairing or enraged people infest the age'.
45 Isomaki, 'Hopkins', pp. 477–8.
46 For the prevalence of this language of evolutionary 'reversion' in late nineteenth-century representations of the working class, see Lucas, 'Hopkins and Symons'.
47 Hopkins read Stevenson's *Dr. Jekyll and Mr. Hyde* soon after its appearance in 1885, and praised it in a letter of 28 October 1886 as 'worthy of Shakespeare' in parts; Phillips, *Hopkins*, p. 265.
48 A point also noted by Zonneveld, *Random Grim Forge*, p. 127.
49 Cp Zonneveld's suggestion that Hopkins' 'complicated syntax' in this poem might be a sign of the 'emotional strain' he felt 'in having to reject any form of action by the unemployed'; *Random Grim Forge*, p. 136.
50 Robert Bernard Martin, *Gerard Manley Hopkins: A Very Private Life* (London: HarperCollins, 1991), pp. 217–8.
51 Zonneveld, *Random Grim Forge*, pp. 138–9.

Chapter 4 The Devotional Sonnet

 1 Arline Golden, 'Victorian Renascence: The Revival of the Amatory Sonnet Sequence, 1850–1900', *Genre* 7 (1974), 133–4.
 2 G.B. Tennyson distinguishes between the 'Tractarian' phase of 1833–45 (culminating in the defection of J.H. Newman and others to the Roman Catholic church) and the Oxford Movement as a broader and longer-lasting cultural phenomenon; see *Victorian Devotional Poetry: The Tractarian Mode* (Cambridge, Mass. and London: Harvard UP, 1981), p. 9.

3 Specifically the repeal of the Test and Corporation Acts preventing Dissenters (Protestants outside the Church of England) from sitting in Parliament (1828), and the various legislative enactments under the heading of Catholic Emancipation (1829) which allowed Catholics the same privilege.

4 The phrase is from John Henry Newman's famous discussion of the origins of the Movement in *Apologia pro Vita Sua* (1864; rpt. New York: Chelsea House, 1983), pp. 116–8.

5 This is somewhat *avant la lettre*; the formal inauguration of the Movement is usually seen as John Keble's Assize sermon on 'National Apostasy' given (symbolically) on 14 July 1833. The 'myth' surrounding this event is analysed by Mark D. Chapman in 'John Keble, "National Apostasy", and the Myths of 14 July': *John Keble in Context*, ed. Kirstie Blair (London: Anthem Press, 2004), pp. 47–57.

6 *Keble's Lectures on Poetry*, tr. (from Latin) E.K. Francis, 2 vols (Oxford: Clarendon Press, 1912).

7 Tennyson, *Victorian Devotional Poetry*, p. 73.

8 First published as *Ecclesiastical Sketches*, and considerably augmented between 1822 and 1845. All references in what follows will be to poems first published in 1822 unless otherwise stated.

9 From Wordsworth's Preface to *Ecclesiastical Sketches* (1822); *Poems*, ii p. 997. The first poems of the series would seem to be III, xxxix–xli.

10 From the sonnet 'Charles the Second'; see above ch. 3, n. 43.

11 The significance of this sonnet is recognised by Wordsworth's biographer Mary Moorman, who describes it as a 'challenge' to which Keble responded; see Brian W. Martin, *John Keble: Priest, Professor and Poet* (London: Croom Helm, 1976), p. 75.

12 Cp II xxviii; and note the change from 'new-born church' to 'Church reformed' in xl, undertaken to mollify those who saw the Reformation as the restoration of the true national church rather than the founding of a new one.

13 Margaret Johnson, *Gerard Manley Hopkins and Tractarian Poetry* (Aldershot, Hants. and Brookfield Vermont: Ashgate, 1997), p. 21.

14 See (eg.) the sonnets on the 'Revival of Popery' and the Protestant martyrs Latimer and Ridley added in 1827 (II, xxxiii–iv).

15 John Keble, Review of 'Memoirs of the Life of Sir Walter Scott', 431; 426–7; 435. Keble's theories are discussed in M.H. Abrams, *The Mirror and the Lamp* (1953; rpt. Oxford: Oxford University Press, 1971), pp. 144–8; Tennyson, *Victorian Devotional Poetry*, ch. 2.

16 *Keble's Lectures on Poetry*, ii pp. 101–2.

17 Keble, 'Sacred Poetry', rpt. in *Occasional Papers and Reviews of John Keble* (Oxford and London: James Parker and Co., 1877).

18 Williams (1802–65) was the author of the famous Tract 'On Reserve in Communicating Religious Knowledge', second in notoriety amongst the *Tracts for the Times* only to Newman's *Tract XC*.

19 In the 'Advertisement' to The Cathedral Williams notes: 'it has been suggested by the author of "the Excursion," in his Preface to that work, that his Poems might be considered as capable of being arranged as the parts of a Gothic Church, of which the minor Pieces might be "likened to the little

cells, oratories, and sepulchral recesses"'; *The Cathedral* (Oxford: John Henry Parker, 1838), p. v. Although the sonnet is used extensively in *The Cathedral*, it is mostly for the peripheral and external parts of the edifice; the aisles and pillars demand more substantial forms.

20 Oddly, the drawing of the Cathedral (which Williams helpfully provides at the beginning of the volume) and the Contents page both represent Repentance as the left-hand door, while the text itself and the illustration on the facing page call it the right-hand door.

21 Williams' 'Advertisement' also mentions 'Herbert's "Temple," where he attaches moral and sacred Lessons to the "Church windows" and "Church floor"', as a similar enterprise to his own (p. v). In advertising his indebtedness in this way, Herbert was manifesting a characteristically Tractarian disdain for originality.

22 See the discussion in chapter 5 below, pp. 108–9.

23 This is number XI of 'The Cloisters', entitled 'Foreign Breviaries'; this section as a whole is subtitled 'Ecclesiastical Sonnets'.

24 Genesis 19:14.

25 This is number CXXXIV of the first edition (*Lyra Apostolica* (Derby: Henry Mozley and Sons, 1836)). Froude (older brother of the historian J.A. Froude) was one of the founders of the movement; his death in early 1836 led Newman to identify individual contributors to *Lyra Apostolica* by letter (Newman is δ, Froude β).

26 Johnson, *Hopkins*, p. 39.

27 Kathleen Jones, *Learning Not to be First: The Life of Christina Rossetti* (New York: St Martin's Press, 1991), p. 37; Jan Marsh, *Christina Rossetti: A Literary Biography* (London: Jonathan Cape, 1994), p. 55.

28 Cynthia Scheinberg, *Women's Poetry and Religion in Victorian England: Jewish Identity and Christian Culture* (CUP, 2002), p. 9.

29 Text taken from <http://lion.chadwyck.co.uk>. The significance of this sonnet in the formulation of a specifically female Tractarian aesthetic is noted by Emma Mason in '"Her Silence Speaks": Keble's Female Heirs' in Blair, *Keble in Context*, pp. 131–2.

30 Tennyson, *Victorian Devotional Poetry*, 198; Joel Westerholm, 'In Defence of Verses: The Aesthetic and Reputation of Christina Rossetti's Late Poetry', *Renascence* 51.3 (1999).

31 Mason, 'Female Heirs', 127.

32 See for instance Germaine Greer, *Slip-shod Sybils* (Harmondsworth: Penguin, 1995), ch. 11, 'The Perversity of Christina Rossetti', in which she sees Rossetti's 'invalidism' as a hysterical symptom caused by her simultaneous indulgence and repression of her own emotional nature. For an argument against this understanding of religious sentiment as sublimation in her work, see Eric Griffiths, 'The Disappointment of Christina G. Rossetti', *Essays in Criticism* 47 (April 1997), 107–42.

33 Barrett Browning revises her earlier assertion in *Sonnets from the Portuguese* XLII; see above, ch. 2.

34 See William Michael Rossetti, 'Memoir', in *The Poetical Works of Christina Rossetti* (1904), p. lxvi. Christina first met her fellow Christian poet Dora Greenwell during a visit to the family of William Bell Scott in Newcastle in 1858.

35 Around a quarter of *The Complete Poems* consists of material unpublished at the time of Christina's death.

36 This is especially true of the Italian-language sonnets, which have of course the additional defence of being written in a foreign language (and an archaic version of that language as well); see for example '"Blumine" risponde' [Blumine answers], which draws on the Dantean notion of the lover meeting her beloved in heaven.

37 There are seven sonnets in *Goblin Market, and Other Poems* (1862) and just five in the first edition of *The Prince's Progress and Other Poems* (1866); in contrast *A Pageant and Other Poems* (1881) contains fifty-six, and Rossetti's last published collection *Verses* (1893) fifty-eight.

38 Griffiths, 'The Disappointment of Christina G. Rossetti', 108.

39 *Monna Innominata* is dealt with in ch. 5 below, pp. 119–24.

40 See above, pp. 92–3.

41 Keble, 'Sacred Poetry' (1825), rpt. *Occasional Papers and Reviews*, p. 81; see also John Griffin, 'Tractarians and Metaphysicals: The Failure of Influence', *John Donne Journal* 4 (2) (1985), 291–302.

42 'Sacred Poetry', p. 95.

43 On the use of repetition in Rossetti's poetry, see esp. Sylvan Esh, 'Not speaking the unspeakable: Religion and repetition in Christina Rossetti's Monna Innominata sequence', *Studies in English Literature, 1500–1900*; Autumn 1994.

44 Wagner, *Moment's Monument*, p. 174; the term 'terrible' sonnets is usually used to refer to the four poems sent to Hopkins' friend Robert Bridges on a half-sheet of sermon paper in 1885 or 1886: 'To seem the stranger', 'I wake and feel', 'Patience', and 'My own heart' (see Edward H. Cohen, 'The Chronology of Hopkins's "Terrible Sonnets"', *Victorians Institute Journal* 21 (1993), 191–200).

45 Gary M. Bouchard notes that critics have become 'preoccupied with constructing a narrative to explain the emotional innards of Hopkins's later sonnets' and have in consequence neglected their formal dimension; 'What Gets Said in a Narrow (ten-by-fourteen) Room: A Reconsideration of Hopkins's Later Sonnets', in Francis Fennell ed., *Rereading Hopkins: Selected New Essays* (English Literary Studies: University of Victoria, 1996), pp. 180–92.

46 See esp. Robert Bernard Martin, *Gerard Manley Hopkins* (London: HarperCollins, 1991); Margaret Johnson, *Hopkins and Tractarian Poetry*.

47 Hopkins met Christina Rossetti at the home of his friend Frederick Gurney in 1864, and claimed in a letter written later in life that 'the simple beauty of her work cannot be matched'; Martin, *Hopkins*, p. 73.

48 He also translated part of the poem into Latin elegiacs.

49 From a letter of 12 October 1881; cited Wagner, *Moment's Monument*, pp. 156–7.

50 The terms are taken from Hopkins' undergraduate essay 'On the Origin of Beauty'; see Wagner p. 155.

51 Hopkins was always producing little mathematical formulae to explain his understanding of the sonnet; the letter to Dixon cited above contains the formula '$(4+4) + (3+3) = 2.4 + 2.3 = 2 (4+3) = 2.7 = 14$' (where the dot is the mathematical symbol for multiplication). See also the discussion of the curtal sonnet below.

52 This is what Hopkins attempts to convey on a theoretical level by his odd language of 'inscape' and 'instress'.

53 J. Hillis Miller, *The Disappearance of God* (New York: Schocken, 1965), p. 280; Miller gives examples from Hopkins' journals of his construction of word sequences by changing consonants or nouns as a way of investigating the hidden relations between words.

54 Jennifer Wagner's suggestion that the relation between octave and sestet is one of 'mirroring' or 'analogy' but also of 'reduction' overlooks the fact that most of Hopkins' sonnets move not from God to man, but from man to God; the 'volta' is less like 'an imaginative bridge between heaven and earth, between divine and human', and more like an optical device radically altering the angle of vision of the reader; see Wagner, *Moment's Monument*, p. 152; and on the significance of perspective in Hopkins see Hillis Miller, *Disappearance of God*, p. 274.

55 Phillips, *Hopkins*, p. 109.

56 As pointed out by Lois W. Pitchford in 'The Curtal Sonnets of GMH', *Modern Language Notes* 67 (3), 1952, 165–9.

57 By 'counterpoint' Hopkins means variation from an expected regular rhythm; for 'sprung rhythm' see above ch. 3, n. 31.

58 Phillips, *Hopkins*, p. 228.

59 Miller, *Disappearance of God*, p. 304.

60 Wagner, *Moment's Monument*, p. 154; on the 'caudated' sonnet see ch. 3 above, p. 79.

61 Bouchard (without referring to 'The Caged Skylark' in particular) notes the 'provocative' nature of Wordsworth's imagery of convents, hermitages and cells for Hopkins; 'What gets said…', 186.

62 See Hillis Miller, *Disappearance of God*, on the idea of 'selving' in Hopkins.

63 The word recurs in 'No worst'.

64 Cp. I Corinthians 5:6: 'a little leaven leaveneth the whole lump'.

65 See 'As kingfishers catch fire', esp. ll. 12–14: 'For Christ plays in ten thousand places,/ Lovely in limbs, and lovely in eyes not his/ To the Father through the features of men's faces'. Joseph H. Gardner notes (in '"Decoding" Rossetti: Sonnets II and III of *The House of Life*', *Journal of Pre-Raphaelite Studies* 1 (1) 1980, 36–44) a resemblance to Dante Gabriel Rossetti's sonnet 'Lost Days' from *The House of Life* (1881): 'I do not seem them here; but after death/ God knows I know the faces I shall see,/ Each one a murdered self, with low last breath./ "I am thyself, – what hast thou done to me?"/ "And I – and I – thyself," (lo! each one saith,)/ "And thou thyself to all eternity!"' In a later article he reveals that this is one of three poems of Rossetti's copied by Hopkins into his commonplace book: see '"But Worse": Hopkins and Rossetti', *ANQ* 15 (2002), 21–23.

66 Martin, *Hopkins*, p. 383.

67 Phillips, *Hopkins*, p. 255.

68 Keble, 'Sacred Poetry', p. 88.

Chapter 5   'Illegal Attachments': The Amatory Sonnet Sequence

1 On the dominance of the Miltonic-Wordsworthian sonnet, see Arline Golden, 'Victorian Renascence', 133–4; Feldman and Robinson, *Century of Sonnets*, p. 8.

2 On Petrarch's proverbial insincerity see above ch. 2, p. 44.

3 Corrigan, *Italian Poets*, pp. 4–5; De Sade's findings became widely known in England through Susannah Dobson's translation (1775).

4 *The Book of the Sonnet*, I, p. 68.

5 'Among the more important cultural trends inspiring this liberation were the studies and translation of Italian and Elizabethan poetry – begun early in the century, neglected while the Wordsworthian sonnet reigned, and now renewed again by Romantic and Victorian interest in the past.' (Golden, 'Victorian Renascence', 134).

6 Corrigan, *Italian Poets*, p. 150; from the second edition of Campbell's *Life* (1843).

7 Ibid., p. 161.

8 'The Victorian domestication of love is reflected even in that stronghold of the courtly-love code, the sonnet sequence. Mrs Browning's popular *Sonnets from the Portuguese* (1850) is the first important sonnet sequence in history to reject the convention of illicit love and portray a happy courtship culminating in betrothal and (implied) marriage' (Arline Golden, '"The Game of Sentiment": Tradition and Innovation in Meredith's *Modern Love*', *ELH* 40 (1973), 265–6)

9 Golden, 'Victorian Renascence', 140.

10 Christopher Ricks cites Shakespeare's sonnets as a source for the poem in his edition of the poems; see *Poems of Tennyson*, pp. 860–1. Ricks' notes also indicate a number of moments of direct indebtedness to Shakespeare's sonnets (eg. i 7–8). Erik Gray has recently suggested that there may be moments of indebtedness to Sidney's *Astrophil and Stella* in the poem, and argues on this basis that 'it is crucial to remember the sonnet precedent when reading Tennyson's elegy, not least because Tennyson himself clearly recalls it'; 'Sonnet Kisses: Sidney to Barrett Browning', *Essays in Criticism* 52 (2002), 133.

11 From *The Times Digital Archive* <http://web5.infotrac.galegroup.com>; accessed 4 February 2004. A similar opinion of the sonnets was voiced before the publication of *In Memoriam* by Henry Hallam, Arthur's father; see Ricks, *Tennyson*, p. 861.

12 See the discussion of the poem's fluid and ambivalent relation to the available languages of sexual orientation in Alan Sinfield, *Alfred Tennyson* (Oxford: Blackwell, 1986), ch. 5; and below pp. 000–00 for the sonnet's role as a vehicle for the coded articulation of homosexuality later in the century.

13 See eg. st XXXIII.

14 Given the biographical emphasis in sonnet criticism, many critics have seen this sequence as a fictionalisation of the failure of Meredith's own marriage; his first wife Mary Ellen Nicholls, the daughter of Thomas Love Peacock, left him for another man in 1858, and died in 1861.

15 Golden, 'The Game of Sentiment', 268; the phrase 'sentimental passion' is Meredith's.

16 On *Modern Love* as an example of the Victorian 'verse-novel', see Dorothy Mermin, 'Poetry as Fiction: Meredith's Modern Love', *ELH* 43 (1976), 100–115.

17 This stanza is, as a number of critics have pointed out, similar to Tennyson's stanza in *In Memoriam*, the principal difference being Tennyson's use of the shorter octosyllabic line.

18 See ch. 6 below, pp. 139–40.

19 It is also worth pointing out the Darwinian undercurrents of this sonnet, and indeed of the sequence's repeated use of animal imagery.

20 There are also similarities with some of Claude's utterances in Clough's *Amours de Voyage* (1858): 'Ah, ye feminine souls, so loving and so exacting,/ Since we cannot escape, must we even submit to deceive you?/ Since so cruel is truth, sincerity shocks and revolts you,/ Will you have us your slaves to lie to you, flatter and – leave you?' (III, ll. 147–50)

21 The relative obscurity of Modern Love is indicated by William Sharp in his notes to *Sonnets of This Century*, p. 306: 'Out of the hundreds who have read and delighted in [his fiction]... there are probably only two or three here and there who before the recent issue of Poems and Lyrics of the Joy of the Earth knew that Mr. Meredith had written verse at all. Yet two very noteworthy little volumes had previously... seen the light. In the second, entitled *Modern Love: and other Poems*, there is a very remarkable sequence of sixteen-line poems comprised under the heading *Modern Love*.... I had always imagined them to have been sonnets on the model of the Italian "sonnet with a tail," but Mr. Meredith tells me that they were not designed for that form.'

22 This is considered in more detail in the next chapter.

23 The poem was originally entitled 'Placata Venere'.

24 Quoted by Rossetti in his rejoinder to Buchanan, 'The Stealthy School of Criticism', published in *The Athenaeum* of 16 December 1871; rpt. Marsh ed., *Collected Writings*, p. 329.

25 Marsh, *Collected Writings*, p. 330.

26 There is an analogy to be drawn here with Kingsley's extraordinary (and even more disturbing) drawings of his future wife as a kind of sacrificial offering, stretched naked on the cross. Kingsley did not, of course, publish these drawings; some of them are reproduced in Susan Chitty, *The Beast and the Monk: A Life of Charles Kingsley* (London: Hodder and Stoughton, 1974). A comparison with Patmore is suggested by Gardner in '"Decoding" Rossetti'.

27 Most modern editions reinsert it as VI (a). Rossetti also completely rewrote 'Love's Testament' to remove all references to the specifically Christian celebration of the Eucharist.

28 Marsh, *Collected Writings*, p. 330.

29 The structure of the poem is analysed in Robert D. Hume, 'Inorganic Structure in *The House of Life*', *Papers on Language and Literature*, 5 (3) (Summer 1969), 282–95; Clyde de L. Ryals, 'The Narrative Unity of "The House of Life", *Journal of English and Germanic Philology* 69 (1970), 241–57.

30 A comparison first made by William E. Fredeman, 'Rossetti's "In Memoriam": An Elegiac Reading of *The House of Life*, *Bulletin of the John Rylands Library* 47 (March 1965), 298–341. The poem's relation to Rossetti's own life, and in particular his relations with his wife Elizabeth Siddall and Jane Morris, wife of William Morris, has been the subject of a good deal of biographical speculation.

31 D.G. Rossetti, *The Early Italian Poets* (1861; rpt. London: Anvil Press, 1981), p. 123.

32 Rossetti, *Early Italian Poets*, p. 125.

33   Ibid., p. 123; Beatrice is of course married to someone else.
34   This formal congruity may also extend to the structure as a whole; Rossetti notes that Dante uses an unorthodox sonnet form from time to time consisting of 'two sextetts [sic] followed by two quatrains', and describes this as 'analogous' to the usual proportions of the sonnet (Ibid., p. 156). *The House of Life* is divided into two sections of sixty and forty-one sonnets respectively.
35   See (eg.) Robert Browning's well-known comment to Isa Blagden about the earlier version of *House of Life* in *Poems* (1870): 'Then, how I hate "love" as a lubberly, naked young man putting his arms there and his wings there, about a pair of lovers – a fellow they would kick away in the reality' (cited Marsh, *Collected Writings*, p. xxv); Marsh's own comments on Joy and Ruth; and Joseph Bristow's attempts to read significance into the personification of Love as male in '"He and I": Dante Gabriel. Rossetti's other man', *Victorian Poetry* 39.3 (Fall 2001), 365–90.
36   *Early Italian Poets*, p. 160.
37   Dante calls love an 'accident of substance' rather than a substance itself in his defence of personification; ibid., p. 187.
38   Rossetti and the other Pre-Raphaelites were all great admirers of Browning's work, and *The House of Life* betrays this admiration through its title (see '"Transcendentalism: A Poem in Twelve Books"', l. 45), its form (see 'One Word More' for Raphael's 'century of sonnets') and through Rossetti's comment that it was intended to be 'a complete *dramatis personae* of the soul'.
39   Joseph Bristow notes (in '"He and I"') that 'Rossetti's passionate "I"' is 'notorious for fetishizing femininity'.
40   Jan Marsh notes in this connection Rossetti's statement in a letter of December 1870 'that the idea "of the perilous principle in the world being female from the first" was "about the most essential notion of the sonnet"'; *Collected Writings*, p. 499.
41   See Michele Martinez, 'Christina Rossetti's Petrarca', *Essays and Studies 2003 Victorian Women Poets*, ed. Alison Chapman (Cambridge: D.S. Brewer, 2003), 99–121.
42   Flowers, *Complete Poems*, p. 294.
43   See for instance Theodore Watts-Dunton's 1890 sonnet on the six-hundredth anniversary of Beatrice's death: 'No eagle-flight past peaks of fire and snow,/ But through Life's leaves the flutter of a dove/ Whose beating wings soothed Dante's air with love – / Struck music from the wind of Dante's woe' (ll. 11–14).
44   Sylvan Esh argues (in 'Not Speaking the Unspeakable') that sonnet 5 constitutes the real 'volta' of Rossetti's sonnet: 'It is at this point that the poem's declared purpose of giving the long-silenced courtly lover's lady a voice is derailed, establishing irremediably the poem's shift toward endless, futile repetition and finally resignation.'
45   The phrase 'pomp of loveliness' occurs in Felicia Heman's poem 'The Restoration of the Works of Art to Italy' – another indication of Rossetti's indebtedness to a specifically female poetic tradition.
46   Scheinberg, *Women's Poetry and Religion*, p. 139.
47   Ibid., p. 140.

48   See the motto to sonnet 10.
49   See for example Krista Lysack, 'The Economics of Esctasy in Christina Rossetti's *Monna Innominata*, VP 36 (4), 1998, which argues that the 'silence' of the final sonnet is actually a radical gesture which takes the poem 'beyond conventional phallocentric speech'.
50   This description was prompted by Hall Caine's misunderstanding of Christina's mention of Elizabeth Barrett Browning in her preface: 'I am much pleased with [Mr Caine's] *Academy* article, though sorry that he seems to have misapprehended my reference to the *Portuguese Sonnets* [sic]. Surely not only what I meant to say but what I do say is, not that the Lady of those sonnets is surpassable, but that a "Donna innominata" by the same hand might well have been unsurpassable. The Lady in question, as she actually stands, I was not regarding as an "innominata" at all, – because the latter type, according to the traditional figure I had in view, is surrounded by unlike circumstances. I rather wonder that no one (as far as I know) ever hit on my semi-historical argument before for such treatment, – it seems to me so full of poetic suggestiveness'. Christina's explanation produced an additional misunderstanding on the part of her brother William Michael, who reads this letter as implying that 'the speaker in her [i.e. Christina's] sonnets was not intended for an "innominata at all"', when clearly Christina is denying that Elizabeth Barrett Browning's 'Lady' is an 'innominata' (*Complete Poems*, p. 954).
51   Flowers, *Complete Poems*, p. 953; William indiscreetly names the addressee as Charles Cayley.
52   Golden notes that both John Addington Symonds and Theodore Watts-Dunton use this metaphor; 'Victorian Renascence', p. 140.
53   John Addington Symonds, *Animi Figura* (London: Smith, Elder and Co., 1882), pp. viii–ix.
54. Phyllis Grosskurth, *John Addington Symonds: A Biography* (London: Longman, 1964); Phyllis Grosskurth ed., *The Memoirs of John Addington Symonds* (New York: Random, 1984).
55   The 'Labouchere amendment' to the Criminal Law Amendment Act of 1885 effectively outlawed homosexuality; see Elaine Showalter, *Sexual Anarchy* (London: Virago, 2001), p. 14.
56   Peter J. Holliday, 'Symonds and the Model of Ancient Greece' in John Pemble ed., *John Addington Symonds: Culture and the Demon Desire* (Houndmills, Basingstoke: Macmillan, 2000), p. 85. The idea that homosexuality was medicalised as a condition in the late nineteenth century derives from Michel Foucault's *History of Sexuality*: 'Homosexuality appeared as one of the forms of sexuality when it was transposed from the practice of sodomy onto a kind of interior androgyny, a hermaphroditism of the soul. The sodomite had been a temporary aberration; the homosexual was now a species'; (Harmondsworth, Middx.: Penguin, 1984), p. 43.
57   See for instance Richard Jenkyns, *The Victorians and Ancient Greece* (Oxford: Basil Blackwell, 1981), pp. 280–93; Linda Dowling, *Hellenism and Homosexuality in Victorian Oxford* (Ithaca: Cornell University Press, 1994).
58   J.A. Symonds, *The Sonnets of Michelangelo* (1878; rpt. London: Vision Press, 1950), p. 11.

59 In his notes Symonds remarks sardonically that the editor has left only one line of this sonnet (the second) untouched, and that '[instead] of the last words he gives *un cuor di virtù armato* [a heart armed with virtue], being over-scrupulous for his great-uncle's reputation' (*Michelangelo*, p. 193).

60 Symonds, *Michelangelo*, p. 13; he records a specific indebtedness to Plato's *Cratylus* in sonnet lxi. Walter Pater also links Michelangelo's sonnets to Platonism in his chapter on Michelangelo in *Studies in the History of the Renaissance*: 'Now it is the Platonic tradition rather than Dante's that has moulded Michelangelo's verse' (Harmondsworth, Middx.: Penguin, 1986), p. 55. Pater in fact included some of Symonds' translations in a footnote to the first edition, but removed them from the revised version; on the complex interaction between the two writers on Michelangelo see Alex Potts, 'Pungent Prophecies of Art: Symonds, Pater and Michelangelo', in Pemble ed., *Culture and the Demon Desire*, pp. 102–21.

61 John Addington Symonds, *In the Key of Blue and other Prose Essays* (London: Elkin Mathews and John Lane, 1893), pp. 61; 66; 75.

62 *Complete Works of Oscar Wilde* (London and Glasgow: Collins, 1990), pp. 1174, 1175.

63 Ibid., p. 1175; the narrator claims to find puns on 'Hughes' throughout the sequence (eg. in sonnet lxxviii).

64 Grosskurth, *Biography*, pp. 241–2.

65 'How sharp this mixed fascination was at the moment when I first saw Angelo, and how durable it afterwards became through the moral struggles of our earlier intimacy, will be understood by anyone who reads the sonnets written about him in my published volumes. These are 'A Portrait' and 'Angelo Ribello' (VL, 1884, pages 119–20); together with the whole of the following series of sonnets: Animi Figura, 'L'Amour de l'Impossible', i, ii, iii, iv, v, vi; VL, 'Stella Maris' i, ii, iii, xii, xiii, xvii, xviii, xix, xx, xxi, xxii, xxiii, xxiv, xxv, xxxv, xli, xliii, xliv, xlx, xlvi, xlvii–lxiii; Animi Figura, 'Self-Condemnation', i–vii, 'O si! O si!', 'Amends', i–iv. Taken in the order I have indicated, and detached from the artificial context framed to render publication possible, these sonnets faithfully describe the varying moods, perplexities and conflicts of my passion before it settled into a comparatively wholesome comradeship' (*Memoirs*, p. 272).

66 John Addington Symonds, *Vagabunduli Libellus* (London: Kegan Paul, Trench, and Co., 1884), p. viii.

67 *Memoirs*, p. 272.

68 Ibid., p. 272. .

69 Symonds, *Vagabunduli Libellus*, pp. ix–xi. There are strong echoes here of Arthur Hugh Clough's *Dipsychus and The Spirit*, another story of temptation to illicit love set in Venice. Symonds was extremely interested in Clough's work, helping his widow to edit his poems for publication and write the 'memoir'; see Howard J. Booth, 'Male Sexuality, Religion and the Problem of Action: John Addington Symonds on Arthur Hugh Clough', in Andrew Bradstock et al. eds, *Masculinity and Spirituality in Victorian Culture* (Houndmills, Basingstoke: Macmillan, 2000), pp. 116–33.

70 The references to 'gold' are explained by the unpublished sonnet detailing Symonds' encounter with Fusato; see below pp. 132–3.

71 Cp. for instance sonnets xxvii–viii (not based on the relationship with Fusato according to Symonds' list).
72 Cp Symonds' own comment in a letter to Henry Graham Dakyns: 'one section [of *Vagabunduli Libellus*] is a very realistic delineation of an improper love liaison... There is some good poetry in the forty or odd sonnets on this topic... [but] the style [of the whole piece] is oddly mixed, in obedience to changing moods'; cited in Grosskurth, *Biography*, p. 218.
73 'Ode: Intimations of Immortality', l. 150.
74 *Memoirs*, p. 274.
75 *Agricola*, 46: 'Id filiae quoque uxorique praeceperim, sic patris, sic mariti memoriam venerari, ut omnia facta dictaque eius secum revolvant, for-mamque ac figuram animi magis quam corporis complectantur, non quia intercedendum putem imaginibus quae marmore aut aere finguntur, sed ut vultus hominum, ita simulacra vultus imbecilla ac mortalia sunt, forma mentis aeterna, quam tenere et exprimere non per alienam materiam et artem, sed tuis ipse moribus possis.' Translation by Alfred John Church and William Jackson Brodribb (London: Macmillan, 1877). The title is reputed to have been suggested by Robert Louis Stevenson, whom Symonds met during a period of convalescence from tuberculosis; Symonds' 'extreme' reaction to *Dr. Jekyll and Mr. Hyde* might have come from his recognition in it of his own extreme and debilitating self-division; see Grosskurth, *Biography*, pp. 211–3.

Chapter 6   'Thought's pure diamond': The Sonnet at the End of the Century

1 In what is admittedly an imprecise measure, a search of Literature Online (Chadwyck-Healey) reveals just under a thousand sonnets published between 1875 and 1885, compared (for example) to just over five hundred between 1855 and 1865.
2 Max Beerbohm, '1880' in *Works* (1896; rpt. London: The Bodley Head Ltd, 1930), pp. 38–9.
3 The first quotation is Lines 7–8 of the sonnet beginning 'Why practice, love, this small economy' in *Sonnets and Songs* by Proteus [Wilfred Scawen Blunt] (London: John Murray, 1875).
4 This is in fact the second in a series of three sonnets on the sonnet; *Vagabunduli Libellus* (1884), p. 114.
5 Pater, *The Renaissance* (Harmondsworth, Middx.: Penguin, 1986), pp. 52–3.
6 Robert Browning, 'One Word More', ll. 63–4; 70–2. On this poem and Rossetti's *House of Life*, see above ch. 5, n. 38.
7 Cp 'Laurence' in W.H. Mallock's *The New Republic* (1877; rpt. Leicester University Press, 1975), p. 194: 'The mind, if I may borrow an illustration from photography, is a sensitised plate, always ready to receive the images made by experience on it. Poetry is the developing solution which first makes these images visible.'
8 Pater, 'Conclusion' to *The Renaissance*, pp. 151–2.
9 *Vagabunduli Libellus*, p. 113.
10 Some of these effects are noted by Yopie Prins, 'Voice Inverse', *Victorian Poetry* 42 (2004) 43–60, although she does not interpret them as an attempt at metrical mimesis.

11 The role of the anthology in developing the theory of the sonnet is examined in Natalie Houston, 'Valuable by Design: Material Features and Cultural Value in Nineteenth-century Sonnet Anthologies', *Victorian Poetry* 37 (1999), pp. 243–272.

12 T. Hall Caine, *Sonnets of Three Centuries: A Selection, including Many Examples Hitherto Unpublished* (London: Elliot Stock, 1882), p. xxii; Watts-Dunton's metaphor is also adopted by William Sharp in his preface to *Sonnets of this Century* (London: Walter Scott, 1886), which states that '[for] the concise expression of an isolated poetic thought – an intellectual or sensuous "wave" keenly felt, emotionally and rhythmically – the sonnet would seem to be the best medium, the means apparently prescribed by certain radical laws of melody and harmony, in other words, of nature: even as the swallow's wing is the best for rapid volant wheel and shift, as the heron's for mounting by wide gyrations, as that of the kite or the albatross for sustained suspension' (p. xxiii; see also pp. lii–liii).

13 Symonds, *Animi Figura*, pp. xi–xii.

14 Ibid., p. ix.

15 Theodore Watts-Dunton, *Poetry and the Renascence of Wonder* (London: Herbert Jenkins, 1916), p. 183; this essay on the sonnet was first published in *Chambers's Encyclopaedia* for 1891.

16 See above ch. 1, p. 11.

17 T. Hall Caine, *Sonnets*, p. 317; Martin, *Hopkins*, p. 330. The two poems in question were 'The Starlight Night' and 'The Caged Skylark'.

18 Hopkins' political affinities with his contemporaries are discussed in ch. 3 above.

19 Symonds, *Animi Figura*, p. x.

20 Richard Chenevix Trench, 'The History of the English Sonnet' in *The Afternoon Lectures on Literature and Art*, 4th series (London: Bell and Daldy, 1867), p. 154.

21 *Animi Figura*, pp. x–xi.

22 The development of the poem is analysed by Robert D. Hume, who concludes that Rossetti's additions to the final 1881 version, such as 'the explicit association of Love with Spring and Summer', are designed to make the poem 'not the story of a crisis but rather the pattern of a life'; 'Inorganic Structure in *The House of Life*', 292–3.

23 As pointed out by William Fredeman; see Clyde de L. Ryals, 'The Narrative Unity of *The House of Life*', 241. It should also be pointed out that the proportions of Rossetti's 'sonnet of sonnets' (59:42) is analogous to the 6:4.5 of Hopkins' 'curtal' sonnets.

24 David G. Riede, *Dante Gabriel Rossetti Revisited* (New York: Twayne, 1992), p. 128.

25 Riede, *Rossetti Revisited*, p. 140.

26 Watts-Dunton, *Renascence*, p. 172.

27 Brigid Boardman ed., *The Poems of Francis Thompson* (London and New York: Continuum, 2001), pp. 384–6; this sonnet sequence was not published during Thompson's lifetime. The text of Swinburne's sonnets is taken from Literature Online (Chadwyck-Healey).

28 Caine, *Sonnets of Three Centuries*, pp. 310–11.

29 Hall Caine is lavish in his praise of Christina Rossetti, and thanks Mathilde Blind at the end of his volume: '[to] her cordial intercession on my behalf

I owe not a few of the noble sonnets by living poets, printed here for the first time' (p. 318).

30 Sharp, *Sonnets of this Century*, p. 314; Sharp later acquired literary celebrity by reinventing himself as 'Fiona Macleod'.
31 Ibid., p. lvi.
32 Augusta Webster, *Mother and Daughter: An Uncompleted Sonnet-Sequence* (London: Macmillan, 1895); this edition is available electronically as part of the University of Indiana's 'Victorian Women Writer's Project'. The quotation is taken from an article by Watts-Dunton in *The Athenaeum* of 24 January 1880.
33 Webster, *Mother and Daughter*, pp. 11–12.
34 The 'New Woman' of the 1880s and 90s was seen as 'dangerous to society because her obsession with developing her brain starved the uterus': Showalter, *Sexual Anarchy*, p. 40.
35 *Brother and Sister* was first published in *The Legend of Jubal and Other Poems* (Edinburgh: William Blackwood, 1874), pp. 183–91. It is a series of eleven Shakespearean sonnets with significant similarities to the early chapters of *The Mill on the Floss*.
36 Also known as Madame Darmesteter and Madame Duclaux; the poem is taken from the 1886 volume entitled *An Italian Garden and Other Lyrics*; rpt. in *The Collected Poems, Lyrical and Narrative, of A. Mary F. Robinson* (London: T. Fisher Unwin, 1902), p. 95.
37 Showalter, *Sexual Anarchy*, p. 40; the definition of neurasthenia is taken from the OED.
38 'The Evening of the Year', l. 4; Mathilde Blind, *Songs and Sonnets* (London: Chatto and Windus, 1893), p. 117. The contribution of women poets like Blind, Rosamund Marriott Watson and 'Michael Field' to *fin-de-siècle* poetry is analysed in Natalie M. Houston, 'Towards a New History: *Fin-de-Siècle* Women Poets and the Sonnet', *Essays and Studies 2003*, 145–64.
39 Boardman, *The Poems of Francis Thompson*, p. 226; the poem was first published in *Merry England* in August 1890, and not reprinted during Thompson's lifetime.
40 E.M. Forster, 'Racial Exercise' in *Two Cheers for Democracy* (London: Edward Arnold, 1951), p. 30.
41 'House of Bondage' I, ll. 9–12.
42 Boardman suggests that a reference of to 'Father Hopkins' by Thompson implies knowledge of his work.
43 Watts-Dunton, *Renascence of Wonder*, p. 172; Bernard Bergonzi, *Poetry 1870–1914* (Harlow: Longman, 1980), p. 185.
44 'Pluck from now on the roses of life'; from the 'Sonnets pour Hélène', Book II, XLIII; Yeats' poem comes from *The Rose* (1893).
45 Holbrook Jackson, *The Eighteen Nineties* (London: Jonathan Cape, 1927), pp. 66–7.
46 Robinson, *Collected Poems*, pp. vii–viii.
47 Text from Chadwyck-Healey, Literature Online; *The Work of Cecil Rhodes: A Sonnet Sequence* (1907), III, ll. 9–14.
48 See ch. 3 above, pp. 74–5; Holbrook Jackson calls the Decadence 'a form of imperialism of the spirit, ambitious, arrogant, aggressive, waving the flag of human power over an ever wider and wider territory', and adds that 'it is interesting to recollect that decadent art periods have often coincided with... waves of imperial patriotism'; *The Eighteen Nineties*, p. 64.

Bibliography

1. Poetry

Alexander, Peter ed. *Shakespeare: Works* (London and Glasgow: Collins, 1979).

Allott, Miriam. *Arnold: The Complete Poems*, 2nd ed. (London and New York: Longman, 1979).

———. *Keats: The Complete Poems* (Harlow: Longman, 1986).

Bergonzi, Bernard. *Poetry 1870–1914* (Harlow: Longman, 1980).

Blind, Mathilde. *Songs and Sonnets* (London: Chatto and Windus, 1893).

[Blunt, Wilfred Scawen]. *Sonnets and Songs* by Proteus (London: John Murray, 1875).

Boardman, Brigid ed. *The Poems of Francis Thompson* (London and New York: Continuum, 2001).

Brooks-Davies, Douglas ed. *Edmund Spenser: Selected Shorter Poems* (Harlow: Longman, 1995).

Bullock, Alan ed. *Vittoria Colonna: Rime* (Roma: Giuseppe Laterza e figli, 1982).

Caine, T. Hall ed. *Sonnets of Three Centuries: A Selection, including Many Examples Hitherto Unpublished* (London: Elliot Stock, 1882).

Campbell, Gordon ed. *John Milton: The Complete English Poems* (London: Everyman (David Campbell Publishers), 1992).

Coleridge, Ernest Hartley ed. *The Poems of Samuel Taylor Coleridge* (Oxford: Oxford University Press, 1917).

Crump, R.W. and Betty S. Flowers. *Christina Rossetti: The Complete Poems* (London: Penguin, 2001).

Curran, Stuart ed. *The Poems of Charlotte Smith* (New York and Oxford: OUP, 1993).

Duclaux, Madame [A[gnes] Mary F[rances] Robinson]. *The Collected Poems, Lyrical and Narrative, of A. Mary F. Robinson* (London: T. Fisher Unwin, 1902).

Dyce, Alexander. *Specimens of English Sonnets* (London: William Pickering, 1833).

Eliot, George. *The Legend of Jubal and Other Poems* (Edinburgh: William Blackwood, 1874).

Feldman, Paula R. and Daniel Robinson eds. *A Century of Sonnets: The Romantic-Era Revival 1750–1850* (Oxford and New York: Oxford University Press, 1999).

Gibson, James ed. *Thomas Hardy: The Complete Poems* (London: Macmillan, 1983).

Hanley, Keith ed. *George Meredith: Selected Poems* (Manchester: Carcanet Press, 1983).

Haydon, John O. ed. *William Wordsworth: The Poems*, 2 vols (Harmondsworth, Middx.: Penguin, 1982).

Hemans, Felicia. *The Poetical Works of Mrs. [Felicia] Hemans* (London: Peacock, Mansfield and Britton, n.d.).

Henderson, George ed. *Petrarca: A Selection of Sonnets from Various Authors* (London: C & R Baldwin, 1803).

Hutchinson, Thomas ed. *Shelley: Poetical Works* (1970; rpt. Oxford: Oxford University Press, 1988).

Johnson, Shirley M.C. and Todd K. Bender. *The Collected Poems of Canon Richard Watson Dixon (1833–1900)* (New York Peter Lang, 1989).

Kenyon, Frederick G. ed. *The Poetical Works of Elizabeth Barrett Browning* (London: Smith, Elder and Co., 1907).

Jones, Alun ed. *Wordsworth's Poems of 1807* (Basingstoke: Macmillan, 1987).

Karlin, Daniel ed. *The Penguin Book of Victorian Verse* (London: Penguin, 1997).

Marsh, Jan ed. *Dante Gabriel Rossetti: Collected Writings* (London: J.M. Dent, 1999).

Mason, Michael ed. *Lyrical Ballads* (London and New York: Longman, 1992).

Maxwell, J.C. *William Wordsworth: The Prelude* (Harmondsworth, Middx.: Penguin, 1982).

McGann, Jerome ed. *The Oxford Authors: Byron* (Oxford: Oxford University Press, 1986).

Newman, John Henry (Cardinal) et al. *Lyra Apostolica* (Derby: Henry Mozley and Sons, 1836).

Percy, Thomas ed. *Reliques of Ancient English Poetry*, 3 vols (London: J. Dodsley, 1765).

Pettigrew, John and Thomas J. Collins eds. *Robert Browning: The Poems*, 2 vols (Harmondsworth, Middx.: Penguin, 1981).

Phelan, J.P. *Clough: Selected Poems* (Harlow: Longman, 1995).

Phillips, Catherine ed. *The Oxford Authors: Gerard Manley Hopkins* (Oxford: Oxford University Press, 1986).

Ricks, Christopher ed. *The Poems of Tennyson* (London and New York: Longman, 1969).

Robinson, Eric, ed. *John Clare: Selected Poems and Prose* (Oxford: Oxford University Press, 1982).

———, David Powell and P.M.S. Dawson eds. *John Clare: Northborough Sonnets* (Ashington: Mid Northumberland Arts Group and Carcanet Press, 1995).

Rossetti, Dante Gabriel. *The Early Italian Poets* (1861; rpt. London: Anvil Press, 1981).

Sharp, William ed. *Sonnets of This Century* (London: Walter Scott, 1886).

Smiles, Samuel ed. *The Poetical Works of Gerald Massey* (London: Routledge, Warne and Routledge, 1861).

Smith, Alexander [and Sidney Dobell]. *Sonnets on the War* (London, 1855).

Symonds, John Addington. *Animi Figura* (London: Smith, Elder and Co., 1882).

———. *The Sonnets of Michelangelo* (1878; rpt. London: Vision Press, 1950).

———. *Vagabunduli Libellus* (London: Kegan Paul, Trench, and Co., 1884).

[Taylor, Thomas]. *Sixty-Five Sonnets; with Prefatory Remarks on the accordance of the sonnet with the powers of the English language: also, a few miscellaneous poems* (London: Baldwin, Cradock and Joy, 1818).

Thornton, R.K.R. ed. *John Clare: The Rural Muse* (1835; rpt. The Mid Northumberland Arts Group and Carcanet New Press, 1982).

Waddington, Samuel ed., *English Sonnets by Living Writers* (London: George Bell and Co., 1881).

Webster, Augusta. *Mother and Daughter: An Uncompleted Sonnet-Sequence* (London: Macmillan, 1895).

Williams, Isaac. *The Cathedral* (Oxford: John Henry Parker, 1838).

Wu, Duncan ed. *Romantic Women Poets: An Anthology* (Oxford: Blackwell, 1997).
Yeats, William Butler. *Collected Poems* (1933; rpt. London: Macmillan, 1978).

2. Critical and contextual material

Abrams, M.H. *The Mirror and the Lamp* (1953; rpt. Oxford: Oxford University Press, 1971).
Armstrong, Isobel. *Victorian Poetry: Poetry, Poetics and Politics* (London and New York: Routledge, 1993).
Arnold, Matthew. *Culture and Anarchy* (London: Macmillan, 1869).
Barber, Marjorie M. ed. *A Dorothy Wordsworth Selection* (London: Macmillan, 1965).
Barrell, John. *The Idea of Landscape and the Sense of Place: An Approach to the Poetry of John Clare* (Cambridge: Cambridge University Press, 1972).
Bate, Jonathan. *John Clare: A Biography* (London: Picador, 2004).
———. *Shakespeare and the English Romantic Imagination* (1986; rpt. Oxford: Oxford University Press, 1989).
Bate, Walter Jackson. 'Keats's Style: Evolution towards qualities of permanent value'. In M.H. Abrams ed., *English Romantic Poets: Modern Essays in Criticism*, 2nd ed. (Oxford: Oxford University Press, 1975).
Beerbohm, Max. *Works* (1896; rpt. London: The Bodley Head Ltd, 1930).
Bhattacharya, Arunodoy. *The Sonnet and the Major English Romantic Poets* (Calcutta, 1976).
Billone, Amy. '"In Silence Like to Death": Elizabeth Barrett's Sonnet Turn'. *Victorian Poetry* 39 (2001), 533–50.
Blair, Kirstie ed. *John Keble in Context* (London: Anthem Press, 2004).
Booth, Howard. *Life of John Addington Symonds*. <http://www.LitEncyc.com>
Bradstock, Andrew et al. eds. *Masculinity and Spirituality in Victorian Culture* (Basingstoke: Macmillan, 2000).
Bristow, Joseph. '"He and I": Dante Gabriel. Rossetti's other man'. *Victorian Poetry* 39.3 (Fall 2001), 365–90.
Brown, Charles Armitage. *Shakespeare's Autobiographical Poems* (London: James Bohn, 1838).
Browning, R. Barrett ed. *The Letters of Robert and Elizabeth Barrett Browning*. 2 vols (London: John Murray, 1899; rpt. 1930).
Bump, Jerome. 'Hopkins and the School of Dante'. *Journal of English and Germanic Philology* 83 (1984), 355–79.
Burke, Edmund. *A Philosophical Enquiry into the Origin of Our Ideas of the Sublime and Beautiful* (London: R. and J. Dodsley, 1759).
Burton, K.M. ed. *Milton's Prose Writings* (London and New York: Dent, Dutton, 1974).
Carlyle, Thomas. *On Heroes, Hero-Worship and the Heroic in History* (London: Chapman and Hall, 1888).
Chapman, Alison ed. *Essays and Studies 2003 Victorian Women Poets* (Cambridge: D.S. Brewer, 2003).
Chitty, Susan. *The Beast and the Monk: A Life of Charles Kingsley* (London: Hodder and Stoughton, 1974).
Church, Alfred John and William Jackson Brodribb. *The Agricola of Tacitus* (London: Macmillan, 1877).

Clough, Arthur Hugh. 'Recent English Poetry'. *North American Review* 77 (1853), 1–30.

Cohen, Edward H. 'The Chronology of Hopkins's "Terrible Sonnets"'. *Victorians Institute Journal* 21 (1993), 191–200.

Coleridge, Samuel Taylor. *Biographia Literaria*. Ed. George Watson (London: J.M. Dent and Sons, 1975).

Cooper, Helen. *Elizabeth Barrett Browning, Woman and Artist* (Chapel Hill and London: The University of North Carolina Press, 1988).

Corrigan, Beatrice. *Italian Poets and English Critics 1755–1859* (Chicago: Univ. of Chicago Press, 1969).

Cox, Philip. *Gender, Genre and the Romantic Poets* (Manchester and New York: Manchester University Press, 1996).

Crisafulli, Lilla Maria and Cecilia Pietropoli eds. *Le poetesse romantiche inglesi* (Roma: Carocci, 2002).

Curran, Stuart. *Poetic Form and British Romanticism* (Oxford: Oxford University Press, 1986).

De Selincourt, Ernest ed. *The Letters of William and Dorothy Wordsworth: The Early Years 1787–1805*. 2nd ed. (Oxford: Oxford University Press, 1967).

———. *The Letters of William and Dorothy Wordsworth: The Later Years* (Oxford: Oxford University Press, 1939).

Donow, Herbert S. *The Sonnet in England and America: A Bibliography of Criticism* (Westport, Connecticut and London: Greenwood Press, 1982).

Dowling, Linda. *Hellenism and Homosexuality in Victorian Oxford* (Ithaca: Cornell University Press, 1994).

Drake, Nathan. *Literary Hours or Sketches Critical and Narrative* (London: Cadell and Davies, 1798).

Eliot, T.S. Ed. *Literary Essays of Ezra Pound* (1954; rpt. London and Boston: Faber and Faber, 1985).

Esh, Sylvan. 'Not speaking the unspeakable: Religion and repetition in Christina Rossetti's *Monna Innominata* sequence'. *Studies in English Literature, 1500–1900* (Autumn 1994).

European Romantic Review 13 (2002), 347–464 (Special Issue on the Sonnet).

Fennell, Francis ed. *Rereading Hopkins: Selected New Essays* (University of Victoria, 1996).

Fletcher, Pauline. '"Trifles Light as Air" in Meredith's *Modern Love*'. *Victorian Poetry* 34 (1996), 87–99.

Foakes, R.A. ed. *Coleridge: Lectures 1808–19 on Literature*. 2 vols (Princeton: Princeton UP, 1987).

Foreman, J.B. ed. *The Complete Works of Oscar Wilde* (London and Glasgow: Collins, 1990).

Forster, E.M. *Two Cheers for Democracy* (London: Edward Arnold, 1951).

Foucault, Michel. *The History of Sexuality* (Harmondsworth, Middx.: Penguin, 1984).

Fredeman, William E. 'Rossetti's "In Memoriam": An Elegiac Reading of *The House of Life*'. *Bulletin of the John Rylands Library* 47 (1965), 298–341.

Gardner, Joseph H. '"But Worse": Hopkins and Rossetti'. *American Notes and Queries* 15 (2002), 21–23.

———. '"Decoding" Rossetti: Sonnets II and III of *The House of Life*'. *Journal of Pre-Raphaelite Studies* 1 (1980), 36–44.

Going, William T. *Scanty Plot of Ground: Studies in the Victorian Sonnet* (The Hague and Paris: Mouton, 1976).
————. 'The Term "Sonnet Sequence"'. *Modern Language Notes* 62 (1947), 400–02.
Golden, Arline. '"The Game of Sentiment": Tradition and Innovation in Meredith's *Modern Love'*. *English Literary History* 40 (1973), 264–84.
————. 'Victorian Renascence: The Revival of the Amatory Sonnet Sequence, 1850–1900'. *Genre* 7 (1974), 133–147.
Gray, Erik. 'Sonnet Kisses: Sidney to Barrett Browning'. *Essays in Criticism* 52 (2002), 126–42.
Greer, Germaine. *Slip-shod Sybils* (Harmondsworth. Middx.: Penguin, 1995).
Griffiths, Eric. 'The Disappointment of Christina G. Rossetti'. *Essays in Criticism* 47 (1997), 107–42.
Griffin, John. 'Tractarians and Metaphysicals: The Failure of Influence'. *John Donne Journal* 4 (1985), 291–302.
Grosskurth, Phyllis. *John Addington Symonds: A Biography* (London: Longman, 1964).
———— ed. *The Memoirs of John Addington Symonds* (New York: Random, 1984).
Hardy, Dennis. *Alternative Communities in Nineteenth-Century England* (London and New York: Longman, 1979).
Havens, Raymond D. *The Influence of Milton on English Poetry* (Cambridge, Mass.: Harvard University Press, 1922).
Hazlitt, William. *Table-Talk* (1821; rpt. Oxford: Oxford University Press, 1910).
Hess, Jonathan. 'WW's Aesthetic State: The Poetics of Liberty'. *Studies in Romanticism* 33 (1994), 3–29.
Hill, Alan G. ed. *Letters of William Wordsworth: A New Selection* (Oxford and New York: Oxford University Press, 1984).
[Hopkins, Manley?] Review of *In Memoriam*. *The Times*, 28 November 1851. Accessed through *The Times Digital Archive* <http://web5.infotrac.galegroup.com>; 4 February 2004.
Houston, Natalie M. 'Affecting Authenticity: *Sonnets from the Portuguese* and *Modern Love'*. *Studies in the Literary Imagination* 35 (2002), 99–122.
————. 'Reading the Victorian Souvenir: Sonnets and Photographs of the Crimean War'. *Yale Journal of Criticism* 14 (2001), 353–83.
————. 'Valuable by Design: Material Features and Cultural Value in Nineteenth-century Sonnet Anthologies'. *Victorian Poetry* 37 (1999), 243–272.
Houtchens, L.H. and C.W. Houtchens eds. *Leigh Hunt's Literary Criticism* (New York: Columbia UP, 1956).
Hume, Robert D. 'Inorganic Structure in *The House of Life'*. *Papers on Language and Literature*, 5 (1969), 282–95.
Hunt, Bishop Jr. 'Wordsworth and Charlotte Smith'. *The Wordsworth Circle* 1 (1970), 85–103.
Hunt, [James Henry] Leigh and S. Adams Lee eds. *The Book of the Sonnet*. 2 vols (Boston: Roberts Bros., 1867).
Isomaki, Richard. 'Hopkins, Community, Functions: "Tom's Garland"'. *Nineteenth-Century Literature* 47 (1993), 472–90.
Jackson, Holbrook. *The Eighteen Nineties* (London: Jonathan Cape, 1927).
Jameson, Anna [Mrs.] *The Romance of Biography; or, Memoirs of Women Loved and Celebrated by Poets*. 3rd ed. (London: Saunders and Otley, 1837), 2 vols.

Janowitz, Anne. *Lyric and Labour in the Romantic Tradition* (Cambridge: Cambridge University Press, 1998).

Jarvis, Robin. 'The Wages of Travel: Wordsworth and the Memorial Tour of 1820'. *Studies in Romanticism* 40 (2001), 321–343.

[Jeffrey, Francis.] Review of *Poems in Two Volumes*. *Edinburgh Review* 11 (1807), 214–32.

———. '*The Forest Sanctuary; with other Poems*. By Felicia Hemans.' *Edinburgh Review* 50 (1829), 32–48.

Jenkyns, Richard. *The Victorians and Ancient Greece* (Oxford: Basil Blackwell, 1981).

Johnson, Lee M. *Wordsworth and the Sonnet*. Anglistica XIX (Copenhagen: Rosenkilde and Bagger, 1973).

Johnson, Margaret. *Gerard Manley Hopkins and Tractarian Poetry* (Aldershot, Hants. and Brookfield Vermont: Ashgate, 1997).

Jones, Kathleen. *Learning Not to be First: The Life of Christina Rossetti* (New York: St Martin's Press, 1991).

Karlin, Daniel ed. *Robert Browning and Elizabeth Barrett: The Courtship Correspondence* (Oxford: Oxford University Press, 1989).

———. *The Courtship of Robert and Elizabeth Barrett Browning* (Oxford: Oxford University Press, 1985).

———. *Lectures on Poetry*. Tr. (from Latin) E.K. Francis. 2 vols (Oxford: Clarendon Press, 1912).

———. *Occasional Papers and Reviews of John Keble* (Oxford and London: James Parker and Co., 1877).

Kent, David A. ed. *The Achievement of Christina Rossetti* (Ithaca and London: Cornell UP, 1987).

Kerrigan, John. 'Wordsworth and the Sonnet: Building, Dwelling, Thinking'. *Essays in Criticism* 35 (1985), 45–75.

Leighton, Angela. *Elizabeth Barrett Browning* (Brighton; Harvester, 1986).

Lewis, Scott ed. *The Letters of Elizabeth Barrett Browning to Her Sister Arabella*. 2 vols (Waco, Texas: Wedgestone Press, 2002).

Liu, Alan. *Wordsworth: The Sense of History* (Stanford, California: Stanford UP, 1989).

Lowry, H.F. ed. *The Letters of Matthew Arnold to Arthur Hugh Clough* (Oxford: Oxford University Press, 1968).

Lucas, John. 'Hopkins and Symons: Two Views of the City'. In *Fin de Siècle/Fin du Globe: Fears and Fantasies of the Late Nineteenth Century*. Ed. John Stokes (New York: St Martin's Press, 1992).

Lysack, Krista. 'The Economics of Esctasy in Christina Rossetti's *Monna Innominata*'. *Victorian Poetry* 36 (1998), 399–416.

Macaulay, Thomas Babington. *Critical and Historical Essays*. 2 vols (London: Longman, 1859).

Maidment, Brian. *The Poorhouse Fugitives: Self-taught poets and poetry in Victorian Britain* (Manchester: Carcanet, 1987).

Mallock, W.H. *The New Republic* (1877; rpt. Leicester University Press, 1975).

Marsh, Jan. *Christina Rossetti: A Literary Biography* (London: Jonathan Cape, 1994).

Martin, Brian W. *John Keble: Priest, Professor and Poet* (London: Croom Helm, 1976).

Martin, Robert Bernard. *Gerard Manley Hopkins: A Very Private Life* (London: Harper Collins, 1991).

Massey, Gerald. *The Secret Drama of Shakespeare's Sonnets Unfolded, with the Characters Identified*, 2nd ed. (London: private publication for 100 subscribers, 1872).

Mellor, Anne. 'The Female Poet and the Poetess: Two Traditions of British Women's Poetry, 1780–1830'. *Studies in Romanticism* 36 (1997), 261–76.

Mermin, Dorothy. 'Poetry as Fiction: Meredith's Modern Love'. *English Literary History* 43 (1976), 100–115.

———. 'The Female Poet and the Embarrassed Reader: Elizabeth Barrett Browning's *Sonnets from the Portuguese*'. *English Literary History* 48 (1981), 351–67.

Miller, J. Hillis. *The Disappearance of God* (New York: Schocken, 1965).

Monckton Milnes, Richard [Lord Houghton] ed. *The Life and Letters of John Keats* (1848; rpt. London: J.M. Dent and Sons, 1927).

Neri, Barbara. 'A Lineage of Love: The Literary Bloodlines of Elizabeth Barrett Browning's *Sonnets from the Portuguese*'. *Studies in Browning and His Circle* 23 (2000), 50–69.

Newman, John Henry (Cardinal). *Apologia pro Vita Sua* (1864; rpt. New York: Chelsea House, 1983).

Newman, Teresa and Ray Watkinson, *Ford Madox Brown and the Pre-Raphaelite Circle* (London: Chatto and Windus, 1991).

Pakenham, Thomas. *The Scramble for Africa* (London: Abacus, 1991).

Pater, Walter. *The Renaissance* (Harmondsworth, Middx.: Penguin, 1986).

Pemble, John ed. *John Addington Symonds: Culture and the Demon Desire* (Houndmills, Basingstoke: Macmillan, 2000).

Phelan, J.P. 'Radical Metre: The English Hexameter in Clough's *The Bothie of Toper-na-Fuosich*'. *Review of English Studies* n.s. 50 (1999), 166–187.

Pitchford, Lois W. 'The Curtal Sonnets of Gerard Manley Hopkins'. *Modern Language Notes* 67 (1952), 165–9.

Prins, Yopie. 'Voice Inverse'. *Victorian Poetry* 42 (2004), 43–60

Radcliffe, Anne. *A Sicilian Romance* (1790: rpt. Oxford: Oxford University Press, 1993).

Reynolds, Margaret. 'Love's Measurement in Elizabeth Barrett Browning's *Sonnets from the Portuguese*'. *Studies in Browning and His Circle* 21 (1997), 53–67.

Riede, David G. *Dante Gabriel Rossetti Revisited* (New York: Twayne, 1992).

Riess, Daniel. 'Laetitia Landon and the Dawn of English Post-Romanticism'. *Studies in English Literature* 36 (1996), 807–828.

Robinson, Daniel. 'Elegiac Sonnets: Charlotte Smith's Formal Paradoxy'. *Papers on Language and Literature* 39 (2003), 185–220.

———. 'Reviving the Sonnet: Women Romantic Poets and the Sonnet Claim'. *European Romantic Review* 6 (1995), 98–127.

———. '"Still Glides the Stream": Form and Function in Wordsworth's *River Duddon* Sonnets', *European Romantic Review*, 13 (2002), 449–64.

———. '"Work without hope": Anxiety and embarrassment in Coleridge's Sonnets'. *Studies in Romanticism* 39 (2000), 81–110.

Roche, Thomas P., Jr. *Petrarch and the English Sonnet Sequences* (New York: AMS Press, 1989).

Roe, Nicholas. *Wordsworth and Coleridge: The Radical Years* (Oxford: Oxford University Press, 1988).

Rossetti, William Michael ed. *The Germ* (1901; rpt. Oxford: Ashmolean Museum, 1992).

————. 'Memoir'. *The Poetical Works of Christina Rossetti* (London: 1904).

Ruskin, John. *Unto this Last* (London: George Allen, 1898).

Ryals, Clyde de L. 'The Narrative Unity of "The House of Life"'. *Journal of English and Germanic Philology* 69 (1970), 241–57.

Sanderlin, George. 'The Influence of Milton and Wordsworth on the Early Victorian Sonnet'. *English Literary History* 5 (1938), 225–251.

Scheinberg, Cynthia. *Women's Poetry and Religion in Victorian England: Jewish Identity and Christian Culture* (Cambridge: Cambridge University Press, 2002).

Schlegel, A.W. von. *Lectures on Dramatic Art and Literature.* Tr. John Black (London: Henry G. Bohn, 1846).

Showalter, Elaine. *Sexual Anarchy* (London: Virago, 2001).

Simpson, David. *Wordsworth's Historical Imagination: The Poetry of Displacement* (London: Methuen, 1987).

Sinfield, Alan. *Alfred Tennyson* (Oxford: Blackwell, 1986).

Smulders, Sharon. '"Medicated Music": Elizabeth Barrett Browning's *Sonnets from the Portuguese*'. *Victorian Literature and Culture* 23 (1996), 193–213.

Spiller, Michael R.G. *The Sonnet Sequence: A Study of its Strategies* (New York: Twayne Publishers, 1997).

Stone, Marjorie. *Elizabeth Barrett Browning* (Basingstoke: Macmillan, 1995).

Sussman, Herbert. *Victorian Masculinities: Manhood and Masculine Poetics in Early Victorian Literature and Art* (Cambridge: Cambridge University Press, 1995).

Symonds, John Addington. *In the Key of Blue and other Prose Essays* (London: Elkin Mathews and John Lane, 1893).

Taylor, Miles. *Ernest Jones, Chartism, and the Romance of Politics 1819–1869* (Oxford: Oxford University Press, 2003).

[Taylor, Sir Henry.] 'The Sonnets of William Wordsworth'. *Quarterly Review* 69 (1841–2), 1–51.

Tennyson, G.B. *Victorian Devotional Poetry: The Tractarian Mode* (Cambridge, Mass. and London: Harvard UP, 1981).

Thompson, E.P. *The Making of the English Working Class* (1963; rpt. Harmondsworth, Middx.: Penguin, 1982).

Trench, Richard Chenevix. 'The History of the English Sonnet'. In *The Afternoon Lectures on Literature and Art*, 4th series (London: Bell and Daldy, 1867).

Wagner, Jennifer A. *A Moment's Monument: Revisionary Poetics and the Nineteenth-century English Sonnet* (London: Associated University Presses, 1996).

Watts-Dunton, Theodore. *Poetry and the Renascence of Wonder* (London: Herbert Jenkins, 1916).

Weinstein, Mark A. *William Edmondstone Aytoun and the Spasmodic Controversy* (New Haven: Yale UP, 1968).

Weller, Earl Vonard. 'Keats and Mary Tighe'. *PMLA* 42 (1927), 963–985.

Westerholm, Joel. 'In Defence of Verses: The Aesthetic and Reputation of Christina Rossetti's Late Poetry', *Renascence* 51 (1999), 191–203.

Williams, Raymond. *Marxism and Literature* (Oxford: Oxford University Press, 1986).

Wolfson, Susan J. *Felicia Hemans: Selected Poems, Letters, Reception Materials* (Princeton and Oxford: Princeton UP, 2000).

Woolford, John. *Browning the Revisionary* (Basingstoke: Macmillan, 1988).

————. 'Elizabeth Barrett and the Wordsworthian Sublime'. *Essays in Criticism* 45 (1995), 36–56.

Zonneveld, Sjaak. *The Random Grim Forge: A Study of Social Ideas in the Work of Gerard Manley Hopkins* (Maastricht: Van Gorcum, Assen, 1992).

Index

Printed in the United States
76288LV00001B/106-195